Praise for *Software Pipelines and*

"*Software Pipelines* uncovers a new and unique way of software design for high-performance development. Where other methodologies and frameworks have previously been describing the problem, *Software Pipelines* is focusing on the solution. Simply put, *Software Pipelines* addresses the developer's needs for parallel computing and uncovers the throughput offered by multi-core processors."

—Filip Hanik, Senior Software Engineer, SpringSource, Inc.

"There are some books that tout vision but provide no pragmatic, hands-on details. *Software Pipelines and SOA* offers a dose of both. Isaacson is an authority and practitioner, who understands that the promise of SOA is not fulfilled simply by embracing an architectural style of loosely coupled, network-based services but in how the applications and services that support this architectural style are developed and deployed. This book will help support a pragmatic approach to SOA."

—Dan Malks, Vice President, Partner Engineering, JackBe

". . . it provides insights on how to efficiently realize scalability on and across multi-core machines in a predictable manner using patterns derived from the best practices in distributed computing and SOA. Written in a conversational manner, one of the pioneering technology leaders of our time provides keen insights on how to build scalable software solutions."

—Ravi Palepu, SOA Consultant and Founder of PREDICT

"*Software Pipelines* paves the road in distributed, SOA, high-performance computing in theory and practice with strong technical background, elegant architecture, and a usable implementation. A revolution in grid computing and service-oriented architecture."

—Nicole Nemer, Ph.D., Superior Consulting

"Multi-core computing offers a unique opportunity to deliver dramatic scalability in modern business applications; but the task is not an easy one, presenting significant challenges to the software developer. *Software Pipelines* provides an easy-to-implement, concrete strategy that enables service-oriented applications to really deliver on the promise of this new hardware paradigm. A must read for any developer or architect stepping up to the challenge of high-performance business transaction processing."

—Henry Truong, Chief Technology Officer, TeleTech, Inc.

"Isaacson offers a fresh approach to componentize and parallelize software applications in a way that is easy to debug and easy to maintain. Using the high-level abstraction of Software Pipelines, development managers need not worry about the complexities of concurrent programming or the challenges in dealing with maintaining threads, interprocess communication or deadlocks. Any software architect dealing with performance and scalability issues with complex transactional flows must consider the Software Pipelines design paradigm."

—Venkat Pula, Field Application Engineer, Telelogic, an IBM Company

"Cory has captured the power of simplicity, enabling business software applications to exponentially leverage the capacity and capabilities of today's advanced chip architectures. Using Software Pipelines, corporate IT groups are able to manage, control and fully utilize the power of multi-core computing to improve scalability and reduce long-term costs."

—Jim Hogan, Cognify, Vice President, Managed Services

"Having projects architected to gracefully scale from a single multi-core box all the way to a cluster of thousands of machines is the new reality. With Software Pipelines, the development organization can easily architect every project—from the summer intern's toy prototype to your flagship technology—as though it might need to scale for worldwide consumption. Embrace this change now and the day you need that scalability will be your biggest success. Ignore it and it will likely be your greatest failure."

—Jackson Gibbs, CTO, Strands

Software Pipelines and SOA

Addison-Wesley Information Technology Series
Capers Jones and David S. Linthicum, Consulting Editors

The information technology (IT) industry is in the public eye now more than ever before because of a number of major issues in which software technology and national policies are closely related. As the use of software expands, there is a continuing need for business and software professionals to stay current with the state of the art in software methodologies and technologies. The goal of the **Addison-Wesley Information Technology Series** is to cover any and all topics that affect the IT community. These books illustrate and explore how information technology can be aligned with business practices to achieve business goals and support business imperatives. Addison-Wesley has created this innovative series to empower you with the benefits of the industry experts' experience.

For more information point your browser to www.awprofessional.com/itseries

Sid Adelman, Larissa Terpeluk Moss, *Data Warehouse Project Management.* ISBN: 0-201-61635-1

Sid Adelman et al., *Impossible Data Warehouse Situations: Solutions from the Experts.* ISBN: 0-201-76033-9

David Leon Clark, *Enterprise Security: The Manager's Defense Guide.* ISBN: 0-201-71972-X

Frank P. Coyle, *XML, Web Services, and the Data Revolution.* ISBN: 0-201-77641-3

Jill Dyché, *The CRM Handbook: A Business Guide to Customer Relationship Management.* ISBN: 0-201-73062-6

Patricia L. Ferdinandi, *A Requirements Pattern: Succeeding in the Internet Economy.* ISBN: 0-201-73826-0

David Garmus and David Herron, *Function Point Analysis: Measurement Practices for Successful Software Projects.* ISBN: 0-201-69944-3

Beth Gold-Bernstein, William Ruh, *Enterprise Integration: The Essential Guide to Integration Solutions.* 0-321-22390-X

John Harney, *Application Service Providers (ASPs): A Manager's Guide.* ISBN: 0-201-72659-9

International Function Point Users Group, *IT Measurement: Practical Advice from the Experts.* ISBN: 0-201-74158-X

Cory Isaacson, *Software Pipelines and SOA: Releasing the Power of Multi-Core Processing,* ISBN: 0137137974

Capers Jones, *Software Assessments, Benchmarks, and Best Practices.* ISBN: 0-201-48542-7

Ravi Kalakota and Marcia Robinson, *e-Business 2.0: Roadmap for Success.* ISBN: 0-201-72165-1

Ravi Kalakota and Marcia Robinson, *Services Blueprint: Roadmap for Execution.* ISBN: 0-321-15039-2

David S. Linthicum, *B2B Application Integration: e-Business-Enable Your Enterprise.* ISBN: 0-201-70936-8

David S. Linthicum, *Enterprise Application Integration.* ISBN: 0-201-61583-5

David S. Linthicum, *Next Generation Application Integration: From Simple Information to Web Services.* ISBN: 0-201-84456-7

Anne Thomas Manes, *Web Services: A Manager's Guide.* ISBN: 0-321-18577-3

Larissa T. Moss and Shaku Atre, *Business Intelligence Roadmap: The Complete Project Lifecycle for Decision-Support Applications.* ISBN: 0-201-78420-3

Bud Porter-Roth, *Request for Proposal: A Guide to Effective RFP Development.* ISBN: 0-201-77575-1

Ronald G. Ross, *Principles of the Business Rule Approach.* ISBN: 0-201-78893-4

Dan Sullivan, *Proven Portals: Best Practices for Planning, Designing, and Developing Enterprise Portals.* ISBN: 0-321-12520-7

Karl E. Wiegers, *Peer Reviews in Software: A Practical Guide.* ISBN: 0-201-73485-0

Ralph R. Young, *Effective Requirements Practices.* ISBN: 0-201-70912-0

Bill Zoellick, *CyberRegs: A Business Guide to Web Property, Privacy, and Patents.* ISBN: 0-201-72230-5

Software Pipelines and SOA

Releasing the Power of Multi-Core Processing

Cory Isaacson

▲▼ Addison-Wesley

Upper Saddle River, NJ • Boston • Indianapolis • San Francisco
New York • Toronto • Montreal • London • Munich • Paris • Madrid
Capetown • Sydney • Tokyo • Singapore • Mexico City

Many of the designations used by manufacturers and sellers to distinguish their products are claimed as trademarks. Where those designations appear in this book, and the publisher was aware of a trademark claim, the designations have been printed with initial capital letters or in all capitals.

Java, JDBC, J2EE, JNI, Javadoc, MySQL and all Java-based trademarks are trademarks of Sun Microsystems, Inc. in the United States, other countries, or both.

Linux is a registered trademark of Linus Torvalds in the United States, other countries, or both. UNIX is a registered trademark of The Open Group in the United States, other countries, or both. Microsoft, Windows, Microsoft .NET Remoting, and Microsoft .NET connection software are either registered trademarks or trademarks of Microsoft Corporation in the United States and/or other countries.

IBM, iSeries, and zSeries are trademarks of International Business Machines Corporation in the United States, other countries, or both.

CORBA is a registered trademark of Object Management Group, Inc. in the United States and/or other countries.

Apache, log4j, JMeter, Ant, and Tomcat are trademarks of The Apache Software Foundation.

dbShards is a trademarks of CodeFutures Corporation, in the United States.

The Software Pipelines Reference Framework includes software developed by the Spring Framework Project (springframework.org). Spring Framework components copyright 2002–2007 by the original author or authors. The Spring Framework is licensed under the Apache License, Version 2.0 (the "License"). You may obtain a copy of the License at: apache.org/licenses/LICENSE-2.0.

Other company, product, or service names mentioned may be trademarks or service marks of others.

The author and publisher have taken care in the preparation of this book, but make no expressed or implied warranty of any kind and assume no responsibility for errors or omissions. No liability is assumed for incidental or consequential damages in connection with or arising out of the use of the information or programs contained herein.

The publisher offers excellent discounts on this book when ordered in quantity for bulk purchases or special sales, which may include electronic versions and/or custom covers and content particular to your business, training goals, marketing focus, and branding interests. For more information, please contact: U.S. Corporate and Government Sales, (800) 382-3419, corpsales@pearsontechgroup.com

For sales outside the United States please contact: International Sales, international@pearsoned.com

Visit us on the Web: informit.com/aw

Library of Congress Cataloging-in-Publication Data

Isaacson, Cory.
    Software pipelines and SOA : releasing the power of multi-core processing
/ Cory Isaacson.—1st ed.
      p. cm.
  Includes bibliographical references and index.
     ISBN 0-13-713797-4 (pbk. : alk. paper)
      1. Parallel processing (Electronic computers)   2. Computer software—Development.
  3. Web services. I. Title.

QA76.58.I82 2008
004'.35--dc22
                                                  2008040489

ISBN-13: 978-0-13-713797-8
ISBN-10:   0-13-713797-4
Text printed in the United States on recycled paper by RR Donnelley in Crawfordsville, Indiana.
First printing, December 2008

Contents

Section I: Pipelines Theory   1

CHAPTER 1   Parallel Computing and Business Applications   3

CHAPTER 2   Pipelines Law   17

Section II: Pipelines Methodology   79

Foreword

Multi-core hardware is the new normal. Major computer chip vendors have essentially halted the regular increase in CPU clock speeds that reigned for almost a half century in response to issues like power consumption, heat output, and unpredictability of quantum physics (to paraphrase Einstein, CPUs shouldn't play dice …).

Instead, they are using multi-core architectures to deliver increased processing power in place of faster clock speeds. Although this is a logical move, a large percentage of existing software applications cannot take advantage of the processing power on the additional cores, and they often run even slower due to reduced clock speeds in multi-core CPUs, setting up what could be called the Multi-core Dilemma.

In general, the Multi-core Dilemma applies across the spectrum of programming languages—Java, C#, C++, etc. This is why major technology vendors are investing heavily in research intended to lead to the next generation of programming environments. But what about the software that has already been written? The reality for any software application is that to benefit from multi-core, the application must either be written to be multi-threaded, or it must be in a container that effectively makes it multi-threaded.

There is no "plug-and-play" solution, but there are development tools and containers available that can help with the Multi-core Dilemma for many use cases. There are not, however, many good methodologies for solving this problem. In *Software Pipelines and SOA,* Cory Isaacson outlines a systematic, logical approach for planning and executing the move to multi-core.

This hardware trend will create a tectonic shift in the software industry as billions of lines of code are migrated, optimized, or rewritten to take advantage of multi-core hardware. Practical, logical approaches will be essential to making this transition smoothly.

Now that parallel computing has moved from being an edge case to being a common requirement for enterprise software, enabling applications to run in parallel can't be limited to only the most experienced programmers. *Software Pipelines and SOA* describes several techniques for bringing parallel computing to mainstream software development.

For example, one technique for making parallel computing happen throughout your development group is to separate your concurrency model from the application logic, much as you have your data and UI layer separate from the main business logic. Doing so allows feature developers to focus on the application functionality without having to worry about explicitly threading at design time. In addition, it can be an effective technique for migrating existing single-threaded applications into multi-core environments.

In addition, *Software Pipelines and SOA* discusses the connection between service-oriented architectures and multi-core. The basic approach is to treat your application as a collection of services and deploy a container that can run multiple instances of those services.

Using this link between SOA and multi-core, services can be a key part of your concurrency model. By separating concurrency from application logic, you can make the migration of existing applications to multi-core much simpler and enable more effective building of new parallel applications. It also makes it much easier to reconfigure (rather than recode) your applications, then continue to optimize them and move to new generations of hardware—from 2 and 4 cores to 8, 16, 32 ... 128, and beyond. Designing enterprise applications in a service-oriented architecture makes it easier to separate concurrency from application logic, so that they work together.

There is work involved if you have a monolithic application, but it is still significantly less than rewriting. If you plan to use a container, make sure that it can handle your business application requirements, which might include message ordering, forks and joins in the business process, human interaction, and long-running processes.

Most parallel computing approaches use traditional multi-threaded programming, a "thread-level" approach. *Software Pipelines and SOA* describes a "service-level" approach that can provide a way to move to multi-core that requires less effort and is more configurable. It complements, rather than replaces, the traditional thread-level approaches.

Moving your existing applications to multi-core takes some planning, but it might not be as much work as you think. Design a solid concurrency model, and your existing applications can continue to serve you for years to come. *Software Pipelines and SOA* provides a great road map for getting there.

Patrick Leonard
VP, Engineering & Product Strategy
Rogue Wave Software
pleonard@roguewave.com

Preface

We're now in the multi-core era. As consumers of computing power, we've all come to expect a never-ending increase in power, and CPU manufacturers are now using multi-core processors to continue that long-standing trend. If we want to take full advantage of this enormous capacity, our business applications must "do more than one thing at a time." However, traditional parallel computing methods (such as multi-threading, SMP, and clustering) are either limiting or extremely difficult to implement—especially when used on top of application components that weren't originally designed for a parallel world.

Software Pipelines architecture is a new architecture that specifically addresses the problem of using parallel processing in the multi-core era. It is a new approach to the problem. Pipeline technology abstracts the complexities of parallel computing and makes it possible to use the power of the new CPUs for business applications.

We wrote this book primarily for software architects, application developers, and application development managers who need high-performance, scalable business applications. Project managers, software quality assurance specialists, and IT operations managers will also find it useful; however, the main focus is software development. Our intention was to make the book as applicable as possible, and to provide tools that you can quickly learn and apply to your own development challenges.

The book is divided into four sections, which we'll describe in this preface.

Pipelines Theory

The Pipelines Theory section, Chapters 1 through 5, covers the following topics:

- How pipelines work, including the fundamental concepts and underlying theory of Software Pipelines
- What pipelines can accomplish
- Methods for applying Software Pipelines
- Pipelines Patterns, including various ways to apply Software Pipelines in business application scenarios, setting the stage for the examples in later chapters

As the foundation for the remainder of the book, this section is appropriate for all readers. If you're a software architect or an application developer, you should definitely study this section first. If you're reading the book from a managerial perspective, or if your interest is more general and less technical, you can focus on just this section.

Pipelines Methodology

The Pipelines Methodology section, Chapters 6 through 13, shows how to implement Software Pipelines by using the step-by-step Software Pipelines Optimization Cycle (SPOC). To illustrate how the methodology works, we use it to solve a business problem for a fictitious example company, the Pipelines Bank Corporation (PBCOR). In each chapter we present a new step, then show you how we used the step in our PBCOR example.

This section will be of interest to all primary audiences of the book, including project managers. The PBCOR examples get into a fair amount of technical detail; therefore, application development managers might want to skip over the more complex examples.

Pipelines Examples

The Pipelines Examples section, Chapters 14 through 22, contains code examples based on the reference Pipelines Framework we developed for the book. We've included examples for each main Pipelines Pattern from the Pipelines Theory section. You can use these as guides for applying Software Pipelines directly to your own real-world applications.

This section is for software architects and application developers, the roles directly involved in pipelines implementation. In addition, IT operations managers will find it helpful to read the configuration sections, which show how to modify the scalability of an application without modifying the actual application components.

We recommend that you read the first three chapters of this section in detail. These basic chapters include Chapter 14, "Hello Software Pipelines"; Chapter 15, "Scaling Hello Software Pipelines"; and Chapter 16, "Additional Pipelines Router Configurations." After that, you might prefer to scan the more advanced examples in Chapters 17 through 22, then concentrate on the ones that most apply to your specific application scenarios.

The Future of Software Pipelines

In the final section we tell you about the future we envision for Software Pipelines architecture. There are plenty of greenfield areas that can be developed, and it is our hope that this section will inspire readers to help move the technology forward into the mainstream.

Conventions

In our examples, when we present a section of code or XML, refer to a command, or refer to a code element, we'll use a monospaced font, for example, `<pipelines-distributor>`. For names of components, such as services, clients, and distributors, we'll use an italic monospaced font, for example, *Distributor1*.

The Web Site

We've established a Web site for Software Pipelines technology at softwarepipelines.org. The site is for readers of the book and for anyone else who is interested in using or advancing the Software Pipelines architecture. You can download the following items from the site:

- Tools and sample report templates for the Software Pipelines Optimization Cycle (SPOC) methodology
- Source code for the reference Pipelines Framework
- Complete source code for all examples in the book
- Articles and discussions on pipelines technology and its applications

We hope you find Software Pipelines as exciting as we've found it, and that you take this opportunity to capitalize on its capabilities and use it to help overcome your own performance and scalability challenges.

Acknowledgments

There are many individuals who have contributed to the evolution of Software Pipelines, and who have helped with the creation of this first book. I am deeply indebted to all of them for the ideas, input, and, most of all, encouragement and support on the project. I cannot mention everyone, but here are some of the many contributors who made this work possible:

Ravi Palepu, great friend and business associate, spent countless hours with me discussing pipelines ideas and helping to develop the initial concepts and outline for the current work.

Patrick Leonard and David Haney of Rogue Wave Software worked with me to formulate the original core pipelines concepts, forming the foundation of the current work.

I also want to acknowledge the entire Rogue Wave Software organization, for its support during and after my tenure there as president of the company.

Barbara Howell was the illustrator and incredibly dedicated editor for my draft of the book; without her I never could have gotten the job done. Her persistence, attention to detail, and talent for helping me communicate the key concepts through the diagrams and graphics you see in the book were invaluable.

Colin Holm provided the majority of development for the code examples, as well as the reference Pipelines Framework presented in the third section. Colin's insight and work on this were critical to the book's final content, and his ability to create the examples from the viewpoint of a "real-world" business application developer helped transform Software Pipelines from concept to reality.

Last, I must thank my family, especially my wife, Kim, for putting up with the enormous amount of work required to complete the book. I also want to thank my talented and understanding children for their cooperation and understanding. In fact, my older son, Devyn (a genuine math whiz), helped clarify the early formulas for Pipelines Law, and my younger son, Tyler, was often a sounding board for the various ideas in the book and how to present them.

About the Author

Cory Isaacson is CEO of Prelude Innovations, Inc., a firm specializing in the incubation and introduction of leading software technology products. Actively involved in leading information technologies for over 20 years, Cory served as technical editor and columnist for *WebSphere Advisor Magazine*, has spoken at hundreds of public events and seminars, and authored numerous articles on architecture and practicalities of employing technology. Cory has provided guidance to hundreds of top architects and professional developers in the financial services, entertainment, telco, and software industries on the development and implementation of powerful business applications.

Most recently Cory was president of Rogue Wave Software, managing the organization for over three years, building new product strategies, and culminating in a successful acquisition in mid-2007 by a leading private equity firm. Cory has focused on efficiently addressing development and deployment challenges of emerging technologies such as SOA, virtualization, and commoditization of resources to support real-world business applications. Cory's expertise with high-performance transactional applications has helped leading IT organizations respond to the challenges of dramatic growth in business and data volumes, while still managing cost pressures. Most recently, Cory has been an active evangelist on the need for using concurrent processing and scalable database techniques in order to improve application performance on multi-core architectures.

Cory received his B.A. degree from the University of California at Santa Barbara.

Introduction

Throughout IT history, professional developers have searched for ways to enhance the performance of critical business applications. The computer industry has tried to provide the answer time and time again, and we've seen plenty of solutions, architectures, and approaches. Obviously, the problem is not a minor one. In today's information-based economy, companies often succeed or fail because of their software performance. There are abundant examples: banking systems, trading systems, call center operations, reporting services, and many others—they all depend on applications with high-performance requirements. In these industries, viability is directly tied to the speed at which a company conducts business. A slow, inadequate, or unresponsive application is damaging to operations and the bottom line; ultimately, it can literally kill or impair the organization that relies on it. And there is no end in sight; as we depend more and more on the exchange of information to do business, performance will lag behind demand even further.

There's an additional problem. Simply achieving faster performance of individual components isn't always enough. If your company installs a new application, if your business expands, or if your data volume rises, you may suddenly need an order-of-magnitude increase in performance—five, ten, twenty times or more.

Another vector is also critical: How fast can you adapt your software to meet new needs and competitive threats? The popularity and rapid adoption of service-oriented architecture (SOA) is hard evidence of the demand for more flexible software systems.

SOA is a superior technology. Compared to earlier trends in IT architecture, SOA delivers better on its promises. But it presents its own challenges. If you're using SOA for development, it's even more important to address performance and scalability, because of the following factors:

- In general observation, SOA demands significantly more computing power from a system than earlier monolithic or tightly coupled designs.

- The very notion of loosely coupled services implies message-centric application development. Developers not only have to write traditional processing logic; they also have to handle message transmission, validation, interpretation, and generation—all of which are CPU- and process-intensive.
- As more organizations use SOA, we can expect messaging volume to explode and put a tremendous load on existing IT systems. The potential for adverse effects will escalate.

Predictions show that over the next year or two, organizations using SOA will run into performance issues. This is nothing new; historically, each time the business world adopts a new software architecture, it suffers through growing pains. In the past twenty years, the shakeout period for each new major paradigm shift in software development has lasted about one to three years for a given evolutionary phase (any early J2EE user can attest to that). During that time, businesses gradually adopt the new design, and while doing so, they face significant performance- and scalability-related problems. In many cases software developers cannot overcome the steep learning curve; many projects end in outright failure when the deployed application doesn't perform as expected.

Until recently, hardware was the saving grace for such immature architectures. Whenever the computer industry made a significant advance, mostly in CPU performance, performance bottlenecks could be fixed by plugging in a faster chip or by using some other mechanical solution. That advantage is now gone. We've hit a plateau in microprocessor technology, which comes from physical factors such as power consumption, heat generation, and quantum mechanics. The industry can no longer easily increase the clock speed of single CPUs. Therefore, for now and the foreseeable future, CPU vendors are relying on multi-core designs to increase horsepower. The catch is that if you want to take advantage of these new multi-core chips, your software must implement parallel processing—not a common capability in the majority of today's applications.

Let's sum up what today's businesses really need from their software architecture:

- A practical approach to parallel processing, for performance and scalability
- Flexibility, to enable the business to adapt to market and other environmental changes

Creating an application with these characteristics is not easy, especially when using traditional means. Further, making such a paradigm shift work in the real world requires the talent, business knowledge, and technical expertise of the professional developer. In short, the professional developer needs a set of tools designed to meet these objectives, enabling a new level of parallel processing for *business* applications.

Therefore, what is needed is a flexible, sensible, and practical approach to parallel processing. The Software Pipelines technology was developed to be that approach, offering the professional developer a usable set of tools and capabilities to enable scalable processing for today's competitive business application environment.

What Do People Think about Parallel Processing?

As part of our research for this book, we wanted to find out what the software community thinks about parallel processing, so we conducted a statistical analysis of associated Web documents. Our analysis tool compares the usage of terms in Web documents, along with their frequency, in order to indicate the overall trend for a given subject. The results are intriguing; they confirm the importance of parallel processing as a solution for modern computing challenges.

To run the analysis, we based our search on the subject "software" and looked for references to related terms in the context of that subject. We started with the following terms:

- Multi-core
- Multi-threaded
- Parallel processing
- Parallel programming

We've included several charts in this section to show you the results. The first chart, Figure I.1, shows how often people use each term. As you can see, *parallel programming* is the most popular term, followed by *multi-core*, and then *parallel processing*. This gives us a good idea of how the software community talks about the subject.

To get a more detailed query, we cross-linked each term with the following attributes:

- Complex
- Hard
- Important
- Knowledge
- Useful

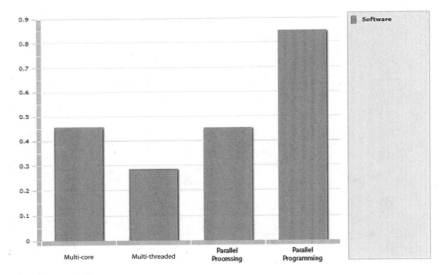

Figure I.1 Software query

In Figure I.2 you can see the relationship of each attribute to *parallel processing*. Parallel processing is perceived as "useful" and "important," its two strongest attributes.

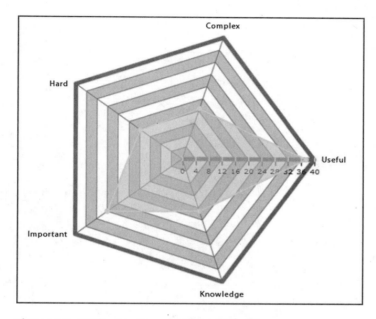

Figure I.2 Attributes for *parallel processing*

Figure I.3 shows *parallel programming* and its attributes. Parallel programming is definitely "important," but a high percentage of documents also mention that it is "hard." It's interesting that "knowledge" has a high rank, which is not surprising, given the difficulty of parallel programming and the general lack of experience with its techniques.

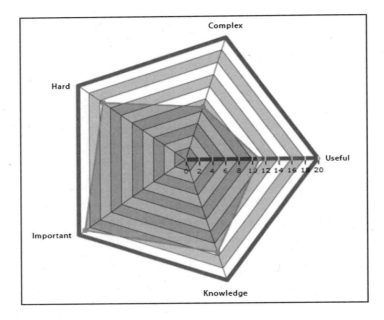

Figure I.3 Attributes for *parallel programming*

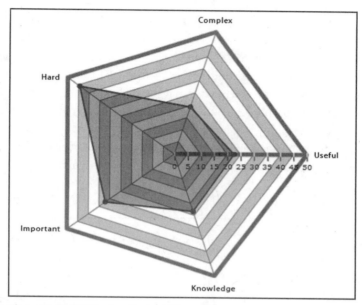

Figure I.4 Attributes for *multi-core*

Figures I.4 and I.5 show the attributes for *multi-core* and then *multi-threaded*. Both charts show responses similar to what we found for *parallel programming*.

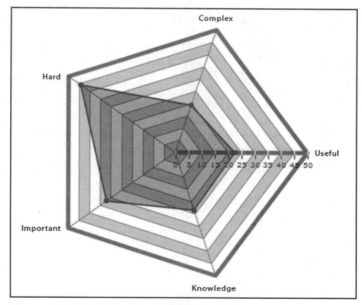

Figure I.5 Attributes for *multi-threaded*

In Figure I.6 we've included a chart with all terms and attributes to show the relative strength of each combination. You can see that parallel processing is considered "useful," and that parallel programming is both "important" and "hard."

What conclusion could you draw from all of this? It appears that people who talk about software are saying that parallel processing is important, but it's not easy. We're hoping we can help make it easier. The goal of Software Pipelines, and our goal in writing this book, is to provide a practical and useful set of techniques to address the challenge, and our intention is that you will find it helpful in your own application development and business management.

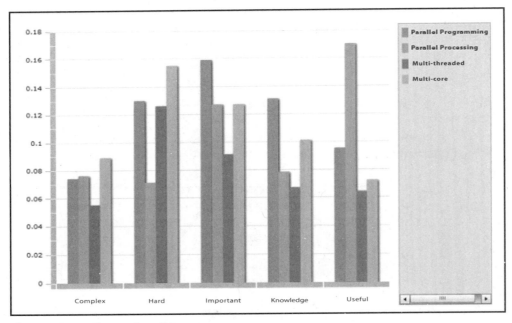

Figure I.6 Attributes for all terms

Pipelines Theory

The first section of this book covers the fundamentals of Software Pipelines.

In Chapter 1, "Parallel Computing and Business Applications," we investigate the existing methods for parallel processing. This beginning discussion is useful as a frame of reference for comparing Software Pipelines to other technologies with which you're familiar. After that, we introduce you to the most basic principles of the pipelines architecture, and then we present our first example of a pipelined application.

The following chapter, "Pipelines Law," describes the basic theory of pipelines and explains how to "do the math" for predicting and managing pipelines performance. We introduce Pipelines Law by drawing an analogy to fluid dynamics, a long-standing engineering discipline that provides insights into gauging the performance of business transaction applications. From these simple principles you'll get the tools for modeling your own applications and for identifying areas where you can improve performance.

Chapter 3, "Pipelines Examples," contains a simplified automated teller machine (ATM) example. We use this basic example to show you how the theoretical foundation fits into a real-world application. In later sections we expand the banking application concept to more detailed, advanced examples.

We've included a number of common, useful patterns for pipelines implementations in Chapter 4, "Pipelines Patterns." You can implement Software Pipelines in many ways. In this chapter you'll learn about several aspects and their options. Later in the book we cover these patterns in much more detail. You'll learn how they work and how you can apply them to solve various problems in performance and scalability.

In the final chapter of the section, "Pipelines: The Organizational Impact," we present the issues with which IT and business organizations must deal when using Software Pipelines technology. We cover all the critical points, including strategy, resources, and budget.

## CHAPTER ONE

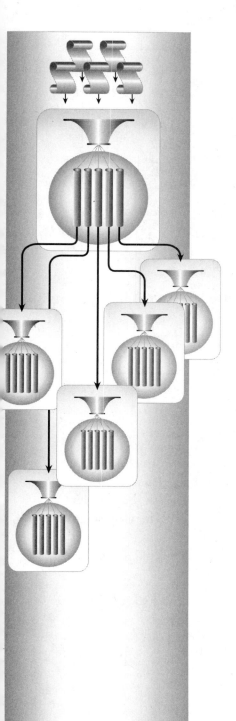

Parallel Computing and Business Applications

If you own, manage, or work with a critical business application, you're most likely dealing with performance problems. The application can't handle the ever-increasing data volume, it can't scale to meet new demand, or its performance is never good enough or fast enough. You need a higher level of performance; or even more daunting, you may need an order-of-magnitude increase so you can multiply the number of transactions your application can handle. In today's computing environment, there's really only one way to get there: Utilize a parallel architecture to run multiple tasks at the same time.

The fundamental concept of parallel architecture is this: Given a series of tasks to perform, divide those tasks into discrete elements, some or all of which can be processed at the same time on a set of computing resources. Figure 1.1 illustrates this process.

To do this, you have to break the application into a series of steps, some of which can run in parallel. However, that's really hard to do if you're working with existing business applications that do not lend themselves to such decomposition. Whether monolithic or object-oriented, most modern applications are tightly coupled, and that makes it hard to decompose a given process into steps.

Over the years, computer scientists have performed extensive research into parallel architecture and they've developed many techniques, but until now they focused on techniques that don't easily lend themselves to busi-

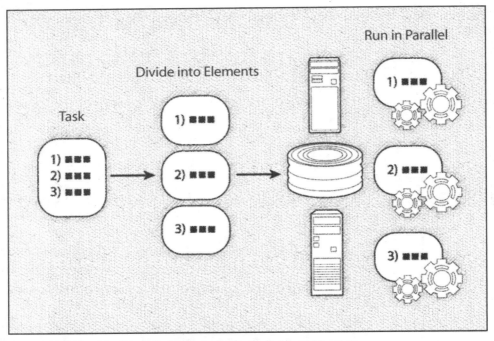

Figure 1.1 The fundamental concept of parallel architecture

ness systems. At the same time, demand for greater performance started over-reaching the limit of most business applications, and the recent trend toward a service-oriented approach has made the challenge even greater. Parallel processing can fix the problem, but common existing techniques are either too complex to adapt to typical business transactions, or they don't even apply to the business arena.

Before we show you the solution, let's look at the existing techniques for parallel computing. The three main approaches are

- Mechanical solutions used at the operating system level, such as symmetric multiprocessing (SMP) and clustering
- Automated network routing, such as round-robin distribution of requests
- Software-controlled grid computing

Mechanical Solutions: Parallel Computing at the Operating System Level

Symmetric Multiprocessing

SMP automatically distributes application tasks onto multiple processors inside a single physical computer; the tasks share memory and other hardware resources. This approach is highly efficient and easy to implement, because you don't need specific, detailed knowledge of how SMP divides the workload.

Mechanical solutions such as SMP are very useful as generic one-size-fits-all techniques. To get the most out of SMP, however, you have to write applications with multi-threaded logic. This is a tricky job at best and is not, in general, the forte of most corporate IT developers. Plus, SMP is a black-box approach, which can make it very difficult to debug resource contention. For example, if you have shared software components and run into a problem, finding the cause of the bug may be very hard and time-consuming.

There's another drawback: Resource sharing between processors is tightly coupled and is not optimized for any particular application. This puts a lid on potential performance gain, and when you start scaling an application, shared resources will bottleneck at some point. So you might scale an application to eight processors with great results, but when you go to 16, you don't see any real gain in performance.

Clustering

In clustering, another widely used mechanical solution, separate physical computers share the workload of an application over a network. This technique provides some capabilities for automatic parallel processing and is often used for fail-over and redundancy.

Clustering techniques are automated and contain some inefficient functionality. If you're not using centralized resources, the system has to copy critical information (or in some cases, *all* information) from one node to another whenever a change in state occurs, which can become a serious bottleneck. As is the case with SMP, clustering is often effective up to a point—then adding hardware results in severely diminished returns.

Automated Network Routing: Parallel Computing by Predetermined Logic

In this technique you use some type of predetermined logic to divide application requests. One common approach is round-robin routing, where the system distributes requests evenly, one after the next, among a set of physical computers. Each computer provides exactly the same application functionality. A good example and use case for round-robin is a Web application, in which the system shunts each Web page request to one of several available processors.

Although this approach is useful for certain applications and can be useful as part of a Software Pipelines design, it is also very limited; the router has no logic for determining the best route for a given request, and all downstream processors perform identical tasks. Further, business applications often demand strict "order of processing" requirements, something that simple round-robin logic cannot accommodate.

Grid Computing: Parallel Computing by Distribution

All of the techniques covered so far have their uses, but you can't use them for massive scalability, and they don't work for transaction-based, message-oriented applications. You can scale them mechanically and automatically to a certain level, at which point the overhead of maintaining shared or redundant resources limits performance gains. If you need greater scalability, grid computing is a better choice.

In grid computing the system distributes discrete tasks across many machines in a network. Typical grid architecture includes a centralized task scheduler, which distributes and coordinates tasks with other computing facilities across the network.

Grid computing can deliver far higher throughput than the automated approaches described earlier, but it puts a significant burden on the developer. You must explicitly write the code for dividing tasks, for distributing tasks, and for reassembling the processed results.

Most importantly, grid computing is primarily designed to solve the "embarrassingly parallel" problem—long-running, computation-intensive processes as found in scientific or engineering applications. Grids are very beneficial for the typical use cases, such as modeling fluid dynamics, tracing the human genome, and complex financial analytics simulations. In each of these applications you divide a massive, long-running computation among multiple nodes. This divides the problem into smaller, similar tasks, which interact predictably with computational resources. However, this is not as useful for business applications, given their transactional nature, mixed workload requirements, and ever-changing volume demands.

Parallel Computing for Business Applications

Business applications are very different from engineering or scientific applications. They have the following traits:

- They process transactions.
- They process tasks with mixed workloads. Quite often you can't predict the size of each task, or what the processing requirements might be.
- The workload varies widely throughout a given time period. It might even change from day to day, or from one hour to the next.
- They often have requirements that defy the very concept of performing multiple tasks in parallel. For example, first in/first out (FIFO) transactions (which are very commonly used) must be done in an exact, ordered sequence.
- They almost always use a database or other centralized resource that bottlenecks and caps off transaction throughput.

Up to now, research on parallel computing concentrated mostly on mechanical solutions with limited scalability, or on grid-based scientific and engineering applications that lie outside the business domain. What we need is a new, simpler way to implement parallel computing for businesses. This new approach must support the following requirements:

- It must handle a wide variety of business application needs.
- It must provide ultimate scalability.
- It must maintain critical business requirements.
- It must be easy to implement by corporate IT developers.

In reality, there's no automagic answer for scaling business applications, because each organization has very different needs and requirements. The ultimate solution requires the right tools, architecture, and approach, and it must focus on business applications. But more importantly, the solution requires the expertise of the professional developer—the invaluable corporate resource who possesses both a full understanding of the technology and an intimate knowledge of the business domain.

The challenge of finding a business-oriented approach to parallel processing is answered by Software Pipelines. The architecture is highly scalable and flexible. It executes business services independent of location, and in such a way as to maximize throughput on available computing resources, while easily meeting a vast array of complex business application requirements.

The Solution: Software Pipelines

Imagine the ideal implementation for a business environment:

> You can divide any application process or portion of a process into discrete tasks or services and perform them anywhere in a given network (local or remote), in parallel with other tasks whenever possible. You can define the granularity of tasks to fit the specific needs of each application; the size can range from coarse-grained (such as Web services) down to fine-grained (such as class/method calls). In addition, the system optimizes resource utilization of all available facilities, because it dynamically shifts available resources to handle current demand.

The idea is simple, but the details are often complex, with a multitude of potential variations and design patterns. The solution is Software Pipelines architecture, which supports the following features and capabilities:

- You can decompose business processes into specific tasks, then execute them in parallel.
- It has virtually unlimited peer-to-peer scalability.
- It's easier on the developer because it provides an easy method for distributing and executing tasks in parallel—on one server, or across many servers.
- It's specifically designed for business applications, particularly those that use, or can use, SOA.
- It handles a high volume of transactions, both large and small, and is therefore ideal for mixed-workload processing.
- The design gives you control of throughput and task distribution, which means that you can maximize your computing resources.
- You can scale upward by using parallel architecture, while still guaranteeing the order of processing—a key business requirement in many mission-critical applications. This is a huge benefit over previous approaches.
- Because the architecture supports so many configurations and patterns, you can create a wide variety of application designs.

These features also allow you to take full advantage of today's multi-core processors, distributing transactions within and across servers at will.

The fundamental component in Software Pipelines is the pipeline itself, defined as follows:

> An execution facility for invoking the discrete tasks of a business process in an order-controlled manner. You can control the order by using priority, order of message input (for example, FIFO), or both.

Essentially, a pipeline is a control mechanism that receives and performs delegated tasks, with the option of then delegating tasks in turn to other pipelines in the system as required. This means you can use pipelines as building blocks to create an unlimited variety of configurations for accomplishing your specific application objectives.

You can group multiple pipelines into fully distributed, peer-to-peer pools; each pipeline processes a portion of an application or process. And because you can configure each pool to run on a specific local or remote server, the system can execute tasks anywhere on a network.

A pipeline can route tasks to other pipelines through a Pipeline Distributor, its companion component. The Pipeline Distributor is defined as follows:

> A virtual routing facility for distributing a given service request to the appropriate pipeline (which in turn executes the request) within a pipeline pool. The distributor is colocated with its pool of pipelines and effectively front-ends incoming service requests.
>
> The distributor routes service requests by evaluating message content. Routing is based on configuration rules, which you can easily modify without changing individual business services. You can route requests by using priority, order of message input (such as FIFO), or both.

In Figure 1.2 you can see how pipelines work with distributors. Requests go to the first distributor, which splits them off onto three pipelines. The second pipeline delegates a request to the third pipeline, and the third pipeline sends a request to another distributor, which in turn splits requests onto five pipelines.

By using pipeline and distributor components, you can build a fully distributed, multilevel series of interlinked pipelines—and achieve massive scalability through parallel processing.

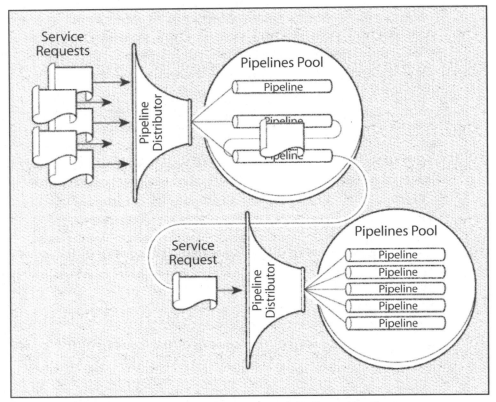

Figure 1.2 The Pipeline Distributor and its relationship to pipelines

Fluid Dynamics

It's easy to visualize Software Pipelines by comparing them to a network of hydraulic pipelines, which transport and direct the delivery of water or oil. Such a system has physical limitations:

- The input source delivers a particular maximum volume to downstream resources.
- Each downstream pipeline or receptacle (including subsidiary downstream pipelines and downstream destinations that process the delivered stream) must accommodate the input volume, or the entire system backs up.

In other words, all channels in the system must accommodate the maximum volume of flow. If they can't, the flow stops or slows down, or even breaks the system.

The same principles apply to Software Pipelines, but it's far easier to avoid bottlenecks. All you have to do is move some of the processing load to other pipelines. The example in the next section shows how to do this.

Software Pipelines Example

To show you how Software Pipelines work, we'll use a banking example. A large bank has a distributed network of ATMs, which access a centralized resource to process account transactions. Transaction volume is highly variable, response times are critical, and key business rules must be enforced—all of which make the bank's back-end application an ideal use case for parallel pipelines. We must apply the following business requirements:

- Make sure each transaction is performed by an authorized user.
- Make sure each transaction is valid. For example, if the transaction is a withdrawal, make sure the account has sufficient funds to handle the transaction.
- Guarantee that multiple transactions on each account are performed sequentially. The bank wants to prevent any customer from overdrawing his or her account by using near-simultaneous transactions. Therefore, FIFO order is mandatory for withdrawal transactions.

Before we cover pipeline design, let's take a look at the traditional design for a monolithic, tightly coupled, centralized software component. You can see the main flow for this design in Figure 1.3.

The simplicity of this design has several benefits:

- It's very easy to implement.
- All business rules are in a single set of code.
- Sequence of transactions is guaranteed.

However, this design forces every user transaction to wait for any previous transactions to complete. If the volume of transactions shoots up (as it does in peak periods) and the input flow outstrips the load capacity of this single component, a lot of customers end up waiting for their transactions to process. All too often, waiting customers mean lost customers—an intolerable condition for a successful bank.

To use Software Pipelines to solve this problem, we'll do a pipeline analysis. The first step is to divide the process into logical units of parallel work. We'll start by decomposing the steps required for processing. Figure 1.4 shows the steps of the ATM process.

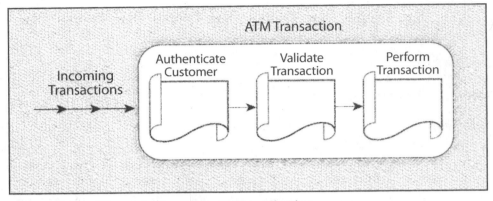

Figure 1.3 Traditional design for an ATM application

The steps are

- Authenticate the user (customer).
- Ensure the transaction is valid. For example, if the transaction is a with-drawal, make sure the account has sufficient funds to handle the transaction.
- Process the transaction and update the ATM daily record for the account.

Now that we understand the steps of the business process, we can identify the pipelines we'll use for parallel processing. To do this, we determine which portions of the business process can execute in parallel.

For the initial ATM design (Figure 1.5), it seems safe to authenticate users in a separate pipeline. This task performs its work in a separate system, and after it

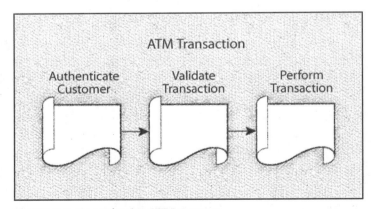

Figure 1.4 Steps in the ATM process

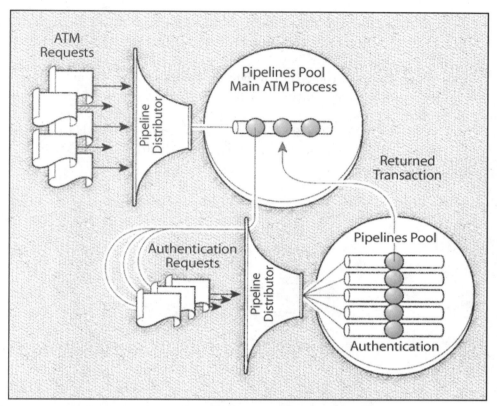

Figure 1.5 Initial pipeline design: Distribute the authentication step.

returns the authentication, the process can perform the next two steps. In fact, because we're not concerned with ordering at this stage, it's safe to use multiple pipelines for this single task. Our goal is simply to process as many authentications as we can per unit of time, regardless of order.

This design speeds up the process, but most of the work—updating the ATM accounts—is still a serial process. You'll still get bottlenecks, because the updating step is downstream from the authentication step. To improve performance by an order of magnitude, we'll analyze the process further. We want to find other places where the process can be optimized, while still enforcing the key business rules.

After authenticating a user, the next step is to validate the requested transaction. The application does this by evaluating the user's current account information. Business requirements allow us to perform multiple validations at the same time, as long as we don't process any two transactions for the same account at the same time or do them out of sequence. This is a FIFO requirement, a key bottleneck in parallel business applications. Our first configuration with the single pipeline guarantees compliance with this requirement; but we want to distribute the process, so we need a parallel solution that also supports the FIFO requirement.

The key to the solution is the use of multiple pipelines, as shown in Figure 1.6. We assign a segment of the incoming transactions to each of several pipe-

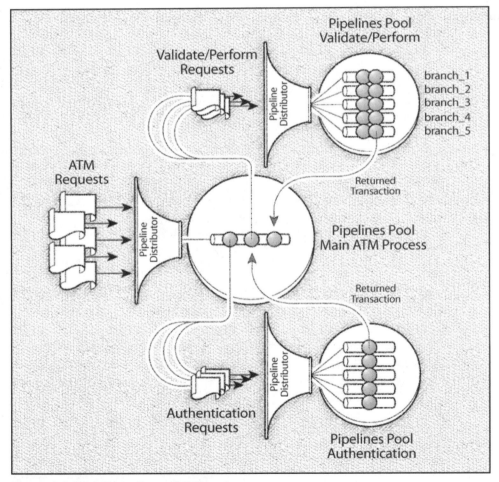

Figure 1.6 Distribute the validation step.

lines. Each pipeline maintains FIFO order, but we use content-based distribution to limit the pipeline's load to a small subset of the entire number of transactions.

To implement the new design, we create a pipeline for each branch of the bank (named branch_1 through branch_5), so that each pipeline controls a subset of accounts. We want the pipelines to handle delegated transactions sequentially, so we specify FIFO order for the new pipelines.

The Pipeline Distributor checks the branch ID in each transaction (which is an example of content-based distribution), then sends the transaction to the matching pipeline.

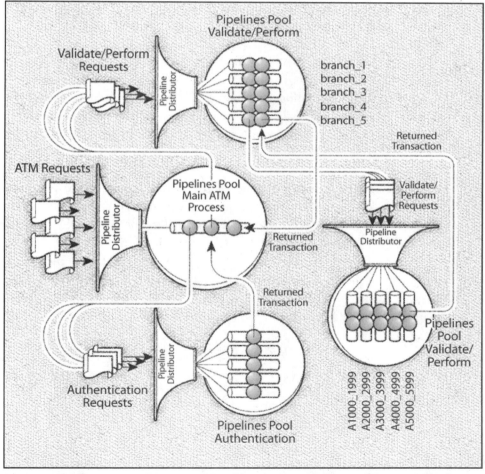

Figure 1.7 Scale the application further by adding downstream pipelines.

Now, by processing many branches in parallel, the system completes many more transactions per unit of time.

You can use this approach to scale the application up even further, as shown in Figure 1.7. Let's assume the bank has a very large branch with more than 100,000 accounts. The branch's peak transaction volume overloads the previous pipeline configuration, so we create additional downstream pipelines. The distributor divides the transactions by using a range of account numbers (A1000_1999, A2000_2999, etc.).

At this point, whenever the bank's business increases, it's a simple matter to build additional pipeline structures to accommodate the increased volume.

To sum up, the ATM example illustrates how you can use Software Pipelines to increase process performance by an order of magnitude. It's a simple example, but the basic principles can be used in many other applications.

Summary

Many of today's organizations are facing a hard reality: In order to meet current demand, their business applications must increase performance by an order of magnitude. And over time the problem only gets more severe—the business sector depends more and more on data, so demand is going to accelerate, not slow down.

In order to meet such daunting requirements, the capability of performing multiple tasks in parallel becomes vital. We have many solutions for improving application performance, but we've never had the technology to create a parallel software environment specifically for business applications.

Software Pipelines architecture answers this challenge at every point. It was designed specifically for business, you can easily scale your application to any size, you can maximize your resources, and best of all, you can do all this and still maintain critical business transaction and integrity requirements.

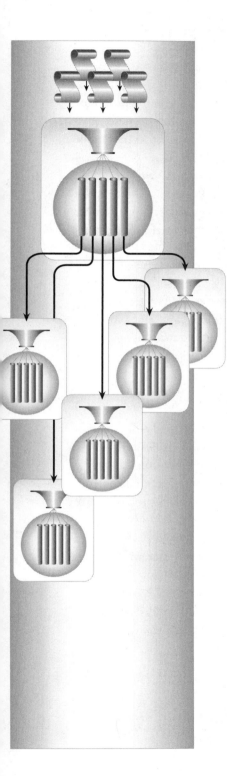

## CHAPTER TWO

Pipelines Law

In the preceding chapter we explained the basics of Software Pipelines. We defined the pipeline and the Pipeline Distributor, and we showed you how to put these components together to create a multilevel hierarchy.

You also learned that Software Pipelines have an interesting similarity to a physical system of hydraulic pipes. In this chapter we further explore that analogy by showing how Pipelines Law, the basic laws of fluid dynamics, translates to Software Pipelines Rules, which you can use to analyze, predict, and optimize the performance of a system.

Although Software Pipelines solutions will vary from application to application, you need to deal with three basic questions for any pipelines application:

- How do I use pipelines to accelerate performance?
- How can I predict and optimize pipelines performance?
- What are the best ways to minimize the constraints and limitations of pipelines?

The basic laws and rules resolve these three questions, and understanding them is key to the development of successful Software Pipelines applications.

The Problem of Wasted CPU Power

"All processors wait at the same speed." That's a famous saying, as old as information technology itself. It describes

17

a fundamental limit on computing performance and usually refers to the hardware limits on a CPU, such as I/O.

As it turns out, this statement is also true for software, and even more so for today's high-performance applications. Many businesses use only 25 percent of their CPU capacity. The reported industry average is even lower, at 15 percent. If you're using multi-core CPUs (with two, eight, or even 32 CPU cores per physical chip), you've got even more unused capacity. Theoretically, this means you could more than quadruple your performance and throughput—if you could find a way to use the other 75 to 85 percent. So, the burning question is: If you can use only a fraction of your *existing* computing power, how can you ever use the vastly expanded capacity of modern hardware?

Using more of your CPU capacity relates to the key goal of every application developer: how to get maximum throughput. When a processor isn't busy, it's waiting while other resources work, it isn't productive, and it creates a performance bottleneck. Reducing the wait time improves throughput and puts your idle processors to work. If you understand Pipelines Law, you can use Software Pipelines to do this.

Fluid Dynamics

You might be familiar with Amdahl's Law,[1] a mathematical formula that predicts to what extent multiple processors can speed up a system. IT professionals have used it since the mid-1960s to predict the performance and limitations of parallel systems, but it's not very easy to apply directly to business application problems. Amdahl's principles apply mostly to the "embarrassingly parallel" problem, or to low-level chip and operating system architectures.

Pipelines Law is similar to Amdahl's Law, but it includes concepts from fluid dynamics—the science of moving fluid through a physical system of pipes. There's a direct parallel between fluid dynamics and software systems, which makes Pipelines Law ideal for analyzing business applications *and* for explaining the principles of Software Pipelines. In the next sections we'll use that analogy to show you how to predict and optimize a Software Pipelines system.

---

[1] See http://en.wikipedia.org/wiki/Amdahl%27s_law for more information about Amdahl's Law.

Pipelines Law: The Basic Rule

In fluid dynamics, the first and most important rule is

Inflow equals outflow.

This is obvious enough, but it is nonetheless your first step when designing a Software Pipelines system. A pipe of a certain size can never output more fluid than its input supply. The inflow volume and rate determine the maximum possible outflow from a system of pipes. Figure 2.1 shows several pipes of different sizes and flow volumes. If a pipe's diameter is too small for the entire inflow, its outflow is restricted.

For Software Pipelines, we can translate this first rule as

Input equals output.

Think of a computing system as a flow of transactions. The rate of input transactions is the raw material for a pipeline. This first rule means you can never process, or output, more transactions than your available input supply.

In practice, input and output transaction rates will always be the same, but let's take this idea further. We know the potential output rate will never exceed the available input rate. Therefore, the input rate is the maximum number of transactions we can process. Of course, one input transaction can generate multiple output transactions. However, the rule still applies; you can't process more than the available number of transactions.

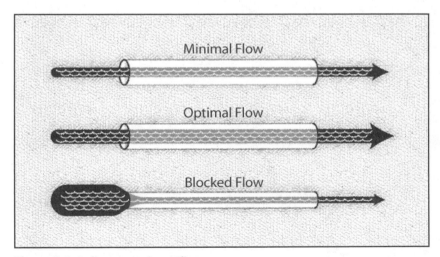

Figure 2.1 Inflow equals outflow.

A system isn't efficient unless it has an adequate supply of input transactions to process. When you design a concurrent processing system, you can determine its potential value by asking, "Are there enough transactions available to justify concurrent processing in the first place?"

Corollary 1: Limitations on the Flow

One of the most important points to understand about a pipeline system is how the flow can be limited. If you can observe and predict the things that might inhibit the flow in a system, you can change its design to fix the problem, and there's a better chance the system will perform as expected. So, the first corollary to the basic rule is

Friction and restriction limit the flow.

Any restriction in a pipe limits the overall flow of fluid through the system and restricts and reduces both inflow and outflow. Restrictions are caused by crimps and bends in a pipe. In Figure 2.2 you can see that a reduced diameter in a pipe restricts the flow.

We can directly translate this corollary into rules for Software Pipelines. If any single component in the middle of a system can't process transactions fast enough to keep up with the input flow, the processing rate of the entire system is reduced accordingly. In other words, the processing rate is always limited by the slowest component in the system.

When a single component can't keep up, transactions back up on the input side. If that goes on long enough, you'll run out of memory or disk space and the system will crash. Therefore, you must evaluate the performance of each compo-

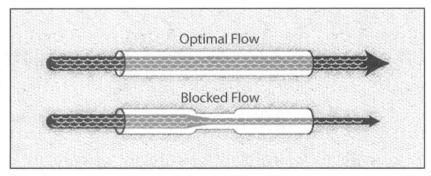

Figure 2.2 Friction and restriction limit the flow.

Figure 2.3 Unwanted debris blocks a flow.

nent in a Software Pipelines application, then balance all components for overall optimum flow. Without this step, optimization of one component might create a bottleneck farther downstream in the system.

Corollary 2: Restrictions on the Output Flow

Another corollary that explains limited flow is

Restriction of the outflow reduces the overall flow.

In a system of pipelines, if anything restricts the output flow, it restricts all flow of fluid through the system.

There's more than one way to restrict an output flow. If unwanted debris gets stuck in the output pipe, as in Figure 2.3, it partially or totally blocks the flow.

Another example is a full reservoir at the end of the pipe system, as in Figure 2.4. If the reservoir overflows, the entire system backs up and the flow stops.

In other words, anything that restricts the output side of a fluid pipeline adversely affects the entire flow.

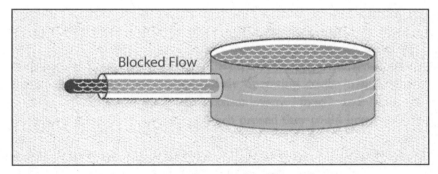

Figure 2.4 A full reservoir overflows and backs up the system.

This rule is also true for a software system. Every developer has seen what happens when an application must use a centralized, external component that can't handle the load. For example, a mainframe system is the final repository for processed transactions, but it's too slow to accommodate the input from many sources. Other common examples are a centralized relational database that can't keep up with transaction rates, and worse, a database that runs out of disk space or becomes locked and simply stops receiving transactions at all.

In each of these cases, the processing rate of the entire system is either hampered or stopped completely. When this happens, transactions back up, users wait, and in some cases the entire application crashes. If you're running a mission-critical business application, that's a sure recipe for disaster.

Software Pipelines Rules

Now that you understand the basics of fluid dynamics, let's take a look at the rules for Software Pipelines:

Rule 1: Input equals output.

Rule 2: The capacity (transaction rate) of any downstream component or process must be greater than or equal to the input rate of any upstream process or component. When this is not the case, you must optimize the downstream component or process, or you must use a Pipeline Distributor to support concurrent processing and handle the load.

Rule 3: The processing rate of the Pipeline Distributor must be far greater than the downstream processing rate.

In the following sections we'll look at each of these rules in more detail. You'll also learn some simple formulas for analyzing a Software Pipelines system.

Rule 1

Input equals output.

This is, of course, Pipelines Law itself, and you can apply everything you learned about Pipelines Law to the design of a Software Pipelines system. To use Rule 1 in your design, do the following actions:

- Make sure an adequate supply of input transactions is available. This justifies the use of Software Pipelines in the first place.

- Identify the slowest component or process in the system. That component/ process governs the overall throughput and performance of the system, so you must optimize it.
- Identify any external system or application that cannot handle the load. That system/application causes a bottleneck, just like a slow component or process, so you must optimize it.
- Predict and remove any other bottlenecks in the system. To do this, identify all the other components in your system. Analyze the performance characteristics of each one, then if necessary optimize it.

The formula for Rule 1 is

$$InputRate = OutputRate$$

InputRate and *OutputRate* will always be the same, no matter how many transactions you process. In other words, a Software Pipelines system, or any software system, can't accept more transactions (*InputRate*) than it can process (*OutputRate*). Another, and more useful, way to say this is

$$AvailableInputRate = PotentialOutputRate$$

For example, if the *AvailableInputRate* is ten transactions per second (TPS), the downstream process can never output more than ten TPS, no matter how fast it processes those transactions.

Let's look at this from the output side. If *AvailableInputRate* is 1000 TPS or better, you can easily determine the *PotentialOutputRate*; it's also 1000 TPS. However, what if the downstream process can output only 500 TPS? You'll get a backlog of queued or lost transactions to the tune of 500 TPS, definitely far from ideal.

In the next section we'll show how to use Software Pipelines Rule 2 to fix the potential bottleneck caused by a slower downstream process.

Rule 2

The capacity (transaction rate) of any downstream component or process must be greater than or equal to the input rate of any upstream process or component. When this is not the case, you must optimize the downstream component or process, or you must use a Pipeline Distributor to support concurrent processing and handle the load.

If you want maximum performance, or have to meet service-level agreements and business requirements, this rule is the key to your success. You can use it to analyze every single point in a Software Pipelines system and identify existing or potential bottlenecks. You can also use it to determine whether you need more capacity. If you do need more capacity, you can use a Pipeline Distributor to add concurrent processing.

The formula for Rule 2 is

$$\text{InputRate must be} <= \text{ProcessRate}$$

In other words, the downstream *ProcessRate* for any component or process must be able to accommodate the *InputRate* of any upstream component or process that supplies transactions. When this is not the case, you must increase the *ProcessRate* by using multiple pipelines or by using another type of optimization.

Consider the simple flow of components in Figure 2.5.

In this example, Step B is the bottleneck. Transactions queue up and backlog when they leave Step A and go to Step B. This cuts down the flow of transactions into Step C, and Step C is underutilized. Furthermore, if there's no buffer in which transactions can queue up before they get to Step B, you can lose transactions—an unacceptable consequence for mission-critical applications such as banking.

To balance the transaction flow, you must increase Step B's throughput. You can use pipelines distribution or some other type of optimization. If you don't

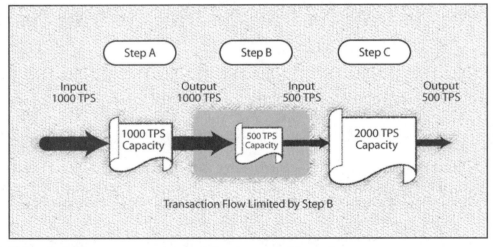

Figure 2.5 Downstream component causes a bottleneck.

handle it one way or the other, the entire flow will top out at Step B's capacity—500 TPS.

If it's safe to distribute Step B, you can simply create two pipelines for it, doubling its capacity, as shown in Figure 2.6. This will resolve the problem and balance the flow.

If you don't have enough hardware resources to handle the increased volume, creating the two pipelines might not double the capacity of Step B. To actually fix the problem, you might also have to add hardware. With two pipelines and sufficient hardware resources, you can take advantage of concurrent processing to double Step B's capacity.

However, if you want a truly effective solution, there's one more missing link: the Pipeline Distributor. Concurrent processing across multiple pipelines requires a way to distribute transactions. In the Software Pipelines architecture, the Pipeline Distributor does that job, across multiple hardware systems or among multiple processors on one system.

In Figure 2.7 you can see the Pipeline Distributor routing transactions and balancing the load for Step B. Figure 2.7 also shows the added hardware resources.

As you may recall from Chapter 1, the Pipeline Distributor routes input messages to individual pipelines. To determine where to send each message, it checks the content of the message, then sends it to the matching pipeline, which executes the transaction. This distributes the load and gives you much more control over

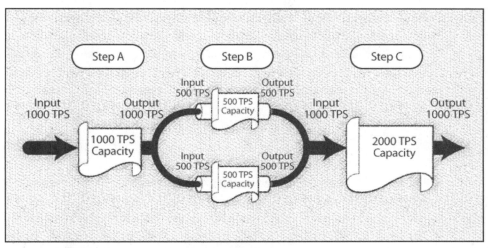

Figure 2.6 Increase capacity by using pipelines.

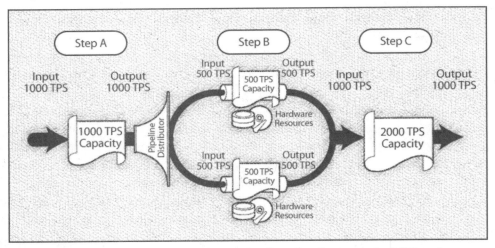

Figure 2.7 Increase capacity by using a Pipeline Distributor and additional hardware resources.

the flow of transactions. In addition, the distributor supports key business requirements, such as FIFO ordering or priority.

Another advantage of using a Pipeline Distributor is scalability. You can assign each pipeline to a specific hardware resource; the distributor sorts transactions into each pipeline, and each pipeline executes its transactions independently and concurrently with other pipelines. If lack of hardware becomes a bottleneck for a pipeline, you can add more resources to that pipeline. Because pipelines are completely independent of each other, adding more hardware resources along with more pipelines enables linear or near-linear scalability.

Taken to an extreme, adding more and more pipelines under a single distributor will eventually create a bottleneck at the Pipeline Distributor itself. In the next section we'll show you how to use Software Pipelines Rule 3 to avoid this problem.

Rule 3

The processing rate of the Pipeline Distributor must be far greater than the downstream processing rate.

To effectively implement a Pipeline Distributor, you must pay attention to Rule 3. The work of distribution always adds overhead to the system, so the Pipeline Distributor must perform its work much faster than the actual process it supplies.

The formula for Rule 3 is

$$DistributorRate \gg ProcessRate$$

In other words, the *DistributorRate* must be far greater than the downstream *ProcessRate*. If it isn't, the Pipeline Distributor will create a new bottleneck in itself, which defeats the entire purpose of the Software Pipelines architecture.

In Figure 2.8 the Pipeline Distributor must have a throughput capacity of at least 2000 TPS to avoid becoming a bottleneck. If it can process 2000 TPS, and it feeds four pipelines that each process 500 TPS, the system works well.

However, what happens if the distributor has very complex logic for routing transactions, so that it processes only 1000 TPS? As shown in Figure 2.9, this simply creates a bottleneck at the Pipeline Distributor. If this happens, there's no benefit from implementing pipelines, and the Pipeline Distributor wastes valuable resources.

You can run into the opposite problem if you distribute to too many pipelines. Assume again that the distributor can process 2000 TPS. However, instead of feeding four pipelines, it routes transactions to eight pipelines in Step B, as shown in Figure 2.10. In this case the distributor can feed only 250 TPS to each pipeline—but each pipeline is capable of processing 500 TPS. Again, this wastes resources, and you haven't optimized the system.

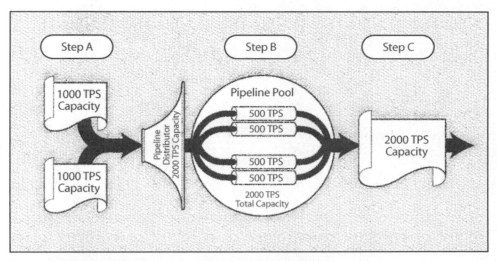

Figure 2.8 The well-balanced system has no bottlenecks.

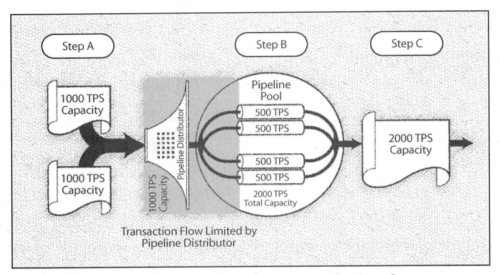

Figure 2.9   A distributor with complex logic can cause a bottleneck.

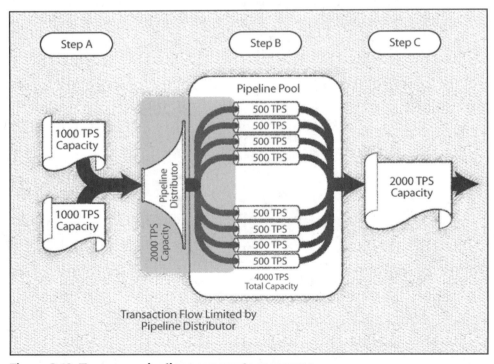

Figure 2.10   Too many pipelines can waste resources.

To avoid both of these problems, use the following formula to determine the optimum number of pipelines for any given part of a system:

$$NumberOfPipelines = DistributorTPS / ProcessTPS$$

NumberOfPipelines is the theoretical maximum number of downstream execution pipelines. You can also think of this as the subdivisions of a given process. *DistributorTPS* is the distribution rate (the rate of the Pipeline Distributor). *ProcessTPS* is the downstream processing rate (the total TPS of the downstream pipelines and components fed by the distributor). The ratio *DistributorTPS/ ProcessTPS* yields the ideal number of effective pipelines for this part of the system.

Of course, real-life systems demand some margin of error, so you should overdesign to some degree. Increase *NumberOfPipelines* by 10 to 20 percent to allow for error and to ensure adequate flow in the system. Used in this way, the *NumberOfPipelines* formula is an excellent guide for properly sizing and optimizing your system.

Let's take a look at a concrete example. If a Pipeline Distributor operates at 1000 TPS, and its downstream process operates at 100 TPS, the maximum number of pipelines is ten:

$$10 \; NumberOfPipelines = 1000 \; DistributorTPS / 100 \; downstream \; ProcessTPS$$

This system should perform up to ten times faster than a comparable system without Software Pipelines. Specifically, the system should process ten times the number of transactions in a given amount of time.

The *NumberOfPipelines* formula is designed to show you an important point: The system must supply transactions to downstream pipelines at a rate comparable to the rate at which they process or consume transactions. Otherwise, the pipelines simply wait as unproductive resources.

Therefore, in the worst possible scenario, if it takes longer for the distributor to evaluate and route one transaction than it does for the pipeline to execute it, you won't get any benefit from concurrent processing. In fact, the distributor just introduces unnecessary overhead into the process. Your goal, when designing a Software Pipelines application, is to minimize the latency of the distributor (increase *DistributorTPS*) while delegating as much work as possible to downstream pipelines.

One more point: Remember from Chapter 1 that you can create multiple levels of distributors and pipelines, where any pipeline can send transactions to another distributor. To get the most benefit from Software Pipelines architecture, it's important to apply Rule 3 and the *NumberOfPipelines* formula to *all* parts of your system.

Summary

Pipelines Law and the rules for Software Pipelines provide an easy, effective method for evaluating a Software Pipelines system. You can use them to predict and improve performance, improve throughput, and better utilize your hardware resources. If you add processors or processor cores while also applying these rules to your design, you can achieve linear or near-linear scalability.

Although other factors can limit performance, these rules provide the basic foundation for your design. We've seen them applied in actual practice, and they provide an excellent way to predict application performance.

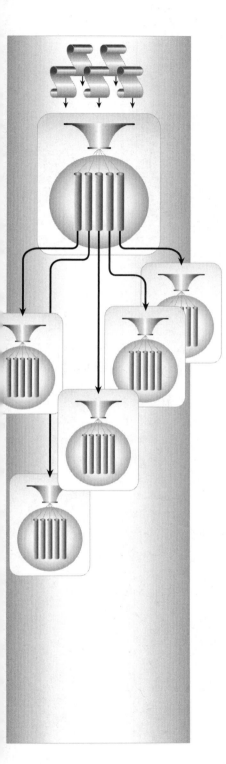

CHAPTER THREE

Pipelines Examples

In the previous chapter we described Pipelines Law—the fundamental rules and formulas for predicting and optimizing a pipelined system. In this chapter we use those concepts to solve some real-world problems, and you'll learn how to apply Software Pipelines Rules and formulas to each step of the design process

Bank ATM System (Single-Tier Distribution)

We'll use our bank ATM application again for the example problems. The main processing flow for each transaction in the ATM application is (1) authenticate the customer, (2) validate the transaction, and (3) perform the transaction, as shown in Figure 3.1.

An ATM application typically has the following critical requirements:

- It must handle a high (and often growing) volume of customers at many locations.
- It must prevent each customer from overdrawing his or her account.
- An ATM system is, by nature, a highly distributed system, so it's vital to maintain FIFO order when processing transactions. FIFO prevents any two users from accessing the same account and overdrawing available funds.

If we use Software Pipelines, we can design an application that will meet all these requirements.

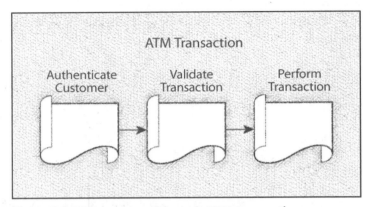

Figure 3.1 Main process for each ATM transaction

Pipelines

To apply pipelines to the ATM application, we need several specific metrics. The metrics help us determine how many pipelines to use. We can use actual measurements of the existing system, which is ideal, or we can use best estimates based on how we believe the system will perform.

In our first design step we'll compare the *InputRate* metric (the rate at which we expect to receive incoming transactions) to the *ProcessRate* metric (the rate of the application's main process). *InputRate* will vary, but we must design for peak loads. Assume the bank has 1000 ATM machines around the country, and, on average, it takes a customer 30 seconds to enter a transaction (insert the bank card, enter the PIN number, key in the transaction, etc.). We want to know the total number of transactions performed each second (TPS) across the whole system. To calculate that, let's first get the TPS for one transaction:

$$\text{One transaction / 30 seconds} = .033 \text{ TPS}$$

The TPS for one transaction is .033, and we have 1000 ATMs. Let's calculate the TPS for the whole system (we'll round it off):

$$\text{1000 ATMs in the system} * .033 \text{ TPS for one ATM} =$$
$$33 \text{ average TPS across the system}$$

Users don't submit their transactions at an even rate, so we'll double the average TPS (from 33 to 66) to cover the potential peak load. We now have our first metric, *InputRate*, which is 66 TPS.

For our second metric, *ProcessRate*, we'll use the TPS for the whole process flow—the authenticate, validate, and perform transaction steps. In other words, we estimate the time to perform the entire monolithic process (this is normally the easiest way to start implementing pipelines). Let's assume we tested the process code and discovered it takes 50 ms to perform. We use the same formula as before to calculate the TPS for one transaction and determine that *ProcessRate* is 20 TPS. We can now compare *InputRate* to *ProcessRate*:

66 TPS InputRate > 20 TPS ProcessRate

The metrics prove we have a bottleneck to handle, because the application violates Rule 2 (*InputRate* must be <= *ProcessRate*). To find out how many pipelines we need to fix the bottleneck and get acceptable performance, we calculate by how much *InputRate* exceeds *ProcessRate*:

66 TPS InputRate / 20 TPS ProcessRate = 3.3

The ratio tells us how many pipelines to use: 3.3. We want to allow for some cushion (about 20 percent), so let's round it up to four pipelines. In our next step we'll make sure the Pipeline Distributor can support this number of pipelines.

Pipeline Distributor

To implement the Pipeline Distributor, we must first decide how we want to split the transaction load among the four pipelines. Each incoming message contains values we can use to sort transactions into groups for routing. The distributor uses the selected value(s), which we'll call input keys, to choose the pipeline for each transaction.

The bank has 1000 branches, each with a `branch_id` numbered from 0001 to 1000, and each customer account (`account_no`) belongs to a particular branch. Since we need only four pipelines, we don't need very complex logic to sort transactions. Using the `branch_id` as the input key, we'll divide transactions into four groups (each group includes a range of branches) and assign an explicitly named pipeline to each group.

Next, we'll do some additional planning to ensure acceptable performance. The distributor must enforce FIFO order, which adds some overhead, so we don't want to use more pipelines than the distributor can handle. To calculate how many pipelines it supports, we use this formula:

NumberOfPipelines = DistributorRate / ProcessRate

We already know the *ProcessRate*. To complete the formula, we need the distributor's TPS, which we plug into *DistributorRate*. Before we calculate the distributor's TPS, let's learn more about its operation. It receives transactions as input messages in the following XML format:

```
<atmtrans>
  <branch_id>222</branch_id>
  <trans_date>01/01/2007</trans_date>
  <trans_time>15:41:01/trans_time>
  <account_no>11111111</account_no>
  <pin>0000</pin>
  <atm_id>456</atm_id>
  <trans_type>withdrawal</trans_type>
  <trans_amount>100.00</trans_amount>
  <currency>USD</currency>
</atmtrans>
```

The distributor's code is very simple; as each message arrives, the distributor parses the XML using a document object model (DOM) or other parsing mechanism, reads the message, then uses a case statement to evaluate the `branch_id` element. Then the distributor routes the transaction to the pipeline assigned to the range in which the `branch_id` falls.

Table 3.1 shows the transaction groups and pipeline names. The evaluation expressions are written in XPath notation.

Let's assume we tested or estimated the distribution algorithm, and we determined that its latency is 2 ms. When we calculate the distributor's TPS for one transaction, we get 500 TPS, which we use for *DistributorRate*. Now we can figure out the maximum number of pipelines:

Table 3.1 Transaction Groups and Pipeline Names

Pipeline Evaluation Expression	Pipeline Name
/atmtrans/[branch_id >= 0001 and branch_id <= 0250]	P_0001_to_0250
/atmtrans/[branch_id >= 0251 and branch_id <= 0500]	P_0251_to_0500
/atmtrans/[branch_id >= 0501 and branch_id <= 0750]	P_0501_to_0750
/atmtrans/[branch_id >= 0751 and branch_id <= 1000]	P_0751_to_1000

25 NumberOfPipelines = 500 TPS DistributorRate / 20 TPS ProcessRate

The distributor's maximum *NumberOfPipelines* is 25, so it can easily support four. We're now done with the high-level design, which appears in Figure 3.2.

The bank will be able to easily manage 1000 ATMs if we use this design for the actual application. To deploy it, we'll use a multi-core server. Since we have only four pipelines, a single CPU quad-core system should be adequate for the load.

Bank ATM System (Multi-Tier Distribution)

Now that we've seen a simple pipelines example and design, let's look at one that's a bit more challenging.

Assume that our pipelined ATM system runs well and performs as expected. We attend a special company meeting, and the executive team makes a surprise announcement: Our bank is merging with another retail bank that has 10,000 ATMs. Because our technology is SOA-based, and theirs is mainframe-based, they've selected our system to run everything for the newly combined bank. Great news—until we're told we have three months to make the switch! As if that wasn't enough, the team announces plans to acquire *more* banks over the next two years, so we might have to run as many as 30,000 ATMs!

We do a quick analysis. If we're handling 10,000 ATMs, our peak input rate jumps ten times from 66 TPS to 660 TPS. However, a single instance of our pro-

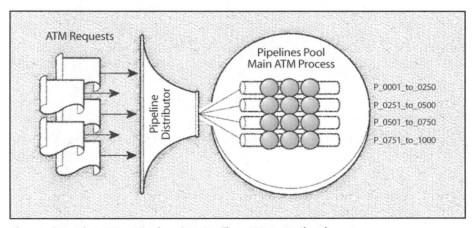

Figure 3.2 High-level design for the first ATM application

cess component still handles only 20 TPS. Once again, the process violates Rule 2 (*InputRate* must be $<=$ *ProcessRate*):

$$660 \text{ TPS InputRate} > 20 \text{ TPS ProcessRate}$$

This time we have a much bigger bottleneck to resolve. We'll start with the same formula; to determine how many pipelines we need for acceptable performance, we calculate by how much *InputRate* exceeds *ProcessRate*:

$$660 \text{ TPS InputRate} / 20 \text{ TPS ProcessRate} = 33$$

That tells us we need 33 pipelines. To add the 20 percent cushion, we'll make that 40 pipelines.

At first glance it's easy to assume we can just add more hardware and pipelines; but wait—from our earlier calculations we know the maximum *NumberOfPipelines* for our current distributor is only 25. That won't handle 10,000 ATMs, and there's no capacity for future expansion. In addition, our server hardware platform supports dual quad-core CPUs. With eight cores per system, it's not realistic to host all 40 pipelines on a single server.

The solution is to distribute *across and within* servers. To do this, we'll implement a multi-tier distribution mechanism, as seen in Figure 3.3.

Using Pipelines Law, we find two areas in this example we should optimize:

- We must increase the primary distributor's throughput.
- We must distribute transactions across multiple levels of pipelines (multi-tier distribution).

Two tiers will handle our new requirements. The best approach to the problem is bottom-up; in other words, we'll analyze and solve the lowest (secondary) tier of distribution and processing, then design the top (primary) tier. The lowest tier provides the actual processing and must handle the ultimate input load, so this is the best place to start our analysis.

Secondary Pipeline Tier

The secondary tier includes the distributors and pipelines that actually perform the ATM process. We already know we need 40 pipelines to handle the load. At this point we must determine the best way to distribute transactions, and we must select the value we'll use as the input key.

We could simply create 40 named pipelines, each supporting a range of `branch_id` values, as we did before. This is acceptable, but the input load might

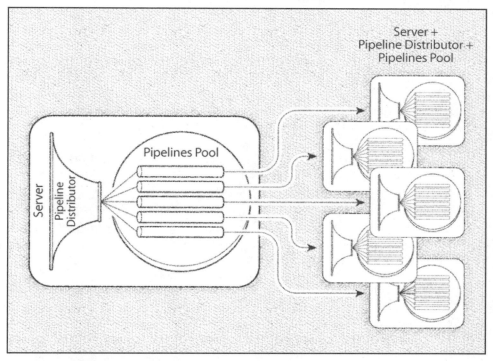

Server +
Pipeline Distributor +
Pipelines Pool

Pipelines Pool

Server

Pipeline
Distributor

Figure 3.3 Multi-tier distribution

not be evenly distributed by branch. Instead, let's use a different technique for the secondary tier: *dynamic* named pipelines, shown in Figure 3.4.

Dynamic named pipelines are virtual pipelines; their names are based on the changing values of the current input key. The server creates each pipeline on the fly as it's needed, allocates it to an individual thread, and then destroys it when it's no longer required. As long as the application is processing transactions for a specific key value, the associated pipeline is "alive." When the key value is no longer present, the system frees the pipeline thread, and it can use that thread to create a new pipeline. This approach provides superior utilization of resources; the server uses a fixed thread pool and constantly shifts pipelines to accommodate the load.

Now let's determine the best input key for the secondary tier of pipelines. Remember, we must support FIFO processing, so we still want to use order-based pipelines. We have two choices: We can distribute by `branch_id` or by `account_no`. The `branch_id` enforces order for each branch, and thus

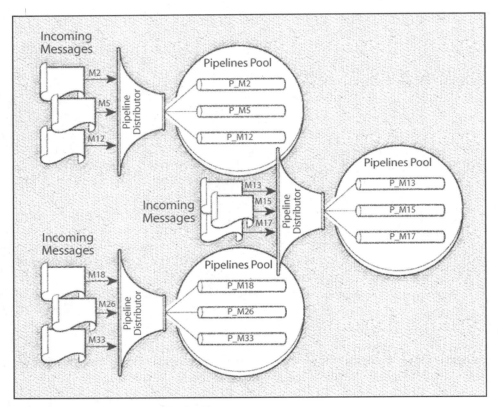

Figure 3.4 Dynamic named pipelines

enforces order for the accounts within that branch. The `account_no` enforces order for each individual account.

There's a trade-off to consider here. If we use `branch_id`, it takes less overhead to allocate dynamic pipelines; however, if there's a burst of transactions for a single branch, we might have a serious wait condition, and users for that branch will see their transactions backing up. Using `account_no` increases overhead for pipeline allocation, but it guarantees almost 100 percent that pipelines will not contend for resources. Based on these factors, `account_no` is our best input key; it provides more scalability and better performance.

Next, let's examine distributor performance at the secondary tier. We know we need 40 pipelines to handle the load, and we have eight cores available per server. We estimate we'll need five servers, and we'll assume we can safely allocate eight threads per server (we're allocating one thread per physical core, although in some hardware architectures you may be able to use more or less than one thread per core). You can see these requirements in Figure 3.5.

The distributor reads each incoming message as it arrives, then performs the following steps:

- It parses the input message into a DOM tree.
- It evaluates the account_no value.
- Based on the account_no value, it routes the transaction to a dynamic named pipeline, as seen in Figure 3.6. If the pipeline doesn't yet exist, the distributor allocates it on an available thread. If the pipeline does exist, the transaction waits until the prior transaction for that specific account_no is complete. (Note that this design does not constrain transactions for other account_no values.)

Using this mechanism, if the distributor receives two or more transactions for the same account_no at or close to the same time, order of processing is guaranteed.

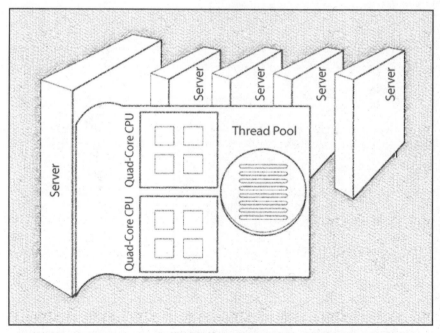

Figure 3.5 Five servers, each with dual quad-core CPUs, and a pool of eight threads per server

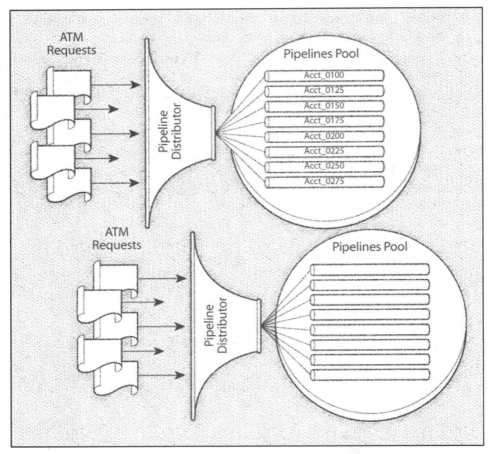

Figure 3.6 Secondary-tier distributor with dynamic named pipelines; pipelines change according to the value of the current input key.

Remember, our *InputRate* is now 660 TPS, so let's find out what the input load is for each server:

660 TPS InputRate / 5 servers = 132 TPS input load per server

The *ProcessRate* for any single instance of the ATM process is still 20 TPS, so eight threads provide an adequate cushion for pipeline allocation. To check if this is true, we calculate the downstream *ProcessRate*; that's the combined rate for each secondary-tier server, including distribution overhead:

$$20 \text{ TPS ProcessRate} * 8 \text{ threads/pipelines per server} =$$
$$160 \text{ TPS downstream ProcessRate}$$

And then we compare it to the input load:

$$132 \text{ TPS input load per server} < 160 \text{ TPS downstream ProcessRate}$$

As you can see, this complies with Rule 2, *InputRate* must be $<=$ *ProcessRate*.

However, when we test the distributor, we find out it's slightly slower than the original one; the overhead for allocating pipelines requires 3 ms per transaction. We calculate the distributor's TPS for one transaction and get 333 TPS, which we use for *DistributorRate*. Now we can determine the maximum number of pipelines (we've rounded down the answer):

$$16 \text{ NumberOfPipelines} = 333 \text{ TPS DistributorRate} / 20 \text{ TPS ProcessRate}$$

The maximum *NumberOfPipelines* is 16, which isn't enough to manage the entirety of the expected load. However, it is more than adequate to support eight concurrent pipelines per server, and we can support the entire load by properly designing the primary pipeline tier. We'll do that in the next section.

Primary Pipeline Tier

We'll now look at the primary pipeline tier, which uses the distributor from the first ATM application we designed. This level must handle the load of all input transactions, then distribute them to the secondary-tier servers for actual processing. Remember from our first example that the *DistributorRate* for this distributor is 500 TPS. However, this time the *InputRate* is 660 TPS, so we have to increase the distributor's performance. And as our bank expands, we know that the required *InputRate* will grow well beyond this level.

The answer lies in a simple design change, which you can see in Figure 3.7. The distributor still routes transactions by `branch_id` as it did before, but we'll optimize its design. Instead of using a DOM model to parse the inbound message, the distributor uses stream-based parsing (such as SAX or other stream-based technology). Instead of waiting until it parses an entire document, the distributor sends the transaction as soon as it finds and evaluates the `branch_id`. Because `branch_id` is near the top of the document, we get a tremendous improvement in distributor throughput.

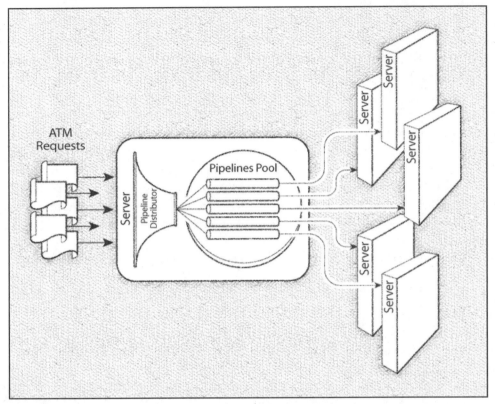

Figure 3.7 Primary-tier distributor, with pipelines routing transactions to five other servers

The new design reduces the distributor's latency to 0.5 ms, including any network latency incurred when forwarding the transaction. Now when we calculate the distributor's TPS for one transaction, we get 2000 TPS for the *DistributorRate*. We've improved our original design by four times, which provides more than enough capacity for 10,000 ATMs. In addition, we've made it possible to add extra capacity when the bank expands in the future.

Let's use the Software Pipelines Rules to validate these conclusions. Using the downstream *ProcessRate* from our earlier calculations, we'll determine the maximum *NumberOfPipelines* for the primary tier (we've rounded down the answer):

$$12 \text{ NumberOfPipelines} = 2000 \text{ TPS new DistributorRate } /$$
$$160 \text{ TPS downstream ProcessRate}$$

The new primary-tier distributor can support 12 secondary-tier servers. To handle our expected load, we require only five servers at the secondary tier. Therefore, our conclusions are correct; the new design will comfortably support our expected load *and* provide the capacity to increase the load when the bank acquires more ATMs.

As for the distribution routing, we'll use the same approach as in the first ATM example, but we'll use five pipelines this time, one to each server. Again, we'll use a range of `branch_ID`s to group transactions, this time dividing transactions into five groups. The distributor reads each message as it arrives, evaluates the `branch_id`, then routes the transaction to the pipeline assigned to the range in which the `branch_id` falls.

Table 3.2 shows the transaction groups and pipeline names. Again, the evaluation expressions are written in XPath notation:

This completes our second ATM application. You can see the high-level design in Figure 3.8.

Summary

We've used Software Pipelines to solve two typical business problems, and we showed you how to apply pipelines theory to application design. Our goal is to give you a predictable methodology for applying Software Pipelines Rules. If you understand this technology, you can design for maximum optimization of avail-

Table 3.2 Transaction Groups and Pipeline Names

Pipeline Evaluation Expression	Pipeline Name
`/atmtrans/[branch_id >= 0001 and branch_id <= 2000]`	`P_0001_to_2000`
`/atmtrans/[branch_id >= 2001 and branch_id <= 4000]`	`P_2001_to_4000`
`/atmtrans/[branch_id >= 4001 and branch_id <= 6000]`	`P_4001_to_6000`
`/atmtrans/[branch_id >= 6001 and branch_id <= 8000]`	`P_6001_to_8000`
`/atmtrans/[branch_id >= 8001 and branch_id <= 10000]`	`P_8001_to_10000`

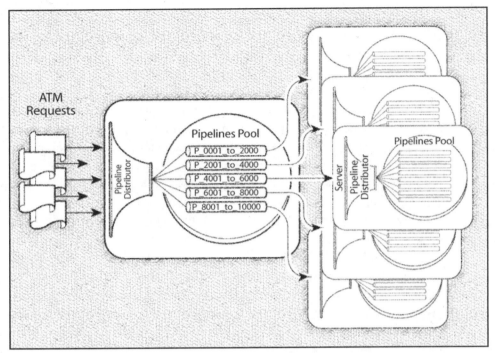

Figure 3.8 High-level design for the second ATM application

able resources, and more importantly, you can predict how your pipelined application will perform.

There are many possible patterns for Software Pipelines and Pipeline Distributor design. In the next chapter we'll show you the basic ones, which you can use to resolve a variety of typical application problems.

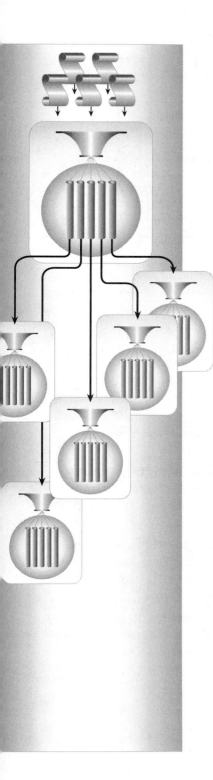

## CHAPTER FOUR

Pipelines Patterns

Now that you have a fundamental understanding of Software Pipelines architecture and its theoretical foundation, let's look at the various patterns in which you can apply pipelines.

The true power and beauty of this architecture is that it gives you the ability to flexibly distribute processing for business applications, and to adapt new and existing software components to ever-increasing performance demands. It follows, then, that Software Pipelines can best be summed up as a method for *distribution of application services*.

There's almost an unlimited number of ways to distribute services and components. You can use virtually any scheme to organize and sequence a set of components to fit a given application problem. To make sense out of these vast possibilities, we developed a set of Pipelines Patterns, reusable schemes that fit a variety of common scalability problems.

To help you understand Pipelines Patterns, let's first review the operation for the Pipeline Distributor, the primary component in Software Pipelines. The distributor receives transactions and distributes the workload to individual pipelines, which in turn invoke individual instances of services to perform the work. Figure 4.1 shows the basic concept.

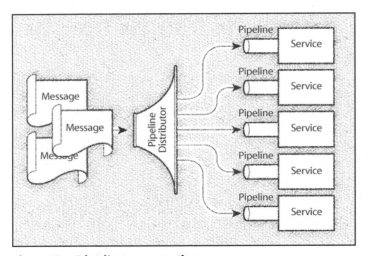

Figure 4.1 Distributor operation

Now let's start looking at the patterns. We've identified several *aspects*, or categories, of pattern types:

- **Service Invocation Patterns:** These patterns define how a calling application (the client) invokes a service, from the viewpoint of the client. The client invokes the service transparently by calling the Pipeline Distributor, which hides the details of pipelining from the client.
- **Message Exchange Patterns:** These patterns define the types of message exchange supported by a distributor. The most common types are One-Way and Request-Response.
- **Routing Patterns:** These patterns define how the distributor routes service invocations after it gets them. There are many ways to do this, from simple round-robin logic all the way to sophisticated logic that makes custom routing decisions.
- **Distributor Patterns:** These patterns define how the distributors are used in an application. You can deploy distributors in many ways, from a single stand-alone distributor on a single server, to several tiers of distributors. You can also deploy them at the client or database level of an application.
- **Distributor Connector Patterns:** These patterns define how the clients invoke the distributor services. Methods include local method invocation and various remote network protocols.

In reality, these aspects overlap each other, and you can use patterns from any given aspect for other uses. In this chapter we explore each aspect and its patterns in depth.

> The third section of the book, Pipelines Examples, contains extensive examples and a reference Pipelines Framework, the element that provides the base distributor used for creating Pipeline Distributors. The Pipelines Framework contains support for much of the pattern functionality, so we refer to it throughout this chapter.

Service Invocation Patterns

In Software Pipelines, a client invokes a service by calling the Pipeline Distributor; this is a fundamental concept in the architecture. The distributor hides the execution and deployment details from the client *and* from the service. Hiding the details makes deployment of service components much more flexible, and you can easily reorganize how the components are executed and how many running instances are available to perform the work.

Service Invocation Patterns define the ways in which the client invokes services. We'll look at the two basic patterns in this aspect: Push and Pull. Almost all distributors use either the Push or the Pull Pattern, combined (when applicable) with suitable patterns from other aspects.

Push Pattern

In the Push Pattern, which is often the most common pattern used, the client pushes transaction messages to the distributor. Figure 4.2 shows how the Push Pattern works.

Pull Pattern

Figure 4.3 shows the Pull Pattern, which uses a message queue between the client and the distributor.

As you can see in the figure, the client interacts only with the intermediate message queue. When messages become available for processing, the distributor pulls them from the queue. This is a good choice if your workload fluctuates widely; you can use the queue as a buffer for the transactions.

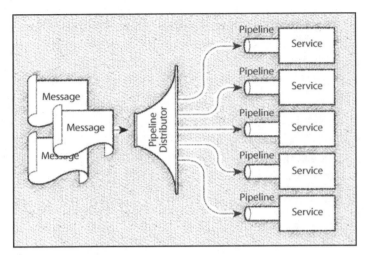

Figure 4.2 Push Pattern

Pipelines use a lightweight, in-memory queue (which you can back with a persistent store) to deliver high-performance, fine-grained transaction control. In a Pipelines Framework, groups of pipelines actually operate like a

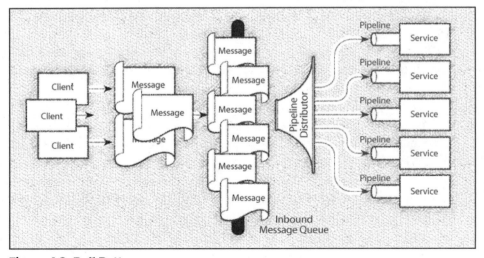

Figure 4.3 Pull Pattern

highly distributed message queue, giving you hundreds or thousands of small, high-performance, distributed "queues" for processing transactions, in contrast with the typical centralized queue.

Message Exchange Patterns

If you've worked with SOA, you're already familiar with Message Exchange Patterns. We'll talk about the two most relevant to pipelines, One-Way and Request-Response, and go over the specifics you'll need to know for using them in pipelines architecture.

One-Way Pattern

Figure 4.4 shows the One-Way Pattern.

This is essentially the same as the Push Pattern, but you can also implement it as a Pull Pattern. The central concept in the One-Way Pattern is the message exchange factor: The client sends messages for processing, and no response is ever returned.

Request-Response Pattern

Figure 4.5 shows the Request-Response Pattern.

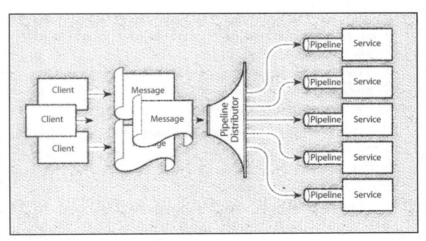

Figure 4.4 One-Way Pattern

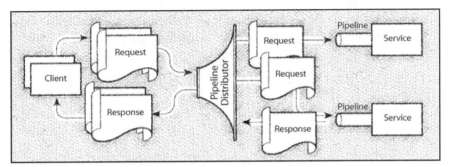

Figure 4.5 Request-Response Pattern

Request-Response is the most common format for exchanging service-oriented messages. There's one very important distinction for a pipelines implementation: You must use asynchronous invocation; otherwise, you'll get no scaling benefit from the pipelines implementation. We built this capability into the distributor for our reference Pipelines Framework; it receives the request from the client, forwards the request asynchronously to the pipelines (and thus the services), and then waits for a callback from the service. When the response is ready, the service sends it back to the client. This mechanism effectively hides the asynchronous complexity from the client, but the effect is the same as it is for other asynchronous or callback execution mechanisms.

You can also use the Request-Response Pattern as a Pull Pattern, as shown in Figure 4.6.

As we mentioned earlier, using a centralized queuing system for message transport gives you a handy buffer for many situations, especially when your transaction loads are unpredictable.

To make the Request-Response Pattern work, you must have two separate queues: one for inbound and one for outbound messages. The pattern uses the following sequence of processing:

1. The client places a message on the inbound message queue. The message usually contains the name of the outbound message queue on which the client will wait for the response. In many messaging systems, including JMS, the outbound queue can be a temporary queue created by the client for this specific transaction.

2. The distributor pulls the message off the inbound message queue, then forwards it to the pipeline and service for processing.

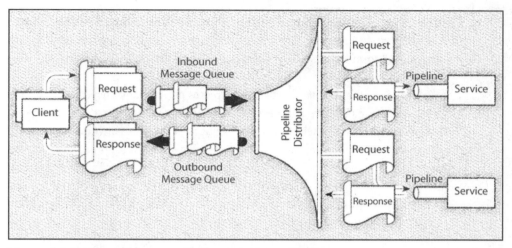

Figure 4.6 Request-Response Pattern used as a Pull Pattern

3. The service prepares and returns the response message to the distributor, which then places it onto the outbound message queue.

4. The client picks up the response message from the outbound message queue.

You can get excellent performance benefits from this approach as long as the message queue implementation doesn't significantly increase processing time. To determine how much benefit you'll get from your pipelines implementation, use Pipelines Law to calculate the overhead from the queue.

Pipeline Routing Patterns

There are many ways a Pipeline Distributor can route a given transaction message to a service for execution. What we're talking about here is the core distribution logic itself, and the pattern you choose directly affects your application requirements.

We'll discuss four basic patterns: the Round-Robin Routing Pattern, the Content-Based Routing Pattern, the Custom Routing Pattern, and the Join Pattern.

The main consideration for selecting a Pipeline Routing Pattern is whether you need to control the order of processing—an issue with a major impact on performance. Guaranteed transaction order and parallel processing are at odds with each other, a fact demonstrated by Pipelines Law and central to Amdahl's Law (from which Pipelines Law was derived). If you enforce sequential order on any group of components, the process can never go faster than the slowest component, and in practice, it usually runs much slower.

It's obvious that order of processing creates performance headaches, but for many applications in banking, securities, inventory management, and payment processing, there's no other choice. The sequential versus distributed processing dichotomy was one of the main factors driving the development of Software Pipelines, and you can now solve the problem with the right Pipeline Routing Pattern.

As we describe each of Pipeline Routing Patterns, we'll cover the impact that each pattern has on sequential processing.

Round-Robin Routing Pattern

Round-Robin Routing is familiar to most developers and operations administrators, who use it for processors, routers, and software scheduling applications.

> The derivation of the term *round-robin* is interesting in itself. It comes from the French for "round ribbon" and referred to the act of signing a petition. When a group of people wanted to petition against someone in authority, but didn't want any one person to be identified as the leader of the group, they signed their names in a circle (as in a ribbon). Signing in this way made it impossible to determine the order in which they signed.
>
> The computing industry uses round-robin to indicate that for a given set of messages, no message has any special priority. The application or service evaluates all messages equally

Figure 4.7 shows the Round-Robin Pattern.

This is the simplest distributor pattern. You can use it when you do *not* require order of processing control. The distributor places each message on the next available pipeline, in no particular order. It usually places messages in the order in which it got them, but there's no guarantee of processing order; each pipeline merely processes each message in turn, as fast as possible. If some messages require more processing time than others, or if any other factors enter into the process, it's entirely possible the application will complete later messages before earlier messages.

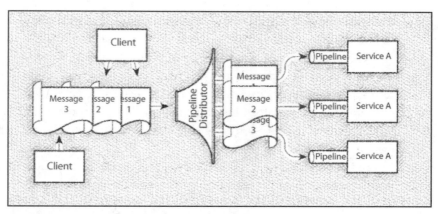

Figure 4.7 Round-Robin Routing Pattern

Content-Based Routing Pattern

In Figure 4.8 you can see the Content-Based Routing Pattern, which addresses the issue of processing order ignored by Round-Robin.

Figure 4.8 shows various incoming messages, each with a different value for "category." We're using "category" as the Pipeline Key, which is the element used by the distributor to make its routing decisions. The application must process transactions for any given category in the order received, one after another. It can process messages for other categories at the same time, but it must maintain order within each category. By breaking transactions down on the basis of con-

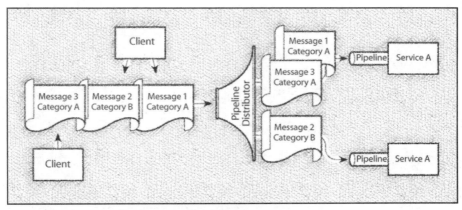

Figure 4.8 Content-Based Routing Pattern

tent, we've gained control over the granularity of sequential processing, and we can now limit our ordered components to much smaller sets of transactions.

The Content-Based Routing Pattern is the pipelines answer to the question of how to preserve order while performing parallel processing, and it is a proven technique for many industries. A good example is securities trading, where order of processing is mandatory. Just think how you'd feel if you were in the middle of buying a hot stock, and someone else beat you to the punch—right before the price jumped by 20 percent!

In Software Pipelines this is the most important pattern, especially for business applications. In order to help you learn how to apply it, we've used it for many of the examples in this book. However, to achieve the best overall performance, your best bet is liberal (but appropriate) use of *all* the patterns. Therefore, feel free to mix and match patterns at will, based on your exact circumstances and requirements.

Custom Routing Pattern

The Custom Routing Pattern is any pattern that you've customized to match your application requirements. In our reference Pipelines Framework, we support pluggable components, so you can tailor the distributor routing logic when the standard methods don't fit.

Figure 4.9 shows customized distributor routing logic.

In this example, messages for Category A and Category X both go to the same pipeline and service in guaranteed order. Why are Category A and Category X related in this way? Only the developer knows for sure ... The point we're making

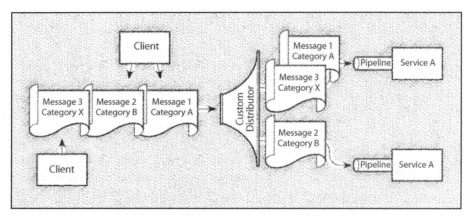

Figure 4.9 Custom Routing Pattern

is that you can implement any arbitrary control you might need for processing transactions or use any logic (for example, complex expressions that evaluate multiple Pipeline Key values) that fits your requirements.

Join Pattern

The Join Pattern is really an extension of either the Push or the Pull Pattern, with an interesting twist. The purpose of the Join Pattern is to enable the Pipeline Distributor to receive two or more related messages, consolidate them, and then forward them to the service instance for processing.

Figure 4.10 shows the Join Pattern in action.

In this pattern the distributor must correlate the incoming messages in order to identify which ones it should consolidate, and it must be able to retain a given message until any correlated messages arrive. It also has to store the evaluation logic and business rules for making these decisions. The distributor has to wait until it receives all the correlated messages, making this the least efficient type of messaging. Use it only when you have no other choice. However, depending on your business requirements, you might not be able to avoid it. On a positive note, the Join Pattern can actually help speed processing if the application can perform many upstream (and process-intensive) steps in parallel before it gets to the join.

Distributor Patterns

There are many ways to deploy distributors. Consider the following factors when you want to make a decision:

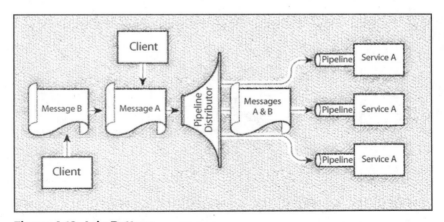

Figure 4.10 Join Pattern

- Scalability and performance requirements
- Available hardware and/or hardware budget
- Pipelines Law calculations, which indicate how effective pipelines will be for your situation

We've developed several Distributor Patterns that should cover most requirements: the Single Distributor Pattern, the Multi-tier Distributor Pattern, the Client Distributor Pattern, and the Database Sharding Distributor Pattern. The following sections cover each pattern in detail.

Single Distributor Pattern

The Single Distributor Pattern, in Figure 4.11, is the most commonly used and the easiest to implement.

In this pattern the distributor receives messages, then routes invocation calls directly to the service instances, which normally run on the same machine. Clients can connect to any point using a variety of connectors, giving you end-to-end flexibility for the environment. You'll learn about connectors later, in the Distributor Connector Patterns section.

Multi-Tier Distributor Pattern

The Multi-Tier Distributor Pattern has the same connection functionality as the Single Distributor Pattern, but it's for more complex tasks that require a greater level of distribution, usually across multiple servers. Since there's more than one level of distribution, you can multiply your performance benefit (use Pipelines Law calculations to validate this effect).

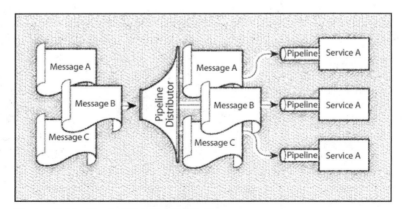

Figure 4.11 Single Distributor Pattern

Figure 4.12 shows how this pattern works; a primary distributor invokes a service on one or more secondary distributors, then the secondary distributors invoke the service instances.

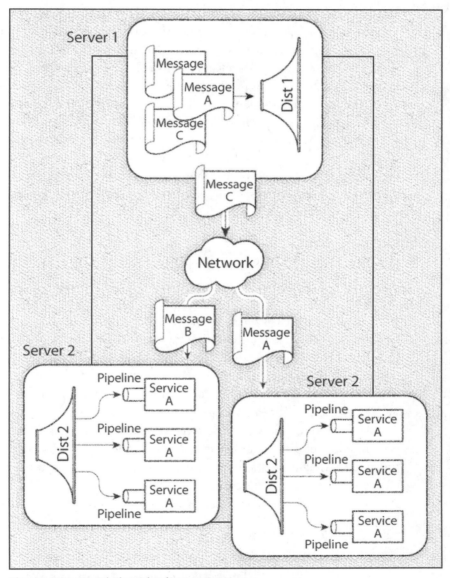

Figure 4.12 Multi-tier Distributor Pattern

In our example the primary distributor, Distributor 1, feeds multiple secondary distributors. Each secondary distributor is an instance of Distributor 2. It's very common to use the Content-Based Routing Pattern for these distributors, with coarse granularity for the primary distributor (for example, using the category as the Pipeline Key) and fine-grained routing for the secondary distributor (for example, using the product number as the Pipeline Key).

You can use several levels of multi-tier distributors; however, you should make sure doing so actually enhances scalability. To check this, calculate the cumulative distributor overhead and downstream processing rates. We'll give you examples of how to do this in later chapters.

Currently, it usually works out best to set up the primary distributor to invoke secondary distributors over the network. This spreads your workload over additional hardware. However, as multi-core processors increase in power and vendors add more cores, this could change, and it might make more sense to implement multiple levels of distribution on the same physical server. For now, though, the most common setup is network-level invocation across machines, which limits your choice of Distributor Connector Patterns.

Client Distributor Pattern

In the Client Distributor Pattern, the application performs distribution at the client level and routes transactions directly to the server. You can see this pattern in Figure 4.13.

Each client is attached to its own distributor, which it usually invokes directly from its own code, and the distributor invokes services directly over the network by using a network-level protocol, such as a Web service. To enable direct invocation of services, you must configure the client so it knows where all service instances reside. The client can be another server, such as an application server, hosting code that calls other back-end services.

This pattern is very direct, and it can yield excellent scalability, because there is no middle-tier distributor between the client and the actual services. If you're thinking of using this pattern for your application, take a look at the number of clients, how manageable the clients are, and the network overhead for invocation. If these factors indicate it's a good match, use it.

Database Sharding Distributor Pattern

Quite commonly, the database is the major bottleneck in a given application, and it's usually the end-of-the-line bottleneck in the downstream flow of transac-

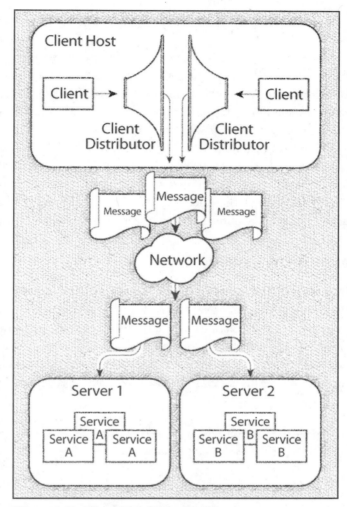

Figure 4.13 Client Distributor Pattern

tional applications. The Database Sharding Distributor Pattern is designed to help in this situation.

Sharding is a term coined by Google in recent years. It means dividing a database into multiple, "shared-nothing" partitions called shards. The concept is very similar to Content-Based Routing but applied at the database level. For example, you can put all customers of a certain group on one database server, and another group on another instance. It's very effective if your application lends itself to such partitioning, and it can greatly improve the overall performance of transactional applications.

Database sharding has been around for quite a while in various forms, but now, with the advent of the dot-com age, it's becoming more common. Some DBMS engines can provide similar capabilities internally, but many large organizations, including most of the major online marketers and social networking sites, are using it across smaller database instances.

Figure 4.14 shows how this pattern works. Services read and write to a special Database Pipeline Distributor, which partitions the SQL calls to several database servers.

To implement this method, use client-level code, a specialized database driver, an object-relational mapping layer, or a middle-tier distributor.

Distributor Connector Patterns

In Software Pipelines the client invokes services by using the service interface on a Pipeline Distributor. Our reference Pipelines Framework supports several of these connectors, each of which allows a different type of interaction between the client and the distributor. We designed our connectors to be as transparent as possible, so that client processes can seamlessly change from one type of connector to another. This is a typical feature for a service-oriented framework; the idea

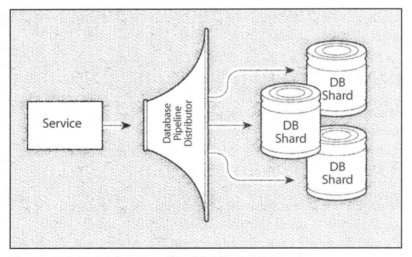

Figure 4.14 Database Sharding Distributor Pattern

is to provide as much independence as possible to the client and service-processing layer.

We'll look at the following Distributor Connector Patterns: the Local Method Invocation Pattern, the Socket Invocation Pattern, and the Web Service Invocation Pattern. This is by no means an exhaustive list of potential connectors. There's a connector for every remote invocation protocol, and one for every customized protocol (such as a hardware device interface) intended for a specialized application environment. You can use any pattern with any service, and you can use any type of invocation, from local invocation to the various types of remote protocols, with any service.

Local Method Invocation Pattern

The Local Method Invocation Pattern is familiar to every developer, but not often in the context of service invocation. For performance reasons, it's often better to invoke services directly, particularly if it makes sense to run the invoking process and service instance within the same environment. We can still treat this as a service invocation, even though it isn't remote, by using standardized message passing for the parameters to and from the "service" (the service is, in reality, the method). This will give you a great deal of independence in service invocation. As a side benefit, it standardizes your service code.

Figure 4.15 shows the Local Method Invocation Pattern, with all service components running in a single containing process.

As you can see in the figure, this pattern is simply a normal method call, except you're invoking a method on the distributor, which then invokes one or more service instances.

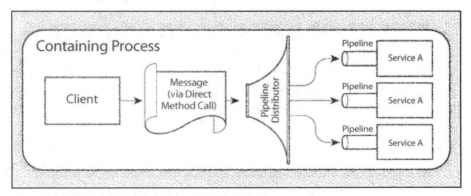

Figure 4.15 Local Method Invocation Pattern

One nice feature of our pluggable Distributor Connector Patterns is that they make the transition from development to QA to production a bit easier, by allowing you to use different invocation methods. While you're developing, you can run a service using the Local Method Invocation Pattern, then deploy and run the same service using a different Connector Pattern.

Socket Invocation Pattern

The Socket Invocation Pattern relies on network socket communications. Most probably you'd use it only for applications that require specialized high-performance remote invocation, for which it's very useful. By using Java and other popular languages, it's getting easier and more efficient to write this type of connector, but you should reserve it for specialized needs, when a more standardized connector doesn't fit the bill.

Figure 4.16 shows the Socket Invocation Pattern.

The mechanism is simple. The client forms a socket-based connection to the distributor over the network, then the distributor invokes the requested service via pipelines in the usual manner.

Web Service Invocation Pattern

This is the most common pattern for remote invocation—highly standardized, but quite straightforward. It uses XML serialization to pass message objects from one service to another. The SOAP protocol is the most popular, but other simpler protocols, such as REST, are now available.

Figure 4.17 shows a typical Web service example.

Other Patterns

There are many other types of Distributor Connector Patterns, including protocols such as CORBA, RMI, Microsoft .NET Remoting, and more. However, their methods for remote invocation are similar to those used in either Socket Invocation or Web Service Invocation, so you can get a good idea of how they work from earlier sections. Again, our intention isn't to list every connector option, but rather to point out the importance of using flexible, transparent methods for service invocation.

Summary

We've covered the basics of Pipelines Patterns, which provide answers for most application problems, and you've now got the technological foundation to start using the principles in a real project. However, before we get into more advanced procedures, we'd like to talk about the impact of pipelines architecture on your organization. In the next chapter we'll look at how you get support for a pipelines project, and how to prepare your organization to start working on it.

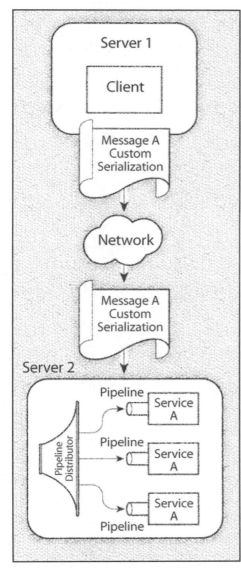

Figure 4.16 Socket Invocation Pattern

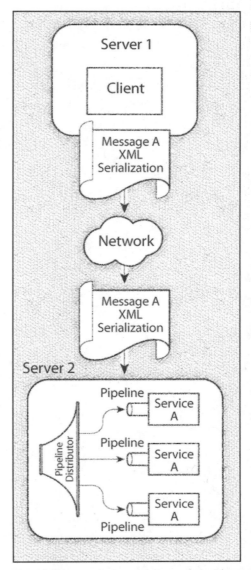

Figure 4.17 Web Service Invocation Pattern

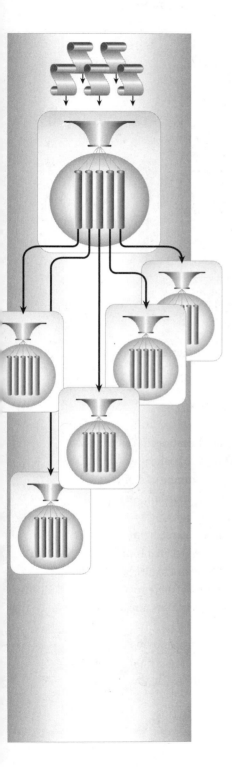

## CHAPTER FIVE

Pipelines: The Organizational Impact

The Software Pipelines architecture is a new way to overcome and manage the challenging performance problems you face when you're building a business application. It's as much a new way to deal with these problems, and predict the outcome, as it is a technology. Therefore, it has an impact on your IT organization and will keep affecting it during the life cycle of your application. You'll need to learn about the technology, and you'll need to create new roles and reshape some of your existing roles, but the advantages far outweigh the time and effort required.

In this chapter you'll learn about the organizational actions you should take to create, implement, and maintain a Software Pipelines project. It's a new technology, so the first step is getting support from your organization, which you're likely to get if the Software Pipelines architecture fulfills a compelling strategic need. To get the budget for your project, show management that it saves money, can increase revenue, and makes sense from an investment point of view. When you've got the go-ahead, make sure the architecture fits easily with your existing technologies and applications, then put the resources and procedures in place to build, implement, and maintain the project. Figure 5.1 shows a breakdown of these tasks.

There's a specific methodology used for implementation and analysis of pipelines applications, the Software Pipelines Optimization Cycle (SPOC). We mention it here

Figure 5.1　Organization actions for a Software Pipelines project

because it's one of your organizational tools. However, it's a subject all on its own, so we'll start covering it in detail in the next chapter.

Strategic Evaluation

Unfortunately, it's all too common for a new idea to fail because no one understands it or supports it, or because nobody figured out how to make it work under existing constraints. When that happens, you lose all the potential benefits you might have gained from the new idea. To help you avoid this pitfall, we'll discuss the first and most critical task, strategic evaluation, in detail.

You must identify the strategic need you want to meet with Software Pipelines, and it must be truly compelling. The highest level in IT makes this evaluation, but it's vital to get other levels—IT executives, software architects, and business unit managers—to participate as sponsors in the process. Their observations and knowledge are essential to the decision to go ahead with a Software Pipelines project.

Take a good look at your current system. What do you need to do in order to succeed? Can Software Pipelines help you with that? The Software Pipelines technology is particularly well suited for business applications with the following requirements:

- **Business flexibility:** Applications that must change quickly in response to market pressure, competition, or some other dynamic force.
- **Scalable performance:** Applications that deal with fluctuating or, more to the point, rapidly growing transaction volume.
- **Core transaction/batch processing:** Applications that are usually central to the operation of the business itself. The flexibility and scalability you get from Software Pipelines will improve this type of application and will help you gain a strategic advantage in the marketplace.
- **Need to reduce cost:** When technology costs determine your success in the marketplace, it's vital to find a way to reduce application costs. The Software Pipelines architecture is an excellent choice for this situation.

Like any new technology, Software Pipelines architecture is only as useful and valuable as the problem it solves for your business. If you don't identify a strategic need as the first step, the success of the project (and the likelihood you'll get financing for it) is doubtful. However, if you clearly define the problem and communicate it so it's understood, you'll get the green light, because your organization will want the project. And because you're solving a real problem, the project will be profitable for your company.

Let's take a look at some of the strategic problems that Software Pipelines can solve:

- Reduce operating costs by 50 percent while multiplying transactional capacity.
  Example: In the search engine market, Google capitalized on this type of capability, and now they're outperforming their well-established competition.
- Offer a new product, a new service, or enhance an existing service. This will push up the data volume. Software Pipelines can help by increasing capacity and/or decreasing processing time.
  Example: A domestic airline installs a pricing engine with the latest software. The application finds the route with the lowest fare, which is delightful for the passenger, but the amount of data it consumes jumps by an order of magnitude.
  Example: A finance company develops a real-time trading system with new, innovative, but very complex rules for evaluating securities transactions. To make any profits, the company has to respond faster than the competition.
- Integrate operations from newly acquired subsidiaries. The goal is to maintain a seamless view of an entirely new organization.

Example: A traditional distribution business acquires several smaller competitors. If the company consolidates all the applications from its new acquisitions into a single high-performance engine, it will gain cost, operational, and service advantages, and it will have a better chance to dominate the marketplace. Customers will like the new system, because their costs will go down, and they'll get more choices when ordering.

- Reduce the processing window (a given amount of time during which an application must complete critical transactions) for a large batch processing application. Batch processing applications are still the lifeblood of many businesses. Reducing the processing window enables the application to handle a higher volume at a lower operational cost.

Example: A bank performs offline check processing before each business day, and its older system has a difficult time keeping up with the load. If the bank applies Software Pipelines to the problem, it can use parallel processing to considerably reduce the time to process transactions, often at a significantly lower cost than that of existing systems.

A very effective way to define the business problem you're trying to solve is to form a small task force. The task force gathers input from IT executives, software architects, and the business unit, then evaluates the options. Very often you can find highly creative people in the business unit who see the true potential of the organization. Seek out these individuals, get their support, and involve them in all stages of the process. These visionaries, and their inherent enthusiasm, are often the drivers you need to get full support from upper management.

When you've figured out the strategic need, and everyone agrees what it is, you've passed the main hurdle on the path toward getting your project approved. Now let's look at how the Software Pipelines architecture affects the budget, and how to get your project financed.

Budget Impact

You need a budget for your project, and the first point you might need to argue is whether IT should get any funding at all. As of this writing, the U.S. economy is facing recessionary pressures, and all too often IT organizations are targets in that kind of environment. A business leader with some tough decisions to make tends to cut IT and reduce everything in sight: new projects, capital expenditures, and head count. However, the real answer is often found in the very department that looks so disposable. Finding and using the right technology intelligently—

especially technology as cost-effective as Software Pipelines—can actually save the company, because it keeps operations running at a competitive level until the economy improves.

The next point is hardware versus software. Relying on hardware to fix problems is tempting. The first and most obvious way to handle a performance problem is to "get a bigger box." It's true! You *can* improve performance with more powerful servers, better network switches, and faster storage solutions, but that's shortsighted, and expensive, and very often only temporary. In one case we studied, a company repeated a hardware "fix" every 18 to 24 months. They knew the volume of transactions would keep going up, but each time they upgraded the hardware, they did it knowing they'd have to get a new "fix" all over again in the not-too-distant future. You don't want to fall into that trap.

It's much more effective to optimize your software to improve performance. It might even be an order of magnitude better than the typical "bigger box" solution. Why is software optimization more successful? Because it forces you to find out where the bottlenecks are, then to fix them by writing better code and using better logic. The application developer who does this gets a full understanding of the application, gains control of the system's dynamics, and delivers a much better product over the long term.

Optimization is a central building block in Software Pipelines, but you can apply it to almost any application. It might take some time to do an optimization, but if you use Software Pipelines, you can componentize the key elements of the process, then use a Pipeline Distributor to enable the elements. These features allow you to keep enhancing performance after you complete the project—a major advantage to this approach.

At the end of the day, what you get from software optimization, especially with Software Pipelines, is significantly reduced cost, which goes a long way toward getting a project approved. We've studied cases where optimization reduced costs (from a combination of factors) by 50 to 70 percent. In one case, a company with IT operating costs fixed at a very high level suffered a serious drop in business. Interestingly enough, they needed to *reduce* their processing capacity in the short term, with full knowledge they'd have to *increase* it again when business turned around. They thought their operating costs—maintenance for expensive hardware and software licenses—were "fixed" and "irreducible." However, the Software Pipelines approach proved they could invest less than a year's budget to reduce the "fixed" costs by as much as 70 percent, allowing them to scale down the transaction load for the immediate situation, but giving them the capability of scaling up rapidly when the business climate improved.

The main point here is that no matter how good a technology is, no matter what benefits it provides, someone has got to fund it. If you clearly demonstrate how your pipelines project will reduce costs (or show how it will provide a new source of revenue, which is less common), more often than not you'll get the funding. So, before you ask for any money, do your homework by getting answers to the following questions:

- How much do we spend right now on the application or process that needs to be optimized?
- How can we increase revenue?
  Can we offer a new product or service?
  Can we enhance an existing product or service?
  Can we add new capabilities or improve existing capabilities?
- How can we reduce costs?
  Can we save money on our hardware purchases or maintenance costs?
  Can we reduce software license costs? Can we use open source in the project?
  How much do operations cost?
  How much do we spend on salaries in the business unit? How much in IT?

The bottom line is that you have to sell the idea to management and get support from the rest of the organization. If you understand the cost structures of your organization (existing and planned) and the cost benefits of your project, you'll be able to communicate what needs to be done, and you'll have your budget.

Organizational Roles and Responsibilities

Several roles, from executive to developer, are vital to a Software Pipelines project. Many of these people will be involved from the start, helping you to identify the strategic business need for Software Pipelines and getting budget approval, and it's important for all of them to understand what this technology can do for the organization. Figure 5.2 shows the organization chart for a typical pipelines project.

We'll describe each role, along with the responsibilities of the role. Some of these roles are commonly found in IT or business organizations, and others are brand-new. Keep in mind that people in existing (and similar) jobs can easily perform the new roles, if their workload is adjusted.

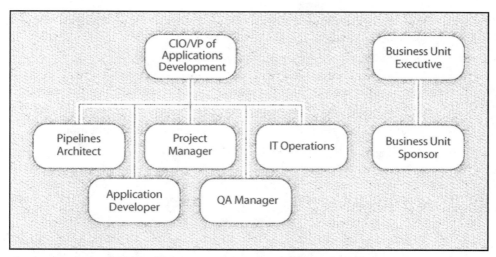

Figure 5.2 Organizational chart for a Software Pipelines project

Pipelines Architect

This is a new role. The pipelines architect provides the main guidance and leadership, both technically and organizationally, for the pipelines project. An existing application architect can take on this job, but whoever fills this position must have a broad view of the organization and its needs and should have an in-depth understanding of Software Pipelines and related technologies.

The person in this role is responsible for and should have knowledge about the following items:

- Software Pipelines theory:
  How can Software Pipelines improve the application(s) we want to optimize?
  How much faster can the application(s) perform?
- Software Pipelines design patterns:
  Can Pipelines Patterns help us? Which patterns should we use?
- Implementation methodology:
  What project management and software development methodologies do we currently use? Which ones are successful?
  How do we incorporate the SPOC into our existing methodologies?

- Business organization:

  How does our business make its profits?

  How do we achieve our organizational goals?

  What are the strategic objectives of the pipelines project?

  Which application(s) does the project include?

  What are the limits of our current application(s)?

  What effect will the project have on the business and its operations?

  Who will fund the project?

  What is the rationale for funding?

- IT organization and standards:

  What standards do we currently have in place?

  How will these coexist with the Software Pipelines architecture?

  Which existing tools and technologies will help us implement the pipelines project?

  How do our IT operations standards and practices fit in with the pipelines project?

  What skills do our application developers have?

- Pipelines infrastructure:

  What hardware components do we need?

  How do we maximize the capabilities of our hardware?

  Can we use open-source components, such as databases and application servers, in the project? If so, will those components be reliable?

  Can we manage the infrastructure properly?

- Management approval processes:

  What is the process to get approval for a pipelines project?

  What are the existing budgets?

  What kind of constraints do we have on our budgets?

  Who will be the executive sponsor for the project?

Business Unit Sponsor

The business unit sponsor is the visionary who helps identify the strategic need for Software Pipelines, plays a vital part in selling the project to management, and helps drive the project through development to completion. This individual works hand in hand with the pipelines architect on the project's strategy, plan, and budget.

The sponsor might or might not be at the executive level but is always the person who fully understands the rationale for the project, in addition to the following:

- Business unit strategy:
  How does our business make its profits?
  Why do we need to improve application performance?
  What financial benefits (revenue and cost reductions) do we get from the pipelines project?
  Are the advantages of Software Pipelines (increased performance and flexibility) compelling to our organization?
  Will the pipelines project benefit our customers?
  Can the project give us a real competitive edge?
- Familiarity with existing application(s):
  What application(s) currently support the business unit?
  What are the strengths and weaknesses of the application(s)?
  Where is the "big need" for improvement?
  What is the impact of changing the application(s)?
  What results can we expect in our day-to-day operations?
  What results can we expect at the tactical level?
- Business unit organization:
  Who will be the business unit executive sponsor?
  Does the project align with our current strategic initiatives and plans?
  Do most of the people in the business unit support the pipelines project?
  What resources are needed from the business unit?
  How do we manage the project without disrupting business?

IT Management

IT managers and executives, who include the CIO, application development managers, and other executives, are extremely important sponsors for a Software Pipelines project, and they're integral to its success. They must be familiar with the existing infrastructure, the business challenges that face their organization, and the expected result of the project. And because pipelines technology is usually used for mission-critical applications, these executives must also understand the potential risks and benefits of the project.

IT management is the backbone of any successful major project. It's their job to put the right team in place and to set realistic, achievable objectives that ultimately benefit the organization.

People in these roles are responsible for and should have knowledge about the following items:

- Business objectives:
  What are the key strategic initiatives and directives the IT organization must support?
  How do we capitalize on Software Pipelines architecture?
  Is the business case for improvement truly compelling?
- Organizational impact:
  What impact will the pipelines project have on our organization, both positive and negative?
  How do we handle change management and ensure reliability without disrupting business?
  Do we have enough IT people to work on the project?
  Do they have the required skills to do the project?
  Should we hire outside consultants?
  Will the business unit executives support the project?
- Budget responsibility:
  How will the project be funded?
  What is the realistic return on investment (ROI) for the project?
  Is the ROI achievable?

Application Developer

Just a comment on the value of the professional application developer. Utilized effectively, the professional developer is a tremendous asset to your company. As modern business moves toward automated high-technology systems, the success of any organization depends more and more on its development team. In fact, a skilled developer who understands the technology, and more importantly understands the business and how to *apply* the technology for strategic and tactical advantage, is one of the most valuable employees in an organization.

If you find sharp, knowledgeable developers in your company, fight to keep them, back them up, and give them enough freedom to accomplish the results of which they're capable. Their business knowledge—plus technology expertise—is often irreplaceable, and organizations suffer when they lose these people and their core skills.

Because the application developer is the one who actually builds the Software Pipelines application, the person in this role must be involved in all phases of the project: planning, development, quality assurance, and implementation.

The person in this role is responsible for and should have knowledge about the following items:

- Familiarity with Software Pipelines and related technologies:
  Which elements of the Software Pipelines architecture will benefit the project?
  What complementary technologies are we going to use with Software Pipelines?
  Can Pipelines Patterns help us? Which patterns should we use?
- Business unit functionality:
  How do our current application(s) perform?
  What are the strengths and weaknesses of our existing application(s)?
  Where does our performance bottleneck?
  Can we fix the bottlenecks with Software Pipelines?
  What are the requirements of the business users?
- Pipeline components:
  Which components should be pipelined? (To figure this out, determine which ones will improve in performance or scalability when pipelined.)
  Can we reuse existing software in the pipelines project?
  Which components should we redevelop?
  Which components should we create from scratch?
  How do we get performance metrics for pipelines?
  Are we going to use a Dynamic Pipelines infrastructure?
- Planning input:
  What are the realistic estimates for development tasks?
  Do we have enough developers to do the project?

Application Project Manager

The application project manager is responsible for delivering the project successfully and making sure it meets the objectives and requirements of the organization. This person coordinates day-to-day tasks and resources and acts as the go-between for all stakeholders.

The person in this role is responsible for and should have knowledge about the following items:

- Business unit strategy:

  What are the key strategic objectives of the business unit?

  How does the pipelines project help meet these objectives?
- Organization:

  Who are the key players in the business unit?

  Do we have enough IT people to complete the pipelines project?

  Do they have the required skills? Do they need additional training? Will it help to get them more training?

  Is our budget adequate to complete the project successfully?
- Project planning:

  Do we have enough reliable input for development? For quality assurance?

  Do we have enough data for a realistic implementation timeline?

  Have we identified all the major tasks? The major components?

  Do we have realistic metrics for measuring project progress?

  Have we allowed for all contingencies in our project plan?

  Have we included enough testing time in the plan? Do we have enough QA people?

  How do we implement the pipelines project without disrupting business?
- Project methodology:

  What methodologies do we currently use? Which ones are successful?

  Do we use agile programming methodologies? If not, should we start using them?

  How do we incorporate the SPOC into our existing methodologies?

Quality Assurance Manager

Application testing, the testing infrastructure, and the quality of the finished application are the responsibility of the quality assurance manager. This person has a tight relationship with the rest of the project team, understands the business goals as well as the technology, and by using this knowledge makes sure the project does in fact meet its objectives.

The person in this role is responsible for and should have knowledge about the following items:

- Software Pipelines fundamentals:

  How do we use pipelines to improve scalability and performance?

- Business application knowledge:
  What are the key requirements of the business unit?
  How do our current application(s) support the business?
  How will the new application improve business operations?
- Testing tools and methodology:
  What tools do we use for unit testing pipeline components?
  How do we validate transaction integrity?
  How do we validate sequential processing (if needed)?
  How do we exercise scalability?
  How do we make sure the implementation delivers the goods as stated in our performance objectives?
- Organization:
  Do we have enough QA staff to do the job?
  What kind of training do they need for this project?
  Who will do the end-user testing from the business unit?

IT Operations

As with any distributed system, it's critical to plan the IT operations for a pipelines application up front. Make sure you've got the people, the tools, and the infrastructure in place for managing and maintaining the completed application.

People in these roles are responsible for and should have knowledge about the following items:

- Software Pipelines monitoring:
  What tools do we use to monitor the Software Pipelines infrastructure?
  Are we building adequate metrics into the application?
- Pipelines infrastructure:
  Can we support pipelines with our current hardware setup—servers, network, and storage?
  What do we need for redundancy? Which components and systems should we include? How do we ensure the application is reliable?
- IT operations tools:
  What tools does IT operations currently use?
  Can we incorporate pipelines runtime statistics into the standard tool set?
  Should we add extensions to our existing tools? Which extensions should we add?

- Organization:
  Do we have enough people to manage and monitor the pipelines infrastructure?
  Do they need more training?
  Did we build a decent disaster recovery plan into the design?

Summary

Creating a Software Pipelines project is a strategic effort. If you plan it well and implement it successfully, you'll get tremendous advantages and cost savings for your organization. You'll need a team of professionals from many levels of your organization, but the results will more than justify the hard work and investment required.

In the next chapter we'll outline the SPOC, which is the key methodology for implementing and analyzing a Software Pipelines project.

Pipelines Methodology

In this section you'll learn about the Software Pipelines Optimization Cycle (SPOC), a special overlay methodology for guiding your implementation of pipelines technology. SPOC is called an *overlay* methodology because it is best used in conjunction with the development methodologies that you're already using. It doesn't replace your standard methodologies; instead, it is tailored to accommodate the special considerations and requirements of a Software Pipelines implementation.

Each of the chapters in this section covers a specific aspect of the methodology. We start with a general view in the first two chapters, "Software Pipelines Optimization Cycle: Overview" and "The Five Steps of SPOC." In Chapter 8 we introduce a fictitious company, the Pipelines Bank Corporation (PBCOR), which we use to illustrate the steps of SPOC.

In the remaining chapters of the section, we walk through each step of SPOC in detail and show you exactly how to apply the methodology to specific application issues. As we go through the procedure, we illustrate each step with sample reports from PBCOR.

## CHAPTER SIX

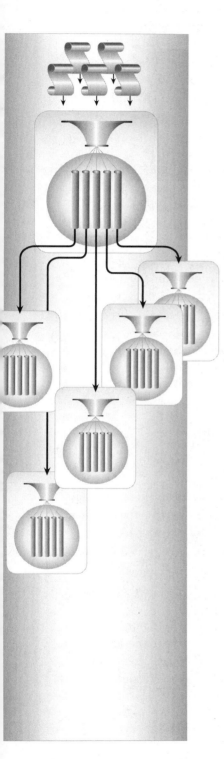

Software Pipelines Optimization Cycle: Overview

Any technology is useful only if it works in your organization, and Software Pipelines technology is no exception. To implement it successfully, you must invest the time to create a good design at the planning stage. For Software Pipelines, this stage is often more critical than any other phase, because it's not just a way to write an application; it's a tool for optimizing the application throughout its life cycle. To take advantage of this fact, and to really use Software Pipelines as an optimization tool, you'll want to use it with its accompanying methodology, the Software Pipelines Optimization Cycle (SPOC).

In brief, SPOC is a step-by-step approach to implementing concurrent computing. As the word *cycle* implies, SPOC is an *iterative* process; to optimize an application, you identify areas where concurrent computing can improve your business transactions, implement the optimization, and look for more areas to improve. An interesting benefit of using SPOC is its effect on your development team; a developer who uses this methodology actually learns how to "think concurrently."

In this chapter we introduce you to the main concepts of SPOC.

Yet Another Software Methodology?

You can find a multitude of valid software development methodologies today, so what's different about SPOC, and why would you use it?

The purpose of SPOC is to enable concurrent computing. It's designed to work with other methodologies, or as an overlay onto other methodologies. It *is* iterative development, and it includes concepts from agile methodologies, but you can easily overlay SPOC onto any development methodology you're already using.

Concurrent computing is a new concept to most developers. It's very hard to do if you don't have a guidebook or step-by-step instructions. SPOC solves this problem by providing a proven set of successful patterns. You can pick the pattern that's right for your application and get it to "do more than one thing at a time" with a fraction of the time, effort, and risk of traditional methods of concurrent computing.

Software Pipelines and SPOC provide a safe, orderly, noninvasive approach, as opposed to other methods, specifically, using a concurrent compiler and redeveloping an application from scratch using hand-coded multi-threaded techniques. Both of these options are high-risk and require a level of expertise that is often unavailable. Ask any developer who has worked on a complex multi-threaded application—it's never easy, and it's usually very frustrating. If you want to run *existing* components concurrently and control business requirements without these drawbacks, use Software Pipelines with SPOC.

SPOC Overview

The two most important characteristics of SPOC are its iterative design and its step-by-step approach.

How does the iterative design of SPOC help you optimize an application? In our experience the best way to optimize software is to do it incrementally. When you increase scalability in one part of a system, you'll see why this is true; fixing one area exposes bottlenecks in other parts of the system, or in related applications on which the system depends. The iterative design of SPOC helps you work with this phenomenon. You improve performance in the most critical areas first, then iteratively optimize the downstream systems and components.

What's the advantage of using SPOC steps? To answer this question, consider what happens when you don't follow a plan. It's pretty common for an organization to take the trial-and-error approach to optimization. You can do it that way, but there's a really good chance you won't like the result, and the outcome might not be what you expected. However, the last thing you want is a performance issue when you go into production, and SPOC prevents that. Just follow the steps: Analyze the application, plan the optimizations, predict the outcome of the optimizations, and validate the pipeline designs *before* you spend the time, effort, and money to implement the project.

Let's take a look at the meat and potatoes of SPOC, the actual elements that make up its methodology. It includes

- A sequence of clearly defined, iterative steps and deliverables with which you can successfully implement your Software Pipelines project. Each step covers a different phase of the project and has its own sequence of sub-steps with specific actions.
- Worksheets for each step, with instructions for applying the relevant portion of Pipelines Law to the associated step. The worksheets show you how to generate or find the key data for each phase of your project.

  For many of the steps, the worksheet includes one or more formulas. You'll use them to generate the key data for each phase of your project and to calculate the expected outcomes of your implementation. The formulas guide your evaluation and design, and they help you predict the potential success of your project.

- A report template: skeleton documents in which you "fill in the blanks." These documents help you build your design and report SPOC deliverables. When you reach the last step, you will have a complete report of the entire project.

  You'll learn more about how the template works in the following chapters; we'll use it to illustrate each step in the SPOC process.

- Sample outputs of SPOC. Use these to guide what you do in your own project.[1]

  SPOC is intended primarily to be used by the professional developer who has extreme performance challenges to crack, and its outputs are part of that process. However, you can also use SPOC reports and outputs to show managers, end users, and business executives what results to expect, and what kind of ROI they'll get from the project.

We'll go over these elements in detail in the next several chapters, which are organized as follows:

- First we'll briefly cover the Five Steps of SPOC and present the overview section of the SPOC report template.

---

[1] SPOC is an open-source methodology, and contributions and enhancements are welcomed. For more information visit the Software Pipelines Web site at www.softwarepipelines.org. All of the examples for this book, including the complete set of SPOC tools and report templates, are available on the site.

- To show how you might actually use SPOC, we'll develop a pipelines project for an example company, PBCOR. We'll start with the company profile for PBCOR, give you some details about its IT problems, and look at why the company wants to use Software Pipelines.

- Each of the next chapters includes a complete explanation of one step of SPOC, including its purpose and what it is intended to achieve. You'll learn how the process works and how to get the expected result and output for each sub-step.

  As we walk through the SPOC cycle, we'll apply each step to the PBCOR project. You can use much the same procedure for your own pipelines implementation.

  Each sub-step ends with the section of the SPOC report template that applies to the current tasks, which we fill in with details from the PBCOR project.

- In the third section of the book, Pipelines Examples, we'll present code samples for the PBCOR implementation.

In the next chapter we'll look at the Five Steps of SPOC.

## CHAPTER SEVEN

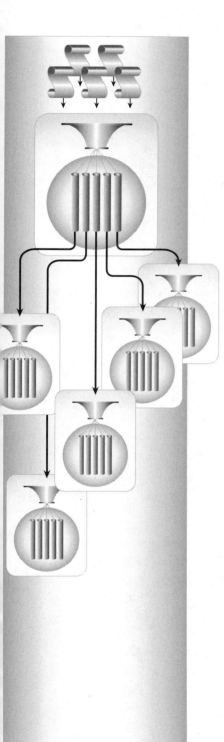

The Five Steps of SPOC

You should now have some orientation on the subject of SPOC, and you're ready to learn more of the details. First, let's take a look at the overview section of the SPOC report template, which will help introduce you to the Five Steps of SPOC.

The SPOC report template provides you with a starting point for preparing documentation for your own pipelines application. In this first section of the template a generic overview is provided along with the top level diagram of the SPOC steps. Just following the template section we drill down into the details of each of the 5 steps.

**Software Pipelines Optimization
Cycle Documentation**

Software Pipelines Optimization Cycle Overview

Software Pipelines architecture is an applications architecture designed to enable flexible performance improvements and to add scalability to business applications. It consists of a proven set of architecture and best practices guidelines, which are based on the physical engineering discipline of fluid dynamics.

To get the maximum benefit from Software Pipelines, we recommend a cyclical, structured approach to implementation. The methodology developed for this purpose is the Software Pipelines Optimization Cycle (SPOC). SPOC is composed of five primary steps, as shown in the following cycle diagram:

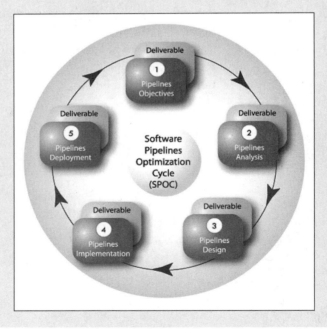

Let's look at the details for each step and its deliverable, in sequence.

- **Step 1: Pipelines Objectives**

    In this step you define the business, technology, and performance objectives of your pipelines implementation. Your objectives *must* be specific, easy to understand, and meaningful to your organization. You'll use these objectives to coalesce and guide the entire project.

    Deliverable: The Pipelines Objectives Assessment, which describes your objectives and includes management information, such as the project's budget and a list of the team members.

- **Step 2: Pipelines Analysis**

    In this step you identify the bottlenecks in your process and pinpoint any other areas you want to optimize. To do this, you map the process flow, review all existing components, and identify constraining elements. The constraining elements are the points where you'll probably want to use pipelines.

    The critical action in this step is the review of existing components. Getting an accurate measurement of their performance is the key to a successful analysis.

    Remember that SPOC is an iterative process! You'll repeat this step each time you apply the methodology to your project. This is the secret to maintaining an optimized system and for keeping up with an ever-increasing number of performance challenges.

    Deliverable: The Pipelines Analysis document, which includes the complete high-level design of the application, the layout of its process flow, all results of the analysis, and a list of the areas you've targeted for optimization.

- **Step 3: Pipelines Design·**

    In this step you lay out the specifics of your pipelines design, based on the factual results of your Pipelines Analysis. You identify any new or modified components that are needed, then calculate the Pipeline Distributor requirements and capabilities, as well as the type of hardware deployment to use.

    Deliverable: The Pipelines Design documents, which detail your pipelines implementation. These documents (and this step) will be extensive in the first iteration, but much shorter in successive iterations, because you'll capitalize on all of your previous work.

- **Step 4: Pipelines Implementation**

  This is where you implement the Pipelines Design. You create the actual pipelines services and components, implement the distributor(s), and certify and test all of your work. Although this looks like a typical development phase, the focus is more on deploying and arranging the pipelines in your system, and less on actual build/test strategies. Many other excellent methodologies cover how to build and test; you should definitely use the process you have in place and overlay the Pipelines Implementation onto that process.

  Deliverable: The Certified Pipeline Service(s)—the actual running pipeline service (or services), fully tested and ready to deploy.

- **Step 5: Pipelines Deployment**

  In this step you put your pipelines service(s) into production. You should use your standard deployment process to do this, but SPOC includes some special actions for this phase. You monitor the results of the deployed components and services, evaluate those results, and feed them into your next SPOC iteration—thus the name "Software Pipelines Optimization *Cycle*."

  The information about your results is vital for a successful operation. You'll use it to verify whether the system meets its objectives and keeps performing as expected into the future.

  Deliverable: The Production Pipeline Application—the deployed pipelined service(s), now successfully handling the required transaction volume.

Summary

Fundamentally, SPOC is a simple process with a logical progression. As you follow the step-by-step procedure to the final result, you learn more about your system and any of its weaknesses, and you'll use that data to optimize it. At the end, not only have you improved performance; you've also created the infrastructure for improving and tweaking performance repeatedly in the future.

In the next chapter we'll introduce you to PBCOR, the fictitious company used in our example pipelines project.

## CHAPTER EIGHT

Pipelines by Example: Introducing the Pipelines Bank Corporation

To illustrate SPOC and the Pipelines Patterns, we'll use a series of concrete examples featuring a fictitious company, the Pipelines Bank Corporation (PBCOR). PBCOR is a new contender in the banking industry, expanding quickly through organic growth and the acquisition of smaller banks. Management is highly innovative, and they want to make dramatic changes by adding new, unique features to attract customers—features, of course, that utilize the high-performance capabilities of Software Pipelines. PBCOR is also facing escalating transaction volume in the near future. However, if it can increase the performance potential in its systems, PBCOR will be able to penetrate new markets and expand services for its existing customers.[1]

Assume we've been chosen for PBCOR's pipelines project team. Our team is responsible for PBCOR's demand deposit account systems, which include consumer checking accounts and savings accounts, and for the ancillary systems that interact with consumer accounts, including the following:

- **Bank teller system (BTS):** Supports live tellers at the bank's branches.

---

[1]   Keep in mind that Pipelines Bank Corporation, our examples, and our example applications are indeed fictitious and are not intended to provide a detailed or accurate picture of how such applications work in the real world—lest any genuine banking experts find flaws in our "creative" examples.

- **Automated teller machines (ATMs):** Automated cash transaction machines.
- **Online banking system (OBS):** Provides Internet account access and service to bank customers.
- **Debit card services (DCS):** Processes all debit card transactions for merchants. Services in this system include authorization, charges, and credits.
- **Batch posting system (BPS):** Overnight batch process. Posts all transactions to accounts on a daily basis.

For the chapters on SPOC, we'll use the BTS, ATM, and OBS online applications in our examples. Later, we'll build on those examples to create an actual (but simplified) working set of pipelines functionality.

Let's take a look at PBCOR's current situation:

- The bank has approximately 10,000,000 consumer accounts.
- PBCOR's network includes more than 2000 ATMs.
- About 30 percent of the bank's consumer customers (and the percentage is steadily rising) use the OBS.
- PBCOR has more than 800 brick and mortar retail branches, each with its own team of tellers. On average, over 3000 tellers are active at any given time.
- PBCOR's management has decided to expand rapidly over the next three to five years by using a twofold strategy: Acquire and integrate several smaller banks, and provide innovative products and services for demand deposit customers.

PBCOR's systems already handle a high volume of transactions, and the expansion plan will increase it dramatically. We're going to calculate the projected growth as we walk through the SPOC process, but we know one thing for sure: The volume increase is going to be major. Potentially, it could double *every year* for the next three years.

Our mission (we don't have a choice; we've already decided to "accept it") is to support the expected volume growth, at the same time reducing the amount of cost, effort, and time it takes to develop new products and services. In fact, we've even heard PBCOR's marketing department muttering about those new products and services; they're expecting them in the next few months! And if this wasn't enough of a challenge, management is demanding that we merge any newly acquired accounts into our systems within one quarter after deal closure.

Let's take a closer look at the problem. Figure 8.1 shows the high-level view of PBCOR's systems in the current environment.

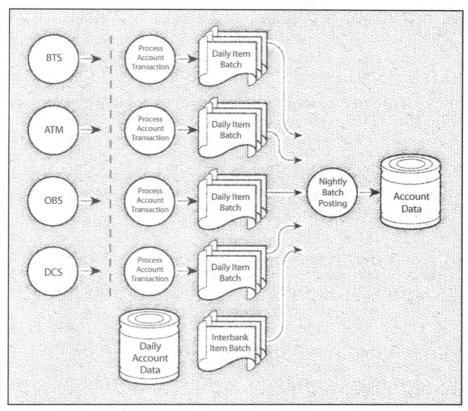

Figure 8.1 High-level view of PBCOR systems

As you can see, PBCOR has several online applications (BTS, ATM, OBS, and DCS) for processing consumer accounts. These applications all share the following characteristics:

- Each application can process any type of transaction (deposit, withdrawal, balance, check, transfer).
- Each application relies on the account data generated from the previous run of the nightly batch posting. It also updates a temporary data store for the daily accounts. The temporary store tracks the current day's transactions, to prevent consumers from inadvertently (or intentionally) overdrawing their accounts.

- Throughout the day, as each application processes its transactions, it generates a posting batch. The system feeds the batch into the nightly batch process, along with any interbank item batch files received from other banks or from clearing processes.

These applications and their workflows are typical of most banks. Unfortunately, as happens in most large organizations, each of these applications was developed over time by different teams using different architectures. Some are still mainframe-based, others use older technologies that are difficult to support, and still others were developed by outside vendors. To top it off, PBCOR used traditional enterprise application integration to sew them all together. The system is functional, but it has a lot of drawbacks:

- The mainframe-based applications are very costly, and it's difficult to find the programming talent to support them. In fact, some applications are older than the developers who work on them! Our long-term plan, which we have to implement gradually, is to move off the older mainframe platforms without seriously risking the bank's operations.
- There's a lot of redundant code in these applications, which makes the functionality inconsistent. It's difficult and expensive to support them. For example, the operation for automated bill payment is the same as the one that fires when customers use debit cards to withdraw funds from their accounts. To change the logic, the business rules, or the validation checks for the withdrawal transaction, we have to change and test *both* applications. Not only is this expensive, wasteful, and time-consuming, but it also opens the door to errors.
- Each application island has its own set of scalability problems and issues. Over the next few years, while PBCOR pursues its acquisition schedule, these scalability issues will complicate the task of integrating new accounts into existing systems. Trying to deal with each of these factors at the same time will put an incredible strain on application and infrastructure resources, not to mention risk service loss and potential downtime.
- It's impossible to quickly add new services or functionality. PBCOR's marketing department is full of bright, energetic people with great ideas for expanding PBCOR's operations. However, they're hampered by a ponderous system; by the time IT incorporates a new product, the window of competitive opportunity is gone.

SPOC Report Template

Now that we've learned about PBCOR and its systems, we're ready to start the project. Our first task is to fill in the company overview section of the SPOC report template, which appears in the next section.

Pipelines Bank Corporation Overview

PBCOR is a national banking organization with operations in approximately half the states in the United States. The company views technology as a key strategic weapon in maintaining its competitiveness. In keeping with this philosophy, PBCOR's top management has directed the IT organization to do the following:

- Enable rapid growth in transaction volume.
- Support the rapid introduction of new products and services, which will allow the bank's marketing team to implement new banking products faster than its competitors.

Our focus is on managing the demand deposit services of PBCOR, which include all products and related services for consumer checking and savings accounts. Related services and systems include the following:

- **Bank teller system (BTS):** Supports all tellers in PBCOR's brick and mortar retail branches.
- **Automated teller machines (ATMs):** Provides customers with access to account information and funds from branch and public locations.
- **Online banking system (OBS):** Provides customers with Internet access to account services.
- **Debit card services (DCS):** Supports and processes all consumer debit card transactions.
- **Interbank processing system (IPS):** Processes all transactions from correspondent banks.

PBCOR plans to expand dramatically through organic growth and acquisitions over the next five years. The following table shows the detailed metrics of this strategy:

Current and Planned Metrics

Metric	Current	Planned (Five Years)
Number of demand deposit accounts	10,000,000	25,000,000
Retail branch locations	1000	1500
ATM locations	3000	9000
Online banking users	3,000,000	15,000,000
Debit card holders	4,000,000	10,000,000

We know the current demand deposit systems cannot handle the load of these high growth projections. We intend to use Software Pipelines to address this issue. The following sections of this document will detail the implementation of our project and will be broken down into five sections, one for each step in the Software Pipelines Optimization Cycle.

Summary

We've introduced you to the Pipelines Banking Corporation, and we've set the stage for the PBCOR project, which will serve as the example for each of the Five Steps of SPOC. Solving PBCOR's problems will help illustrate how to use this methodology in your own company.

We're now ready to start the SPOC. In the next chapter we'll begin with the first step, Pipelines Objectives.

## CHAPTER NINE

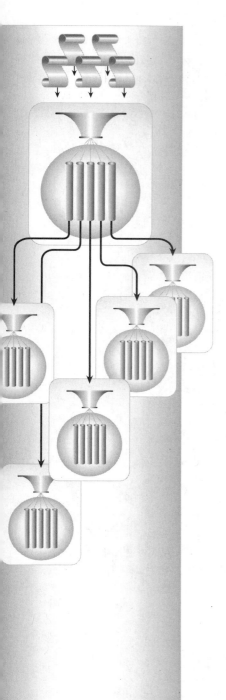

SPOC Step 1: Pipelines Objectives

In SPOC Step 1, Pipelines Objectives, you set the groundwork for a successful pipelines implementation. In many software projects this step is often skimped or overlooked entirely. But without a clear set of objectives—objectives that relate to your business—you'll have no guidepost for your project, no way to focus your organization's efforts, and no measuring stick to verify if you succeeded. This is all the more true when you're considering an optimization methodology such as SPOC.

This step doesn't have to be time-consuming. The time it takes depends on your project and its scope. However, it is critical, and not only will it ensure the success of your project, it will also ensure the long-term success of your pipelines architecture and applications.

Step 1 is broken out into several sub-steps. The report overview for this step, as seen in the next section, shows the overall process and the sequence of the sub-steps. We'll go into the details of each sub-step in the following sections.

Step 1: Pipelines Objectives

In any software project, one of the keys to success is defining the right objectives. This is even more important for a Software Pipelines project than for other types of projects, because Software Pipelines technology is performance-related. Understanding how the project impacts the business, then setting clear targets for it, is critical to the project's success.

The following cycle diagram outlines the sub-steps for this phase of SPOC:

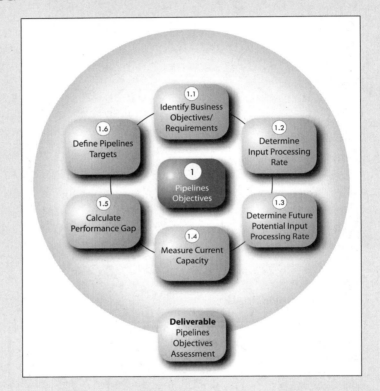

The final output of the Pipelines Objectives step is the Pipelines Objectives Assessment, which appears in the following sections of this report.

Step 1.1: Identify Business Objectives/Requirements

We discussed this step earlier when we described the organizational impact of pipelines projects. To recap, there are three critical elements you must include when planning any major effort:

- **Strategic impact:** Define the strategic objectives and impact your project has for the organization. This is where you translate business objectives into technology objectives.
- **Budget impact:** Identify budgetary requirements and how your project will fit into the overall budget of the organization.
- **Organizational roles and responsibilities:** Name the required sponsors, stakeholders, and members of your pipelines project team.

This step can be a lot of work for a new pipelines implementation. You'll probably spend most of your effort for this phase in generating support for the project and its rationale. But without support from all of the key stakeholders, you may never get your project off the ground, so do your homework and develop a compelling case.

If you're using SPOC as a follow-on iteration for an existing pipelines implementation, this step is much easier to do. Simply look at your current functionality, compare it to any new performance and business requirements, and develop a set of clearly stated objectives for the current iteration.

The following section from the SPOC report shows the PBCOR results for this step.

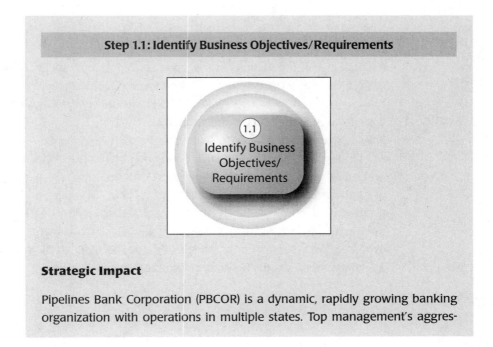

Step 1.1: Identify Business Objectives/Requirements

Strategic Impact

Pipelines Bank Corporation (PBCOR) is a dynamic, rapidly growing banking organization with operations in multiple states. Top management's aggressive acquisition plan, which is expected to outpace earlier growth trends, includes the following strategic objectives:

- Increase PBCOR's size to the super-competitor level through strategic acquisitions.
- Expand PBCOR's range of offerings by releasing innovative new products and services to customers. The products and services must have higher quality than competing products, and they must hit the market faster.
- Use technology in order to become the most customer-responsive banking organization in existence.

Management has also issued directives for the speed with which the company implements the changes:

- Integrate newly acquired banks within one quarter after deal closure. This target includes moving the new customers onto PBCOR's demand deposit systems before the stated deadline.
- Marketing has been charged with developing new products and services as compatible offerings to demand deposit accounts. IT must support and deliver the new services and products within one quarter after product definition.

PBCOR also wants to implement new features for its customers:

- Post all deposit transactions in real time, so that account balances are always current. With this in place, whenever customers come into a branch, use an ATM, or use the PBCOR Web site, they will always see a current, consistent picture of their accounts.
- Provide new services from ATMs and from the PBCOR Web site.

    On average, a single PBCOR ATM services hundreds of customers and other users per day, and more than one million users might be using the online banking service at any given time. This traffic provides a lucrative opportunity for promoting new services or for marketing nontraditional services, such as insurance and stock quotes, and could even provide income through advertising sales. PBCOR wants to take advantage of these underutilized revenue sources.

The demand deposit team will play a key role in supporting this expansion, and we plan to use a Software Pipelines implementation to meet the challenge. There are several other factors we must consider to ensure a successful outcome:

- The transaction volume for core demand deposit systems will grow dramatically over the next five years, and the Pipelines Implementation must provide adequate capacity for this growth. We will provide specific details later in this document.
- Currently, many systems feed data into demand deposit transactions. These applications were developed over many years, and they use different platforms and programming languages, which makes them difficult to support. Supporting the mainframe-based systems is particularly difficult, because the expertise for older environments is becoming scarce.
- Each demand deposit application feeds a separate daily transaction batch, and all batches (including interbank item batches) are fed into the overnight batch posting system. This system updates the master daily database, which is used on the following day by each of the independent demand deposit applications.
- The various demand deposit applications contain many redundant functions. For example, each application must be able to retrieve a bank account balance, apply a deposit, or process a withdrawal. Because the applications were written in various languages for different environments, developers must update each of these functions across all platforms whenever a business rule changes.

This architecture was less of an issue in the past, but it becomes a major problem in the modern business environment. PBCOR, like all other businesses today, has to contend with stringent regulatory requirements and increasing oversight. In addition, today's market pressure is much more intense; survival depends on rapidly developing and releasing new products (which is the rationale for PBCOR's aggressive new product strategy). These factors require a swifter response to change.

The ideal solution for this complex problem is to move all demand deposit applications to a single platform, consolidating all common functions within a single, easily supported environment. A major architectural shift like this must be phased in over time. Our team will get this started by completing the Software Pipelines implementation, which constitutes the first phase of the process.

- With each new acquisition, PBCOR must be able to migrate all data into its systems within a predictable time period. Our team must ensure the system can accommodate the additional data, and we must predict and plan for the increase in transaction volume.

The following table shows a list of the applications supported by the demand deposit team, each of which interacts with demand deposit accounts:

Applications Interacting with Demand Deposit Accounts

Application	Description	Language	Platform
Bank teller system (BTS)	Supports all tellers in PBCOR's brick and mortar retail branches	RPG	IBM iSeries
Automated teller machines (ATMs)	Provides customers with access to account information and funds from branch and public locations	Java/J2EE	x86 servers, Windows operating system
Online banking system (OBS)	Provides customers with Internet access to account services	Microsoft .NET connection software	x86 servers, Linux
Debit card services (DCS)	Supports and processes all consumer debit card transactions	C++	UNIX servers
Interbank processing system (IPS)	Processes all transactions from correspondent banks	COBOL	IBM zSeries-mainframe

Technology Objectives

The demand deposit team must support a diverse set of applications and platforms that have a significant amount of redundant functionality. This increases maintenance costs, development costs, and (more importantly) development time. Furthermore, management has issued a directive that

PBCOR use technology to become the most responsive banking organization in existence. Based on these objectives and factors, our team has translated management initiatives into a set of technology objectives:

- Flexibly accommodate the increased transaction volume as the bank expands.
- Enable rapid delivery of new products and services as requested by the marketing organization.
- (Medium-term) Move all demand deposit systems to a common, easily supported platform, with maximum reuse and minimum redundancy.
- (Long-term) Implement a real-time demand deposit transaction system, in which all demand deposit applications interact with up-to-the-second data.

The current phase of the Software Pipelines implementation will focus on the following areas:

- Use pipelines in the ATM application to accommodate the expected increase in ATM transactions.
- As the first step toward eliminating redundancy and promoting code reuse, consolidate the ATM and DCS systems onto a single platform. We will use Software Pipelines to accommodate the transaction volume from the newly combined application. Combining the systems is also the first step toward a real-time suite of integrated demand deposit applications for PBCOR. This foundation will prove the concept and make it possible to incorporate the remaining applications over time.

Budget Impact

The demand deposit team has analyzed the budget impact and ROI for the pipelines project. We have found several key factors that will improve ROI from the demand deposit systems over the long run:

- Consolidating all demand deposit applications onto a distributed platform will be very cost-effective; it will allow PBCOR to operate and scale its critical systems on efficient, low-cost commodity servers.
- The pipelines architecture makes it possible for PBCOR to deliver new services and products faster than other banking organizations. This means PBCOR will have new, accelerated opportunities for revenue

that the competition (which uses the traditional IT approach) does not have.

- As we gradually move common functionality onto the pipelines architecture, application support will become much more efficient. Developers can concentrate on functionality, using the language of their choice, while the Pipelines Framework manages scalability and performance.
- Integrating systems from newly acquired banks will be faster and cheaper using the streamlined pipelines architecture.

[If the project requires budget details, insert them into this section.]

Organizational Impact

The following organization chart shows the demand deposit pipelines team:[1]

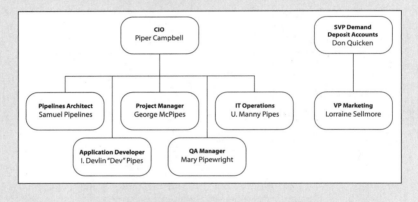

---

[1]   These names are purely fictitious. Any similarity to actual names or actual people is accidental.

Step 1.2: Determine Input Processing Rate

In this step you thoroughly examine your input transaction rates—the rates for the core business transactions you need to process. Examples include customer orders, batch transactions, trading transactions, and account activity.

This step is very straightforward. You simply need an accurate count or a range estimate for your current transaction volume. Use any valid method to determine your volume. For example, you could use your own monitoring tools, track your application processing logs, gauge your call center volume, or count your application transactions.

The following section from the SPOC report shows the PBCOR results for this step.

Step 1.2: Determine Input Processing Rate

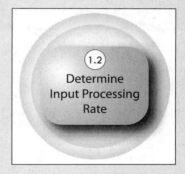

In the first iteration of the PBCOR Pipelines Implementation, the demand deposit team will be working with the ATM and DCS systems. The following lists show the transaction types for both applications.

ATM

A single-user ATM session consists of an average of three transactions, which can be any of the following:

- Authorization (always required)
- Check balance
- Withdraw cash (requires check balance)
- Account transfer (requires check balance)
- Deposit
- New product/service transaction types

DCS

Each user-initiated session consists of an average of three transactions, which can be any of the following:

- Authorization (always required)
- Check balance
- Debit payment (requires check balance)
- Credit

Our team used known values to determine the current input rates for both systems. The following table shows the current input rates:

Current Input Rates

Application	Current Number of Users	Current Average TPS	Current Peak TPS
ATM transactions	3000 ATM locations	150	750
DCS transactions	4,000,000 debit card holders	2500	7500
Total		2650	8250

Step 1.3: Determine Future Potential Input Processing Rate

Now the process gets a bit more interesting. This step answers the key question "How much is your input processing rate going to increase?" It's important to predict this as accurately as you can, in terms of transaction volume *over time*. Admittedly, you're going to get only an estimate of your projected volume, and it's impossible to predict the future perfectly. But it's important to get the most realistic estimate you can; you don't want to overdesign your system (everyone has budget constraints), and your project will fail if you underdesign it.

Let's look at some ways you can predict future processing rates:

- **Historical volume growth:** This is probably the best and most reliable metric you can find. Find the input transaction volume for the past two to three years, from the sources we listed in Step 1.2, and project these past growth rates into the future for the next two to three years. Get additional data from some of the other listed sources, and use that to temper your estimates.

- **Business projections:** Ultimately, you'll have to tie in any prediction with the projections of the business unit that drives the application. Meet with your business analysts and colleagues and go over their current business plans and budget forecasts. This will give you an idea of how the business is expected to perform. When you've gotten enough information, translate it into your predicted transaction volume. Use historical metrics if they apply. For example, look at how many transactions your company is using for each customer order, then find out how many transactions will be required in the future.

- **Plans for new products or new services:** Find out if your business is planning to introduce new products and/or services during your projection period. If so, work with the business team to predict how the new items will affect the transaction volume.

   This area is the most difficult to predict accurately; business studies are full of stories in which someone over- or underprojected sales of a new product. Customer feedback can be an excellent way to find out for sure if there's a demand for a new product. This is, of course, the job of the business unit, but you should review any such studies and form your own opinions.

- **New business requirements:** In some cases the business would like to do more with a given application, and this factor alone will increase transaction volume. For example, a company wants to target consumer behavior more precisely, so the business unit asks IT to add a lower level of granularity to existing transactions. For this type of scenario, once you've understood the requirement and designed the implementation, it's pretty easy to "do the math" and compute the projected transaction rates.

- **Customer or partner online access:** You can find plenty of applications today that provide online access for customers and partners in new, original ways. Sometimes the added feature is completely new, and sometimes it's just an enhancement of existing functionality. Either way, it almost always causes a tremendous volume increase. To predict how much it will increase, look for customer rollout plans or other documents that might help you gauge the impact.

   As an aside, adding this type of capability on top of an existing application has helped many companies succeed against competitors.

- **Acquisitions:** If your company is growing through acquisitions, integrating the systems of acquired organizations is always a challenge—and is almost certain to raise transaction throughput requirements. All too often the business thinks about the IT integration plan too late in the process, and there's no time to accurately plan for the impact.

The main reason enterprise application integration (EAI) was so popular in the 1990s and early 2000s was because of the high volume of business consolidation. However, using EAI by itself results in stand-alone application "islands," each one of which you have to support separately. If at all possible, your company should consider doing a true business integration. Integrating your systems and applications usually results in better customer service, and your company is better able to compete. Integration also makes the environment easier for IT to support.

In any case, if your business is planning any kind of integration effort, it's important to investigate the impact of the additional transaction volume.

From these sources, put together your best estimates over time for high/ medium/low transaction volumes. It's important to get the *peak* input transaction load, not just the average, because your application must be able to process the maximum expected volume at any given time in the daily, monthly, or yearly cycle. You'll use this information in later steps to develop a cost-effective, flexible design.

The following section from the SPOC report shows the PBCOR results for this step.

Step 1.3: Determine Future Potential Input Processing Rate

1.3

Determine Future
Potential Input
Processing Rate

In this step we extrapolated from current values to predict the future input rates for the ATM and DCS systems. The prediction is approximate and is based on the projected increase in users, as shown in the following table:

Current and Planned Numbers of Users

Metric	Current TPS	Planned TPS (Five Years)
ATM locations	3000	9000
Debit card holders	4,000,000	10,000,000

The ATM system is a prime candidate for new products and services. Therefore, we expect the number of transactions per session to increase. To include this factor in our estimates, we raised the estimate for the average transactions per second to six-plus.

The following table shows the current input rates (from Step 1.2) against the planned rates:

Current and Planned Input Rates

Application	Current Average TPS	Current Peak TPS	Planned Average TPS	Planned Peak TPS
ATM transactions	150	750	1000	5000
DCS transactions	2500	7500	6500	32,500
Total	2650	8250	7500	37,500

These figures show that we can expect a sixfold increase in ATM transactions and a fourfold increase in DCS transactions over the next five years. However, these transactions are currently processed by individual systems, and we will be integrating them in the first phase. The combined increase is approximately five times the current rate; that is the rate we must accommodate in the Pipelines Implementation.

Step 1.4: Measure Current Capacity

This step answers the question "What is your current capacity?" Measure the throughput of your entire system today, at a gross level, and compare that to your current transaction load and your future estimates. You'll find that your system falls into one of the following slots:

- The system handles the current transaction volume adequately and can accommodate the expect growth in volume.
- The system meets the current transaction volume without problems, but it can't handle the expected growth in volume without overly taxing hardware and other resources.
- The system fails to meet current transaction volume requirements, and application processing is lagging behind input transaction rates.

If you're lucky enough to find your system in the first slot, you may not have any need for pipelines at all; your system is handling current and predicted volumes.

The second slot is also good news, because you have time to plan for the future. For example, your company's overnight batch processing application barely completes within its allotted processing window. When transactions increase (as expected), the application immediately exceeds the time limit. This is a great opportunity for Software Pipelines, and you can use the lead time to carefully design and implement a long-term solution.

The third slot is the least desirable, but it's also the most common. In this case you have to go into emergency mode, because your application is failing to handle the current load—let alone the future predicted load. For example, you've got an order entry application that slows to a crawl at peak times of the day. Users start complaining, customer orders are getting lost, and it's frustrating for everyone. You need to do something now!

What do you do if your system is in the third slot? Find out, as quickly as you can, where the key bottlenecks are by using SPOC Step 2 (which we'll cover in the next chapter). When you've found the constricted points, implement pipelines for one or two of the most significant ones. This will speed things up so you can handle the current workload, and later you can backtrack to do a more thorough design and implementation.

Remember that Software Pipelines and SPOC are flexible, and they're intended to help you adapt and respond to a variety of situations. The tools are only as good as the use to which they are put, so make sure you apply them in a way that makes sense for your organization and for the situation you're handling.

The following section from the SPOC report shows the PBCOR results for this step.

Step 1.4: Measure Current Capacity

To get the current capacity for the ATM and DCS systems, we measured the processing of actual transactions. The two systems are performing adequately for the existing load; however, we do know that ATM users can experience a delayed response by as much as a few seconds at peak times.

We sampled the systems at peak periods and looked at server utilization for both applications. We found that CPU, memory, and disk utilization have reasonable levels of efficiency (CPU is running at 60 to 80 percent). Therefore, the current hardware is performing at near maximum.

The following table shows the current capacity:

Current Capacity

Application	Current Peak Capacity (TPS)
ATM transactions	500
DCS transactions	5000
Total	5500

Step 1.5: Calculate Performance Gap

This step is very straightforward: Compare your overall current capacity to your current and planned loads. The difference is your performance gap.

The following section from the SPOC report shows the PBCOR results for this step.

Step 1.5: Calculate Performance Gap

We used several elements to calculate the current and future performance gaps for the ATM and DCS systems:

- ATM application as a stand-alone process (current and future)
- DCS application as a stand-alone process (current and future)
- Combined ATM/DCS service (current and future)

We will integrate the two systems using the Java platform (the ATM application is already on this platform), because it is the easiest architecture to support as we go forward. We can reuse much of the DCS C++ infrastructure to receive and validate incoming transactions, but we plan to write all of the demand account processing in Java. Using Java enables us to reuse common functions and makes it easier to support the function over the long term.

Our integration plan significantly affects the performance gap, because the ATM application is currently not quite keeping up with peak volume requirements. We plan to use Software Pipelines and additional multi-core servers to address this issue.

The following table shows the performance gap estimates for both systems:

Performance Gap Estimates

Application	Current Peak Capacity (TPS)	Current Peak TPS	Performance Gap (TPS)	Planned Peak TPS	Performance Gap (TPS)
ATM transactions	500	750	(250)	5000	(4500)
DCS transactions	5000	7500	(2500)	32,500	(27,500)
Combined	5500	8250	(2750)	37,500	(32,000)
Combined (Java)	500	8250	(7750)	37,500	(37,000)

As the table shows, we need to scale significantly in order to accommodate the expected load. In addition, when we combine ATM and DCS into an integrated system, even the current performance has a substantial gap.

Step 1.6: Define Pipelines Targets

At this point you have the raw material for setting pipelines targets that you can actually achieve. Using the calculated performance gap, set throughput targets that bridge the gap. Keep in mind that you are working at the aggregate level, not at the detailed component level.

Table 9.1 shows some current example values and what happens to the performance gap as load demand increases over time. You can easily see that you run out of capacity within the first 12 months, and you're seriously overloaded within two to three years. To fix this, you'll set pipelines targets to handle the gap, plus a reasonable cushion. Note that this table contains a purely hypothetical example, and is not tied to the PBCOR example application.

Table 9.1 Example Pipelines Targets

Time Period	Requirements (TPS)	Capacity (TPS)	Performance Gap (TPS)	Pipelines Target (TPS)
Current	750	800	None	None
Predicted: 12 months	1000	800	200	1100
Predicted: 24 months	1500	800	700	1700
Predicted: 36 months	2000	800	1200	2500

By doing this step, you can see what you have to achieve and when. You can design your pipelines implementation so that you can keep scaling it up to meet future loads, without having to add the entire capacity now. This approach enables you to prepare for the future without overspending in the short term.

The following section from the SPOC report shows the PBCOR results for this step.

Step 1.6: Define Pipelines Targets

The following table shows the pipelines targets for the initial phase of the demand deposit implementation:

Pipelines Targets

Application	12-Month Target (TPS)	24-Month Target (TPS)	36-Month Target (TPS)	60-Month Target (TPS)
ATM transactions	750	1500	2250	5000
DCS transactions	7500	15,000	22,500	32,500
Combined	8250	16,500	24,750	37,500

We will translate the transactions-per-second targets into the number of required pipelines later, in SPOC Step 3.

Summary

SPOC Step 1 is vital to the success of your pipelines implementation. When you finish, you've put the resources for doing your project in place, and you have a very good idea of the project's scope. You know where you're going, and you have an accurate estimate of what to do in order to get there.

In the next chapter you'll learn about Pipelines Analysis, the second SPOC step, in depth. In the first step you compile information about your overall system. In Pipelines Analysis you'll find out what your system is doing on a very detailed level, and you'll discover the exact points where the process flow is backing up.

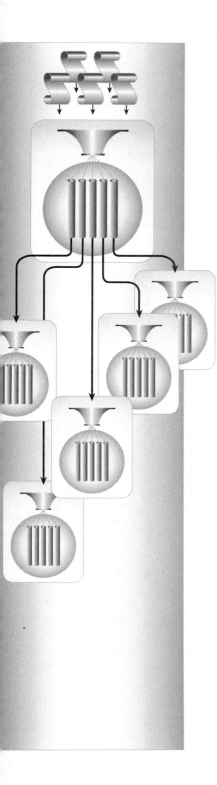

## CHAPTER TEN

SPOC Step 2: Pipelines Analysis

In SPOC Step 2, Pipelines Analysis, you compile the detailed information that is required for applying Pipelines Law to your Pipelines Design. This is the phase where you gain a full understanding of your application, its makeup, and its requirements. Most importantly, you'll identify the performance characteristics of each main component in your application. When you find out how well each component performs, you'll know exactly where the key constraints—the bottlenecks—are located, and you'll be able to fix them by applying Software Pipelines.

As with any analysis, especially one that is performance-centric, the end result is only as good as your data. In many systems you'll have to instrument the application before you can figure out how each component behaves (which means you can then find ways to improve it). This type of instrumentation is very often lacking or nonexistent, and in some cases you'll have to add it to the application before you can do a competent job of analysis. Later, in the Pipelines Examples section of the book, we provide an example of an instrumentation component that will give you a good start toward adding this capability to your applications.

Step 2 is broken out into several sub-steps. The report overview for this step, as seen in the next section, shows the overall process and the sequence of the sub-steps. We'll go into the details for each sub-step in the following sections.

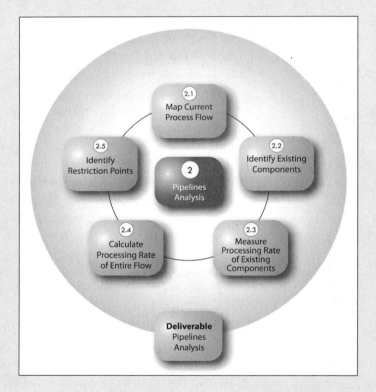

Step 2: Pipelines Analysis

In this step we performed a detailed analysis of the application and its processes, and we identified the performance characteristics of each component. By doing this analysis, we found the application's bottlenecks, which are the points where we plan to apply Software Pipelines.

The following cycle diagram outlines the sub-steps for this phase of SPOC:

The final output of the Pipelines Analysis step is the Pipelines Analysis document, which appears in the following sections of this report.

Step 2.1: Map Current Process Flow

Your first task is to draw or map out the current process flow for your application. You can do this on paper or by using a process modeling tool. It's very important to draw the correct flow so that you can use the map in later steps. You will be using it to analyze and identify individual components, find the bottlenecks in the application, and discover places where pipelines can improve scalability and performance.

The following section from the SPOC report shows the PBCOR results for this step.

Step 2.1: Map Current Process Flow

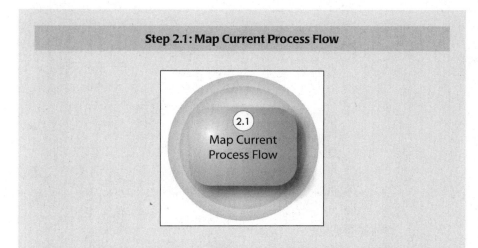

In this step we mapped the process flows for the ATM and DCS applications. Each application has an independent process flow.

ATM Process Flow

The following diagram shows the process flow for the ATM application:

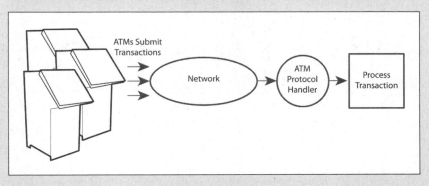

The ATM Protocol Handler is a low-level component that interacts with the ATMs. It was designed efficiently and will continue to perform well for the ATM system into the future, so we do not plan to change it.

We are going to revamp the Process Transaction component. The following diagram shows its flow details:

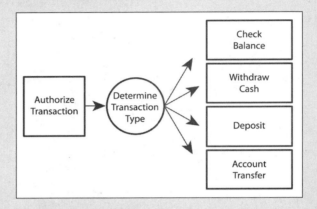

The following diagram shows the flow details for the Withdraw Cash transaction, the most common type of transaction supported by the ATM application:

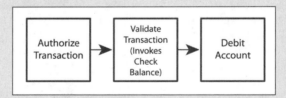

DCS Process Flow

The following diagram shows the process flow for the DCS application:

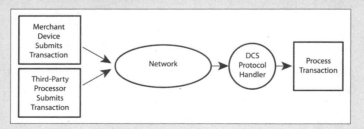

All the components in this application, including the specialized DCS Protocol Handler, are built in C++. The Protocol Handler will continue to perform well for the DCS system into the future, so we do not plan to change it.

We will consolidate the common functions in the Process Transaction component and port it to the same platform as the ATM application. The following diagram shows its flow details:

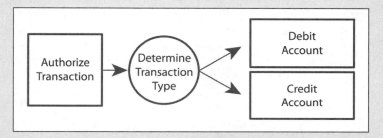

The Debit Account transaction is the most common type of transaction processed by DCS. Its functionality and flow details are similar to those for the ATM Withdraw Cash transaction.

In our PBCOR example, for the sake of simplicity, we've decided to consolidate common functions onto the Java platform. However, you can build pipeline services in any language or environment, and you can invoke pipelines across a network or locally between environments. Pipelined environments can interoperate over a number of different protocols, including Web services, CORBA, proprietary protocols, and various local invocation mechanisms, such as the Java Native Interface. Therefore, when you create your own pipeline designs, go ahead and use the language and environment that make sense for your services.

Step 2.2: Identify Existing Components

After you create your flow map, it's time to identify the service (processing) components for each type of input transaction and for each process flow in your application.

To do this, examine your current process and its code, then isolate the individual service components. You may have to deal with a lot of procedural-style code—big, monolithic programs into which the developer embedded all the processing steps for a transaction. If this is your situation, you can still identify the components. It's usually possible to recognize the primary process steps; look for individual methods or portions of code that act as the logical service steps, then label each one as a service.

When you're done with this step, you'll have a list of the components that constitute your transaction flow. In a later step you'll reorganize these components into a service flow that you can use in your pipelines implementation.

The following section from the SPOC report shows the PBCOR results for this step.

Step 2.2: Identify Existing Components

When we identified the components for ATM and DCS transaction processing, we included only the ones that actually process each transaction. Components for the network, protocol, and originating applications are beyond the scope of this project.

ATM Components

```
Transaction.authorize
Account.checkBalance
Transaction.validate
Account.credit
Account.debit
Account.transfer
```

DCS Components

```
DCS.authorizeTrans
DCS.checkAccountBalance
DCS.validateTransaction
DCS.applyDebit
DCS.applyCredit
```

The ATM components are currently implemented as Java classes, and the DCS components are implemented using C++. Despite a few naming differences, it is obvious that there are redundant functions between the two applications. We plan to eliminate this redundancy during the first phase of the project.

Step 2.3: Measure Processing Rate of Existing Components

The secret to getting the most benefit from Software Pipelines is gaining an understanding of how your application performs right now. If you know the processing rate of each component and function, you can estimate the processing rate of the entire flow (which you'll do in the next sub-step), and just as importantly, you can find the restricted points in the process (which is the last sub-step).

In this step you need precise performance measurements for individual components. There are several methods for doing this. Application logging and code profiling are the two most popular, but they have limited use when you're trying to measure realistic performance.

- Most applications today do a good job of logging by using common frameworks such as Apache log4j. The typical logger is excellent for tracing functionality and debugging, but completely inadequate for measuring performance. It's almost as if logging follows the Heisenberg Uncertainty Principle[1] from quantum mechanics. In quantum mechanics, when you

---

[1]   See http://en.wikipedia.org/wiki/Uncertainty_principle for more information on the Heisenberg Uncertainty Principle.

locate a particle precisely, you can't measure its momentum with certainty, and if you precisely measure its momentum, you can't get its position with certainty. What's happening is that the act of measuring physically changes the thing you're measuring—and the closer you get while measuring, the more you change it. The same thing happens in logging. Logging consumes cycles, and it can perform only at a specified rate. Therefore, if you're using logging to get performance metrics, you're affecting the performance by the act of writing the log record!

There are ways to get around this. For example, you can write log records at carefully selected points that minimally impact the performance you're trying to measure. However, we've found that it's more productive to use a separate instrumentation system for performance metrics.

- Code profiling is good for identifying inefficiencies and other problems in your code, but it adds far too much overhead to provide realistic figures.

The best method for measuring performance is a specialized performance instrumentation utility. We've included an example performance metric utility, the *Instrumentor*, in the Pipelines Examples section of the book. If you go with this type of utility, it's easy to aggregate and report statistics from any component, with minimal distortion and overhead.

After you've decided which tool to use for measurement, the next question is how to measure the performance of an individual component and get it expressed as transactions per second. The standard method we've developed is to determine the processing time, either in milliseconds or in transactions per second, for each major method call. You can easily translate milliseconds to transactions per second. For example, if a given component requires 200 ms to process a single invocation, it is capable of processing 5 TPS. Similarly, a component that requires 20 ms for processing is capable of 50 TPS. The formula for converting transactions per second to milliseconds is in Step 2.4.

The following section from the SPOC report shows the PBCOR results for this step.

Step 2.3: Measure Processing Rate of Existing Components

In this step we measured the processing rate of each individual component in the ATM and DCS transaction flows. To get the rate for each component, we measured its processing time for 10,000 iterations and used the resulting value to calculate the average transactions per second.

ATM Components

The following table shows performance measurements for the ATM components:

ATM Components

Component	Estimated TPS
Transaction.authorize	4500
Account.checkBalance	4800
Transaction.validate	3800
Account.credit	550
Account.debit	550
Account.transfer	300

DCS Components

The following table shows performance measurements for the DCS components:

DCS Components

Component	Estimated TPS
DCS.authorizeTrans	72,000
DCS.checkAccountBalance	12,500
DCS.validateTransaction	11,000
DCS.applyDebit	9800
DCS.applyCredit	7500

The DCS application performs better than the ATM system, because it is written in a native language and uses a proprietary in-memory database with optimized memory caching. Furthermore, the DCS authorization transaction performs far better than its ATM counterpart, because it can use a mathematical card number verification algorithm. However, the C++ platform and proprietary database make the DCS application difficult to maintain and enhance.

Step 2.4: Calculate Processing Rate of Entire Flow

In this step you're just double-checking the processing rates of the individual components in each service flow. Use the following sequence of formulas:

1. Using the TPS values from Step 2.3, figure out how long it takes for each component to process one transaction, in other words, its time per transaction in milliseconds (tT). The formula for converting TPS to tT is

$$tT = 1/TPS * 1000$$

Using this formula, calculate the tT for each component.

2. When you've calculated this value for each component, add them all up, then convert the answer back into TPS. This gives you the TPS rate for the entire flow. The formula is

$$FlowTPS = (1/\sum (tT1, tT2, \ldots tTn)) * 1000$$

If you like, you can combine the first two steps in this sequence by directly calculating *FlowTPS* from the component values:

$$FlowTPS = 1/\sum(1/TPS1, 1/TPS2, \ldots 1/TPSn)$$

3. Compare *FlowTPS* to the current capacity of the whole system—the value from Step 1.4—to ensure that your new calculations are reasonable and make sense.

The following section from the SPOC report shows the PBCOR results for this step.

Step 2.4: Calculate Processing Rate of Entire Flow

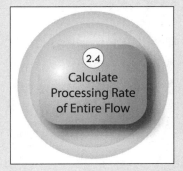

In this step we estimated the processing rate for the entire application flow in both the ATM and the DCS systems. We calculated only the most common transactions, because they are the most critical for our performance requirements.

ATM Withdraw Cash Transaction

The following diagram shows the flow for Withdraw Cash, with the transactions per second for each component:

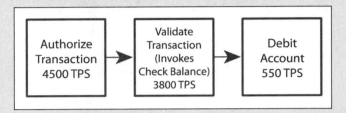

The following table shows the time per transaction in milliseconds (tT) for each component in the flow, using the formula tT = 1/TPS * 1000:

ATM Components—Time per Transaction

Component	tT
`Transaction.authorize`	0.222 ms = 1/4500 * 1000
`Transaction.validate`	0.263 ms = 1/3800 * 1000
`Account.debit`	1.812 ms = 1/550 * 1000

We calculated the processing rate for the entire flow by using the formula

$$FlowTPS = (1/\sum(tT1, tT2,...tTn)) * 1000$$

So

$$434 \text{ TPS} = (1/\sum(0.222, 0.263, 1.812)) * 1000$$

The following calculation combines the two formulas in one step:

$$434 \text{ TPS} = 1/\sum(1/4500, 1/3800, 1/550)$$

We compared the final value, 434 TPS, to the current peak TPS from Step 1.4, 500 TPS, and found it to be reasonable. We do expect some anomalies when the system is deployed to the test and production hardware systems.

DCS Debit Account Transaction

The DCS Debit Account transaction has a similar detail flow to the ATM Withdraw Cash transaction.

The following table shows the time per transaction in milliseconds (tT) for each component in the flow, using the formula $tT = 1/TPS * 1000$:

DCS Components—Time per Transaction

Component	tT
DCS.authorizeTrans	0.013 ms = 1/72000 * 1000
DCS.validateTransaction	0.090 ms = 1/11000 * 1000
DCS.applyDebit	0.102 ms = 1/9800 * 1000

We calculated the processing rate for the entire flow by using the combined formula:

$$4834 \text{ TPS} = 1/\Sigma(1/72{,}000, 1/11{,}000, 1/9800)$$

We compared the final value, 4834 TPS, to the current peak TPS from Step 1.4, 5000 TPS, and found it to be reasonable. Again, we do expect some anomalies when the system is deployed to the test and production hardware systems.

Step 2.5: Identify Restriction Points

This is the final step of the Pipelines Analysis phase. Using the information from the preceding steps, you can now identify the restriction points in your transaction flows. This is critical information for your pipelines implementation.

Look over your calculations from Step 2.4. You'll see that the slowest component in the flow has a major impact on overall process performance. When you identify the slowest component, you've found the restriction point for that flow—and that's where you apply pipelines during the next phase, Pipelines Design.

The following section from the SPOC report shows the PBCOR results for this step.

Step 2.5: Identify Restriction Points

By examining the detailed transaction flows for the ATM and DCS applications, we identified the key restriction points.

ATM Withdraw Cash Transaction

The following diagram shows the ATM Withdraw Cash transaction flow:

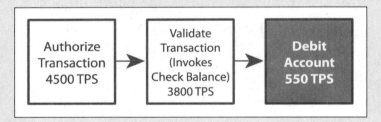

The obvious bottleneck is the Debit Account component, which restricts the processing volume of the flow. This is an ideal initial target for a pipelines implementation.

DCS Debit Account Transaction

The DCS Debit Account transaction is bound by the Debit Account component, which processes 9800 TPS. It is also restricted by the Validate Transaction component, which processes 11,000 TPS. Both of these components are far slower than the Authorize Transaction component, which clocks in at 72,000 TPS.

As a final remark, it is now obvious that we have a major performance gap to handle. We must close this gap to achieve our goal, which is to integrate the back-end transaction processing for both ATM and DCS onto the Java platform, using our standard relational database. Therefore, we consider this gap to be the major technical challenge our team is facing, and we plan to address it in the next phase of the SPOC process.

Summary

In SPOC Step 2 you learn about your system on a detailed level. When you finish this step, you'll have a thorough understanding of your application flows, and you will know where they're running into bottlenecks. The end result shows you exactly where to deploy your pipelines.

In the next chapter we'll show you how to design your pipelines implementation, using all the data gathered in Steps 1 and 2.

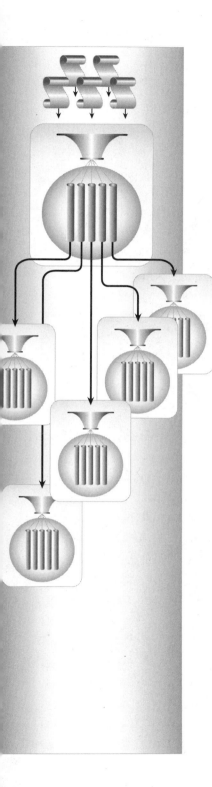

## CHAPTER ELEVEN

SPOC Step 3:
Pipelines Design

In SPOC Step 3, Pipelines Design, all the pieces come together to form the detailed technical foundation for a pipelines implementation. And in your organization, the pipelines architect now takes center stage as the role with the primary responsibility for this step.

This is the most important phase of the entire SPOC process. You're now going to put pipelines theory and Pipelines Law into action and apply the technology directly to your application. As such, it is crucial to "do the math" so you can successfully define exactly how your implementation will operate.

Step 3 is broken out into several sub-steps. The report overview for this step, as seen in the next section, shows the overall process and the sequence of the sub-steps. We'll go into the details for each sub-step in the following sections.

Step 3: Pipelines Design

In this step we present our technical design for the demand deposit Pipelines Implementation, based on our Pipelines Objectives and Analysis. The purpose of Pipelines Design is to determine the best method for implementing the pipelines architecture.

The following cycle diagram outlines the sub-steps for this phase of SPOC:

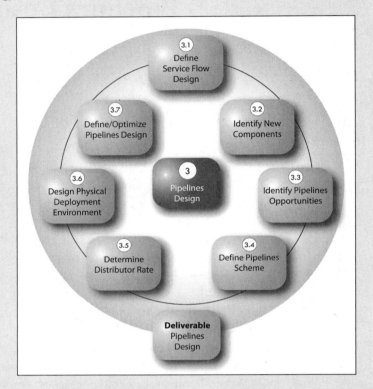

In this step our main goal is to design for performance and scalability, for which we need parallel computing. However, we are dealing with business applications. Business applications present unique challenges when compared to other types of computing:

- Business applications must often process transactions in a certain sequence.
- Short-lived transactions are the backbone of most business applications and must often be completed in milliseconds. This is very different from typical computation-intensive parallel applications, which often deal in processes that require hours (or even days) to complete.

- Business applications must be able to change rapidly to accommodate new market and economic conditions. Therefore, they require a higher level of flexibility than other computing applications.

There are many approaches to parallel computing, such as multi-threaded application servers, grid computing, and clustering. However, these mechanical "automatic" methods are not suited for the unique requirements of business applications. Our target applications are business applications, with all of the requirements in the preceding list. Therefore, to meet these requirements, we will use the Software Pipelines architecture.

Another goal for our team is to be able to predict ultimate application performance during the design phase. All too often, organizations optimize their applications in crisis mode, addressing one bottleneck at a time, only to be faced with another one somewhere else in the system. To address this issue, we are using the SPOC methodology, which will enable us to plan for the future as we go through the design process.

The final output of the Pipelines Design step is the set of Pipelines Design documents, which appear in the following sections of this report. These documents detail our recommended approach to applying pipelines to the ATM and DCS systems.

Step 3.1: Define Service Flow Design

Software Pipelines is a service-oriented approach to business applications. To explain how this works, we should first clarify what we mean by "service-oriented." Our definition of a service goes well beyond the paradigm for a typical Web service:

A service is any discrete software component that can be independently invoked by whatever method is appropriate for a given application. It uses messages for its input and output. When a service component receives a message, it consumes and processes the message, then invokes the next service in the flow, to which it sends the processed message. You can run a service locally on a single server by using a direct method call, or across a network by using one of a variety of protocols (Web services, RMI, CORBA, sockets, etc.).

Figure 11.1 shows a system using a service-oriented approach. The system has service components that exchange messages within one server. It also has a service that exchanges messages between servers across the network.

A given service can run on any computer platform, or on many platforms at the same time. It can also run as a single instance or across thousands of instances. Figure 11.2 illustrates this last point.

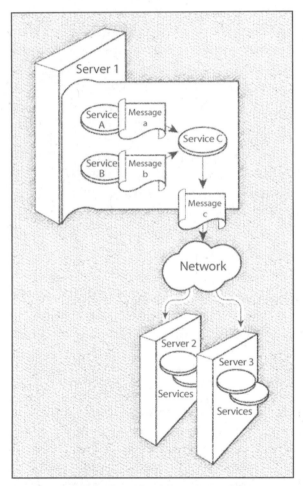

Figure 11.1 System using a service-oriented approach

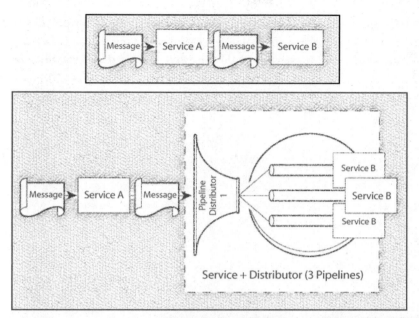

Figure 11.2 Services can run as single instances or as multiple instances.

Earlier, in Step 2.1, you mapped the current *process* flow of your application. In the current step you're going to define the *service* flow. What's the difference? There are only a couple of differences, but they're important:

- The current process flow is just that—the way your application works today, not necessarily how you want it to work in the future.
- The process flow typically shows only the components, not the messages that pass between the components.

Messaging is what defines a service-oriented architecture. That may not sound like a huge difference, but it brings a whole new set of capabilities into the arsenal of the development team, and it allows them to do what they do best— build functionality without getting mired down in the details of deployment and operations. This approach resolves for the first time the apparent conflict between the goals of flexibility and scalability for business applications.

Because of its service orientation, Software Pipelines allows a great degree of independence between the components that do the work (the services) and the framework that executes the components. In other words, service processing is independent from service invocation, and you can easily execute service components in parallel, completely independent of the services themselves.

The following section from the SPOC report shows the PBCOR results for this step.

The demand deposit team plans to consolidate the ATM and DCS transaction processing onto the Java platform. By making this change, we can use one service flow design for each transaction type. The service flow will use a single message type, a Java class (POJO, Plain Old Java Object) named `com.pbcor.message.AccountTrans`.

The `AccountTrans` message contains the transaction type, the authentication information, and fields for the actual transaction. By using a generic message type, we can perform any type of transaction and use any protocol to invoke the service from our Pipelines Framework.

The following diagram shows the high-level service flow for the ATM and DCS applications:

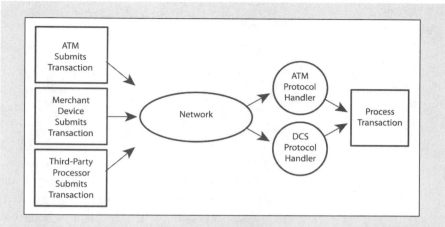

The specialized protocol handlers for ATM and DCS transactions are providing satisfactory performance. We expect this performance to continue into the future; therefore, we are leaving these components intact. Instead, we are focusing on the Process Transaction step. The following diagram shows our new service flow for Process Transaction:

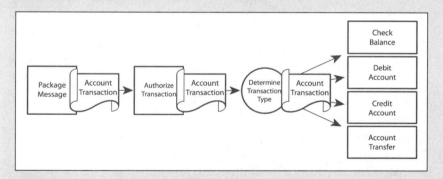

In this new flow, the Debit Account and Credit Account components support both the ATM and DCS applications. Account Transfer applies only to ATM transactions. Check Balance is used as a single transaction by the ATM application, but both ATM and DCS use it to validate each transaction when required.

The sequence of the service flow is as follows:

1. Protocol handlers deliver their messages in proprietary formats.
2. Incoming messages are packaged into the `AccountTrans` message.
3. `AccountTrans` is sent to a downline component.
4. The receiving component processes the transaction.

Because the Debit Account transaction is the most frequently used transaction, we will focus our optimization efforts on it during the design phase. It will be the first service flow we implement using the pipelines architecture.

The following diagram shows the details for Debit Account's service flow, which uses the `AccountTrans` message as input/output between services:

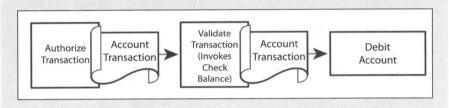

Step 3.2: Identify New Components

In any pipelines implementation, it's common for the new service flow to require new or modified components. Frequently the existing components aren't constructed as "services" with the ability to accept and send messages. This is especially true when you implement pipelines the first time.

This step is very straightforward.

- Review the service flow from Step 3.1.
- Identify any new or modified service components you'll need for your implementation.
- Estimate the processing rate for the new/modified components. Determine whether they will significantly impact the performance of your service flow.
- List the requirements for each new/modified component. You'll use the list later, in Step 4, Pipelines Implementation.

You will only be able to estimate how these components will perform, because you haven't developed them yet. A new component can adversely affect the overall performance of your service flow, so it's important to predict how it will perform. The following techniques might help you make a realistic estimate:

- If the new/modified component has similar functionality to any existing component (for example, it accesses the same database table as an existing component), you may be able to extrapolate performance based on the similarities.
- For a component with net new functionality, it may be necessary to create a test case that performs the component's critical, performance-intensive tasks. Be sure to incorporate any processing that is both required and intensive, such as I/O processing, in your test. By measuring the performance of the test case, you can usually get an idea of how the actual component will perform. This won't be perfectly accurate, but it should give you enough working knowledge to proceed with the Pipelines Design.

The following section from the SPOC report shows the PBCOR results for this step.

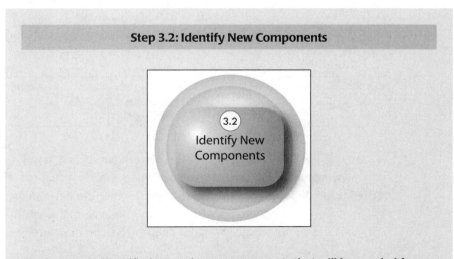

Step 3.2: Identify New Components

3.2
Identify New
Components

In this step we identified several new components that will be needed for our service flow, and several that must be modified. The following table shows each new/modified component, along with its requirements:

New/Modified Components Needed for Service Flow

Service	Requirements
ATM Protocol Handler	Modify the handler to pass transactions asynchronously to the Process Transaction service and wait for a response, which is returned to the ATM device.
DCS Protocol Handler	Modify the handler to pass transactions asynchronously to the Process Transaction service and wait for a response, which is returned to the DCS client device.
`AccountTrans` message	New component. Message class must be developed. Required fields include Transaction type Account number Authorization credentials Amount Any other transaction-specific details
Package message	New service component. Receives the raw transmission from the ATM/DCS Protocol Handlers and packages it into the `AccountTrans` message.
Authorize Transaction	Modify the existing `Transaction.authorize` functionality. Package it as a service, and modify it to handle both ATM and DCS authorizations.
Validate Transaction	Modify the existing `Transaction.validate` functionality. Package it as a service, and modify it to use the `AccountTrans` message.
Debit Account	Modify the existing `Account.debit` functionality. Package it as a service, and modify it to use the `AccountTrans` message.

Moving the DCS functionality to the Java platform will create the primary performance impact in our implementation. We know that our existing performance characteristics are inadequate to meet the performance gap. However, we will be able to address these performance challenges by using pipelines, and we anticipate no major impact from the new/modified components.

Step 3.3: Identify Pipeline Opportunities

You're now at the point where you can apply Pipelines Law directly to your bottlenecks, and you can finally take full advantage of all the homework and analysis you performed in Steps 1 and 2, including

- Pipelines targets
- Performance metrics
- Restriction points (bottlenecks)
- Service flow
- Service components

The key question for Step 3.3 is "Where should I apply pipelines?" To answer the question, use the following pipelines rules:

Rule 1. Input equals output.

Rule 2. The capacity (transaction rate) of any downstream component or process must be greater than or equal to the input rate of any upstream process or component. When this is not the case, you must optimize the downstream component or process, or you must use a Pipeline Distributor to support concurrent processing and handle the load.

The formula for Rule 2 is

$$\text{InputRate must be} <= \text{ProcessRate}$$

Look over all the individual service components you've defined, and review the performance characteristics and requirements of each one. What you're looking for is any downstream component that can't accommodate the current or predicted input rate.

Use the following workflow to figure out which service flows will benefit from pipelines:

- Compare the input rate (from Step 1.2) to the stand-alone processing rate (from Step 2.4) for each service flow you defined.
- The processing rate will be one of the following: (a) higher than the input rate, (b) lower than the input rate, or (c) approximately equal to the input rate. If either (a) or (c) is true, you don't need pipelines. If (b) is true for any flow, that's where you should implement pipelines.

After working over the service flows, follow the next steps to find out exactly where you can and should use pipelines:

- Review the performance gaps you identified in Step 1.5 and your pipelines targets from Step 1.6. The gaps are what you're trying to bridge. When you increase the capacity of the associated service flows, you'll close the gaps.
- Match each performance gap with the restriction points from Step 2.5. The restricting components are your first pipeline opportunities; they're performing at less than the required level, and they're slowing down the entire flow.
- Look at the processing rate for each service component in each service flow (from Step 2.3). Identify *any* component that performs at less than the target input rate. Each of these components (or perhaps the entire service flow) provides an opportunity for pipelines.

The following section from the SPOC report shows the PBCOR results for this step.

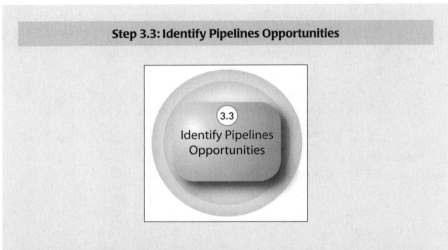

Step 3.3: Identify Pipelines Opportunities

The following table shows the ATM and DCS performance gaps (identified in Step 1.5):

Performance Gap Estimates

Application	Current Peak Capacity (TPS)	Current Peak TPS	Performance Gap (TPS)	Planned Peak TPS	Performance Gap (TPS)
ATM transactions	500	750	(250)	5000	(4500)
DCS transactions	5000	7500	(2500)	32,500	(27,500)
Combined	5500	8250	(2750)	37,500	(32,000)
Combined (Java)	500	8250	(7750)	37,500	(37,000)

We plan to implement the PBCOR pipelines project in two phases:

- ATM stand-alone
- ATM and DCS running as an integrated set of services on the Java platform

We will implement the transaction processing for the service flows in both applications by using the Java platform. Therefore, the ultimate performance gap that we must address is the combined (Java) figure, which has a shortfall of 37,000 TPS in five years. To cover the shortfall, we must multiply the performance by one to two orders of magnitude.

However, because it is difficult to accurately predict a five-year horizon, we intend to concentrate on the 12-month and 24-month targets, which are more manageable. The following table shows the TPS targets for these time frames:

Pipelines Targets for 12-Month and 24-Month Periods

Application	Current Peak Capacity (TPS)	12-Month Target (TPS)	Performance Gap (TPS)	24-Month Target (TPS)	Performance Gap (TPS)
ATM transactions	500	750	(250)	1500	(1000)
DCS transactions	5000	7500	(2500)	15,000	(10,000)
Combined	5500	8250	(2750)	16,500	(11,000)
Combined (Java)	500	8250	(7750)	16,500	(16,000)

The gaps for the ATM application in the first and second years are manageable. We need to achieve 1.5X and 3X performance improvement respectively to close these gaps. The combined (Java) targets are still a major challenge; we must achieve 16X and 33X improvements in that area.

We examined the restriction points in our service flow and determined that the ATM Withdraw Cash flow is our most challenging requirement. It is also the same flow that will ultimately support the most common DCS transaction type. The following diagram shows the bottleneck in this flow:

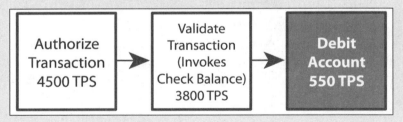

The Authorize Transaction and Validate Transaction components can handle our 12- and 24-month requirements for ATM, but the Debit Account component falls short. And after we integrate ATM and DCS on the Java platform, all of these components fall short. Accordingly, we identified the following pipelines opportunities and scheduled them by implementation stage:

Pipelines Schedule

Pipeline Opportunity	ATM-Only Stage	ATM/DCS Stage
Authorize Transaction		X
Validate Transaction		X
Debit Account	X	X

Step 3.4: Define Pipelines Scheme

You're now ready to formulate your pipelines scheme. The scheme is a high-level design for applying pipelines and Pipeline Distributor(s) to your application and is based on Pipelines Patterns. So the main task in this step is to choose the pattern(s) that is the best fit for the project. Here's the sequence of actions you should follow:

1. Select the Pipelines Pattern(s) that is most appropriate for your application requirements. Table 11.1 can help you make your decision.

2. Modify your service flow diagram from Step 3.1 to show the Pipeline Distributor(s) in your flow.

3. Annotate the diagram by describing the relevant details and assumptions.

Table 11.1 shows the Pipelines Patterns according to distributor aspect, with options and additional comments. Use the table to select the most appropriate pattern(s) for your application.

Table 11.1 Pipelines Patterns

Distributor Pattern Aspect	Pattern Options	Comments
Service Invocation Pattern	Push	Pushes messages directly onto the service execution stack.
	Pull	Places messages on a centralized message queue. Distributor pulls messages from the queue.
Message Exchange Pattern	One-Way	Sends the message and "forgets" it.
	Request-Response	Service must return a response when it finishes its task.
Routing Pattern	Round-Robin	Unordered routing across multiple instances of the service.
	Content-Based	Ordered routing based on the value of the Pipelines Key in the message.
	Custom	Customized routing method for specialized requirements.
Distributor Pattern	Single Distributor	Services are hosted and executed within the distributor instance.
	Multi-tier Distributor	Tiered set of distributors, which route invocations across distributor instances. Increases performance gains.
	Client Distributor	Distributes from the client tier. Directly invokes the service using any protocol for remote method invocation.
	Database Sharding Distributor	Specialized client or middle-tier distributor. Routes invocations to a set of partitioned database "shards."
Distributor Connector Pattern	Local Method Invocation	Client invokes the service locally (via the distributor), using a direct method call.
	Socket Invocation	Client invokes the service (via the distributor) using a TCP/IP socket-based protocol.
	Web Service Invocation	Client invokes the service (via the distributor) using a Web service.
	Other Remote Method Invocation	Client invokes the service (via the distributor) using another remote method invocation model.

The following section from the SPOC report shows the PBCOR results for this step.

Step 3.4: Define Pipelines Scheme

3.4
Define Pipelines
Scheme

In this step we present the pipelines scheme for each phase of our project:

- ATM stand-alone service
- ATM and DCS running as an integrated set of services on the Java platform

ATM Stand-alone Service

The following diagram shows the service flow for the ATM stand-alone phase. We added a Pipeline Distributor (Distributor A), which supports the Debit Account transaction.

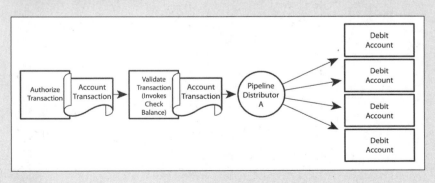

Distributor A improves the throughput of the Debit Account service and makes it possible to achieve our target for 3X scalability in the ATM application over the next 24 months. The following table shows the selected options for Distributor A:

Distributor A Options

Pipeline Distributor A	Pattern Options
Service Invocation Pattern	Push
Message Exchange Pattern	Request-Response
Routing Pattern	Content-Based
	Routing key: `branch_id`
Distributor Pattern	Single Distributor
Distributor Connector Pattern	Local Method Invocation

Integrated ATM/DCS Service

The following diagram shows the service flow for the integrated ATM/DCS phase, which presents much greater scalability challenges. We added multiple Pipeline Distributors (Distributors B, C, D, and E) to support the Debit Account transaction.

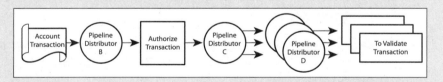

The following diagram shows the Validate Transaction service (detail from the "To Validate Transaction" component in the flow diagram):

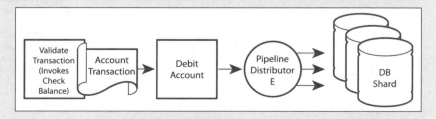

The Multi-tier Distribution Pattern is required to accommodate the tremendous increase in volume we expect from integrating the ATM and DCS transactions. The selected options for each distributor appear in the following tables.

The following table shows the selected options for Distributor B:

Distributor B Options

Pipeline Distributor B	Pattern Options
Service Invocation Pattern	Push
Message Exchange Pattern	Request-Response
Routing Pattern	Round-Robin
Distributor Pattern	Single Distributor
Distributor Connector Pattern	Local Method Invocation

The following table shows the selected options for Distributor C. Distributor C is a multi-tier distributor, which relays transactions to multiple instances of Distributor D.

Distributor C Options

Pipeline Distributor C	Pattern Options
Service Invocation Pattern	Push
Message Exchange Pattern	Request-Response
Routing Pattern	Content-Based
	Routing key: `branch_id`
Distributor Pattern	Multi-tier Distributor
Distributor Connector Pattern	Local Method Invocation

The following table shows the selected options for Distributor D:

Distributor D Options

Pipeline Distributor D	Pattern Options
Service Invocation Pattern	Push
Message Exchange Pattern	Request-Response
Routing Pattern	Content-Based
	Routing key: `account_no`
Distributor Pattern	Single Distributor
Distributor Connector Pattern	Socket

Because Debit Account is the slowest task in the service flow (we identified it as the main restriction point), we investigated methods of making it perform faster. The primary bottleneck is caused by the next downstream component, the back-end relational database, which is very slow.

To resolve this issue, we designed Distributor E as a Database Sharding Distributor, which automatically distributes transactions from the service to the database using shards. Each shard will contain a segment of the customer account records. This pattern will improve overall throughput and thereby increase the performance of the Debit Account service.

The following table shows the selected options for Distributor E:

Distributor E Options

Pipeline Distributor E	Pattern Options
Service Invocation Pattern	Push
Message Exchange Pattern	Request-Response
Routing Pattern	Content-Based
	Routing key: `account_no`
Distributor Pattern	Database Sharding
Distributor Connector Pattern	JDBC Connector

Step 3.5: Determine Distributor Rate

When you get to this step, you've selected the Pipelines Pattern(s) and distributor(s) for your application. We'll now show you how to calculate the maximum number of pipelines for a flow, which you'll get by measuring the rate of the distributor. This task uses the third rule of Pipelines Law:

> **Rule 3.** The processing rate of the Pipeline Distributor must be far greater than the downstream processing rate.

There's no question that the Pipeline Distributor adds overhead to your process. Therefore, it must use far less overhead than the service you intend to pipeline, and its processing rate will have to be much higher.

Distributors for the various Pipelines Patterns can have many possible configurations, and each one has its own performance characteristics. Furthermore, the way your application-specific distributor(s) perform will depend on a number of factors that you must test and evaluate. In other words, the age-old advertising disclaimer definitely applies: "Actual results may vary ..."

Let's look at some of the more important factors that can affect performance:

- What communication protocol do you use to invoke the distributor service?
- Does the distributor use content-based routing? (This requires the distributor to evaluate the content of the message.) If so, how large is the message? Where does the Pipeline Key appear in the message? Placing the key in the header or near the front of the message can make a huge difference in performance (speeding up the distributor operation).
- What protocol does the distributor use to invoke the underlying service? Local method invocation is the fastest, and Web service invocation is usually the slowest.

By far, the most certain way to measure distributor rate is to set up a test framework, using the actual protocol and distributor configurations, and perform actual measurements. With this type of setup, you can simulate production operation and send actual messages to the distributor.

After you determine the Pipeline Distributor rate, you can evaluate the appropriate number of pipelines required for your service. Use the following formula from Pipelines Law:

$$NumberOfPipelines = DistributorTPS / ProcessTPS$$

This formula shows you the maximum number of pipelines the distributor supports and will give you a very good estimate of the potential throughput in your pipelines implementation. You can also use it to plan future modifications and enhancements of your pipelines architecture.

The following section from the SPOC report shows the PBCOR results for this step.

Step 3.5: Determine Distributor Rate

To determine the distributor rates in the ATM and DCS applications, we prepared a test harness for each Pipeline Distributor. To do the tests, we developed the `AccountTrans` message and used an actual sample set of messages. After we determined the rates, we calculated the maximum number of pipelines for each distributor using the formula

NumberOfPipelines = DistributorTPS / ProcessTPS

The following table shows the test results:

Distributor Rates

Distributor	Downstream Process	Process Rate (TPS)	Distributor Rate (TPS)	Maximum Number of Pipelines
Pipeline Distributor A	Debit Account	500	89,000	178
Pipeline Distributor B	Authorize	4500	110,000	24
Pipeline Distributor C	Distributor D	89,000	92,000	1
Pipeline Distributor D	Validate	3800	89,000	23
Pipeline Distributor E	Database	500	38,000	76

Our results indicate that our Pipeline Distributors can handle the expected load for even longer than the 24-month target.

We'd like to elaborate on the PBCOR results for this step. Most of the Pipeline Distributors well outperform the downstream service they support. This high ratio is reflected in the maximum number of pipelines for each distributor; the number in each case is quite adequate.

However, Distributor C (the multi-tier distributor that feeds Distributor D) maxes out at one! This may seem to indicate a problem. However, this configuration works very well. It makes it possible to distribute the load across machines in the network. As long as this setup doesn't slow things down too much, it's definitely advantageous. Distributor D's rate is much faster than that of its downstream services, and Distributor C distributes the workload of the components that do the actual processing, so the final result is a dramatic improvement in total throughput. Furthermore, this configuration makes deployment much easier, and it adds flexibility for scaling upward in the future.

Step 3.6: Design Physical Deployment Environment

There isn't any cut-and-dried procedure for designing your hardware environment. What you do in this step depends on your existing standards, the hardware you already have, and, of course, your budget. It is beyond the scope of this book to get into specific hardware recommendations, but we can give you some general guidelines to help with the process:

- Study and understand the current hardware standards for your organization.
- Evaluate the hardware you're currently using for your target application, and determine if you can use it in your pipelines implementation.
- If you need to buy more hardware, review what's available as thoroughly as you can, and do careful research. Vendors are continually coming up with new and attractive packaging, server configurations, and pricing.
- Consider using multi-core technology. Software Pipelines architecture is designed to work well with multiple commodity servers utilizing multi-core chips. We recommend that you take advantage of the massive amount of processing power available on multi-core servers. If you can do this, you'll get the best performance from your pipelines implementation. As of this writing, servers with eight processing cores are standard, and we'll see chips with 16 cores, 32 cores, and more in the not-too-distant future. So there's a tremendous amount of untapped computing resources at your fingertips. The big question is how to take advantage of this power and put it to productive use in your business applications.

    Multi-core chips are generally inexpensive enough to yield cost-effective scaling for your organization, but typical business software hasn't yet capitalized on their capabilities. The biggest selling point for these chips is their built-in support for multi-threading. The goal of your pipelines implementation is to get the most out of this facility—which will be easy, since the architecture is designed to take advantage of it.
- Determine your reliability requirements. Include fail-over in your designs for critical services.
- Identify the servers you'll need for your services and Pipeline Distributors.
- Use the measurements and processing statistics you've been compiling throughout the SPOC process to determine the number of servers you'll need. Get this figured out for your initial implementation, then estimate how many you'll need as your organization (and your pipelines implementation) grows.

- Fully evaluate your network capabilities, performance, and reliability. The network is the most critical component in any scalable distributed system such as a pipelines implementation.

   We can't stress enough how important it is to verify your network's condition. It must be reliable and fast if you want your implementation to succeed. It's even more important to verify it if you're running business transactions, and you're dealing with an ever-increasing number of small transactions distributed across your infrastructure. In fact, we predict that network condition will ultimately govern how fast a given business application can perform.

   When you use a distributed architecture such as Software Pipelines, you're using the network like the internal bus of a massively parallel or mainframe machine. Therefore, as your pipelines implementation grows over time, you must pay attention to your network and invest in it. Right now, 1GB networks are standard issue, and 10GB Ethernet will soon be affordable.

- Set up a test lab, ideally with the exact systems you intend to deploy. If the systems are substantially different from your current environment, you should run performance benchmarks throughout both the design and the development phases.

Step 3.7: Define/Optimize Pipelines Design

In the final step of Pipelines Design, you'll combine the results from all previous steps into a practical, concrete design you can deploy. You're going to accomplish two goals in this phase:

- Design the final layout of your services, Pipeline Distributors, and pipelines.
- Use Pipelines Law to validate your design for each service flow.

To do this step, you'll need the ability to confirm and predict the flow rate of your application. We'll show you how to do that with a set of formulas very much like the ones you used in Step 2.4, in which you calculated the processing rate of the entire flow. You'll calculate the rate again, but this time you'll take your Pipeline Distributors into account. To create a precise design, you must include the impact from the distributors. You're using them to improve performance, but they can also cause more overhead.

We'll use the service flow in Figure 11.3 to illustrate how the formulas work.

Figure 11.3 Example service flow

In our example flow, Service A receives input messages and sends them to Service B. Order of processing is mandatory; the application must call Service A before it calls Service B. Notice that Service A can process 1000 TPS, whereas Service B has a capacity of only 400 TPS. Let's use the formulas from Step 2.4 to see how this service performs without pipelines. The formula for individual components is

$$tT = 1/TPS * 1000$$

And the formula for the entire flow is

$$FlowTPS = (1/\sum(tT1, tT2,\ldots tTn)) * 1000$$

Let's do the calculations:

[Service A rate at 1000 TPS] 1 ms = 1/1000 * 1000

[Service B rate at 400 TPS] 2.5 ms = 1/400 * 1000

[FlowTPS without pipelines] 285 TPS = (1/(1 ms + 2.5 ms)) * 1000

We'd like to increase the rate of our example flow, which is pegged at 285 TPS, so let's look at some ways to optimize it. We'll use the following three methods:

- Pipeline the downstream service.
- Pipeline each of the services independently.
- Pipeline the entire service flow.

Pipeline the Downstream Service

The simplest way to optimize our flow is to pipeline Service B. We'll add a Pipeline Distributor, which you can see in Figure 11.4.

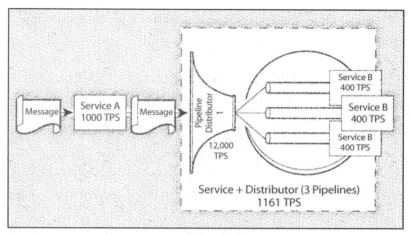

Figure 11.4 Pipeline the downstream service.

In our new design, Pipeline Distributor 1 receives messages from Service A and distributes them to Service B. Order of processing is still mandatory; the application must call Service A before it calls each instance of Service B.

Now we want to know what the rate is when the flow includes Distributor 1, which increases the flow's overhead. First, we'll get the rate for the distributor plus one instance of Service B, but without Service A (you'll see why we do this shortly):

[Distributor 1 rate at 12,000 TPS] .083 ms = 1/12,000 * 1000

[Service B rate at 400 TPS] 2.5 ms = 1/400 * 1000

[Distributor 1 + Service B rate] 387 TPS = (1/(.083 ms, 2.5 ms)) * 1000

If you look at Figure 11.4 again, you'll see we designed the service with three pipelines; each pipeline runs an instance of Service B. We want to know the distributor's pipelined rate, in other words, the rate for the distributor plus its downstream services. The downstream services are the three pipelines, each going to one instance of Service B. To get the pipelined rate, we multiply 387, the TPS for the distributor plus one service, by three, the number of pipelines. The formula is

ServiceTPS = TPS * NumberOfPipelines

Therefore, the *ServiceTPS* for the distributor plus its downstream services is

$$1161 \text{ TPS} = 387 * 3 \text{ pipelines}$$

And now we can calculate the rate of the entire *pipelined* flow. To do this, we'll use the combined formula:

$$\text{FlowTPS} = 1/\textstyle\sum(1/\text{TPS1}, 1/\text{TPS2},\ldots 1/\text{TPSn})$$

We won't use individual values for the distributor and Service B; instead, we'll use the *ServiceTPS* (distributor plus three downstream services) we just calculated. Therefore, the rate of the pipelined flow, with Service A (at 1000 TPS) and *ServiceTPS* (at 1161 TPS) is

$$[\text{FlowTPS with distributor + pipelines}] \ 537 \text{ TPS} = 1/\textstyle\sum(1/1000, 1/1161)$$

Notice that even when we added three pipelines for the slowest component, throughput increased only from 387 TPS to 537 TPS. That's because the flow is sequential, and because each component adds processing time. Table 11.2 shows how more pipelines affect the rate.

As you can see, even when we add ten pipelines, we still increase the rate by only 2.8X. Service A hasn't changed; its rate is 1000 TPS. Therefore, no matter how fast we push Service B (toward a theoretical rate of zero), we can't ever go beyond Service A's speed; we can only approach it. You can see how this works in Figure 11.5, which shows the performance curve for adding more pipelines.

This solution might be acceptable for some applications, but we're illustrating a specific point here: Potential scalability depends on the relative performance of your components. For example, if Service A has a capacity of 10,000 TPS, the

Table 11.2 Performance Improvements from Pipelining

Number of Pipelines	Distributor 1 + Service B (TPS)	*FlowTPS*	Performance Improvement
0	400	285	1X
3	1161	537	1.8X
5	1935	659	2.3X
10	3870	794	2.8X

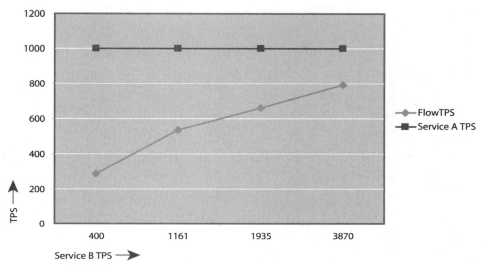

Figure 11.5 Performance for pipelining single service

effect of adding pipelines to Service B is much greater. Without pipelines, *FlowTPS* is 387 TPS. With three pipelines, *FlowTPS* is

[FlowTPS with three pipelines] 1040 TPS = $1/\sum(1/10{,}000, 1/1161)$

We've increased the rate 2.6X. With five pipelines, we can increase the rate to over 4X.

Keep this point in mind as you design your implementation. When you apply pipelines to a service component, remember that the other service components in your flow will affect your result. This is the principle originally quantified in Amdahl's Law, which we're now using in pipelines theory to solve problems in multi-core computing.

If the upstream component performs 1X to 2X faster than the downstream component, pipelining the downstream component makes a bigger impact. In the same vein, your Pipeline Distributor should run 1X to 2X faster than the component(s) it supplies. This will give you plenty of room for adding more pipelines in the future as your demand increases.

Pipeline Services Independently

Independent pipelines are justified when there's a great disparity between the upstream and downstream components. In Figure 11.6 we've pipelined each service independently.

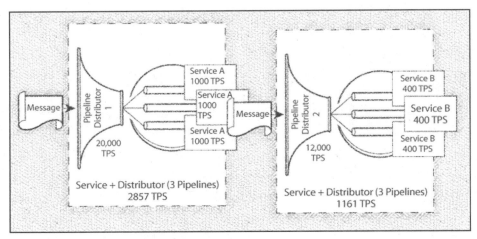

Figure 11.6 Pipeline services independently.

Table 11.3 shows the results from adding more pipelines. We're using the same number of pipelines for each service.

You can see the performance curve for this method in Figure 11.7.

There's a caveat to this approach, however. You won't improve performance if the application has to preserve order of processing for input transactions. If your requirements include sequential processing, you can still use this method by using content-based routing for the distributors. Content-based routing adds a layer of complexity and some redundancy to the process, so you should use it only if you must preserve input order, and if it really looks like you can benefit from independent pipelines.

Table 11.3 Performance Improvements from Pipelining

Number of Pipelines	Distributor 1 + Service A (TPS)	Distributor 2 + Service B (TPS)	*FlowTPS*	Performance Improvement
0	1000	400	285	1X
3	2857	1161	825	2.8X
5	4761	1935	1376	4.8X
10	9523	3870	2752	9.6X

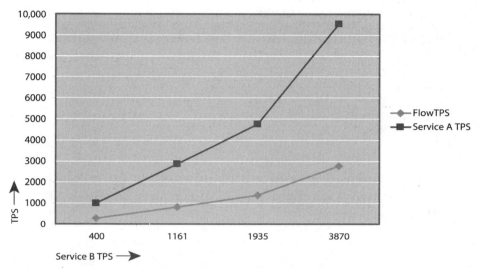

Figure 11.7 Performance for pipelining services independently

Pipeline the Entire Service

In Figure 11.8 we've pipelined the entire service.

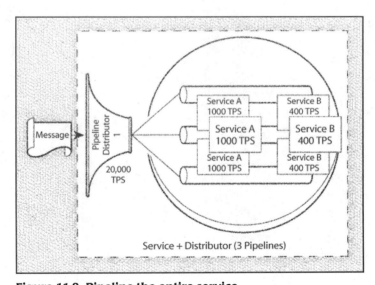

Figure 11.8 Pipeline the entire service.

Table 11.4 Performance Improvements from Pipelining

Number of Pipelines	FlowTPS	Performance Improvement
3	845	3.0X
5	1408	4.9X
10	2816	9.8X

When you pipeline a whole service, you include the distributor's rate directly in the formula for calculating *FlowTPS,* then multiply the result by the number of pipelines. So the formula is

$$\text{FlowTPS} = (1/\Sigma(1/\text{TPS1}, 1/\text{TPS2},\ldots 1/\text{TPSn})) * \text{NumberOfPipelines}$$

And for our example, the *FlowTPS* is

$$[\text{FlowTPS}]\ 845 = (1/\Sigma(1/20{,}000,\ 1/1000,\ 1/400)) * 3$$

Table 11.4 shows the results from adding more pipelines.

You can see the performance curve for this method in Figure 11.9.

Our performance is the same as or better than it was for independent pipelines, and this approach is easier to implement.

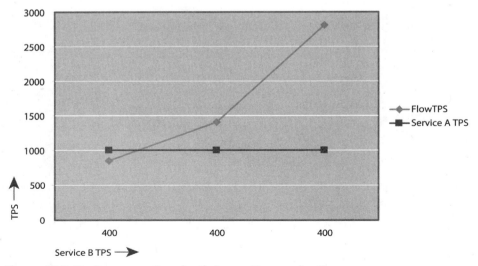

Figure 11.9 Performance for pipelining entire service flow

So which approach should you use? The answer is: "It depends …" You have to evaluate the options, do the calculations, and use the design that best fits your application and the problem you're trying to solve.

The following section from the SPOC report shows the PBCOR results for this step.

Step 3.7: Define/Optimize Pipelines Design

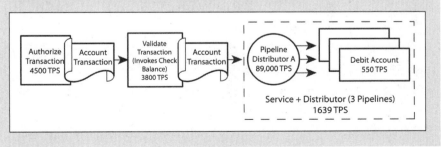

In this section we present the detailed Pipelines Design, with calculations for the predicted performance of each service.

ATM Stand-alone Service

The following diagram shows the flow for the ATM stand-alone service, using our recommended pipelines scheme. We have annotated the diagram with metrics for the predicted performance.

The flow uses a single Pipeline Distributor, which will speed up the Debit Account service, the slowest component in the flow.

The predicted processing rate for Debit Account, using three pipelines, is

$$[\text{DebitAccountTPS}]\ 1639\ \text{TPS} = (1/\textstyle\sum(1/89{,}000,\ 1/550)) * 3$$

The predicted rate for the service is

$$[\text{ServiceTPS}]\ 913\ \text{TPS} = 1/\textstyle\sum(1/4500,\ 1/3800,\ 1/1639)$$

Using three pipelines, the rate is 913 TPS, which is inadequate to meet our 24-month target (1500 TPS) for the stand-alone ATM service, so we calculated rates using more pipelines. The following table shows that if we use ten pipelines, we can meet the 24-month target. The performance improvements are based on the current capacity of 500 TPS.

Performance Improvements from Pipelining

Number of Pipelines	*FlowTPS*	Performance Improvement
3	913	1.8X
5	1174	2.3X
10	1496	3.0X

Integrated ATM/DCS Service

The following diagram shows the design for the integrated ATM/DCS service:

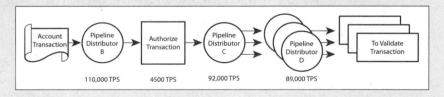

The following diagram shows the Validate Transaction service (detail from the "To Validate Transaction" component in the flow diagram):

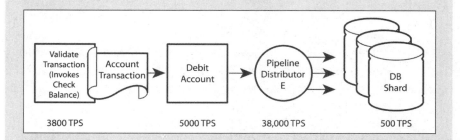

We must scale this service flow up to handle much higher transaction rates; therefore, we are using several Pipeline Distributors. Our 24-month target is 16,500 TPS, an increase of more than 33X over the current levels of peak performance.

Due to the complexity of this flow, we analyzed the predicted performance one segment at a time. We started with the database layer, which is the primary bottleneck in the flow.

Database Tier: Distributor E

The Debit Account transaction accesses a stand-alone instance of the database, which performs at 500 TPS. To handle this, we added Pipeline Distributor E as the database distributor. Distributor E distributes transactions using `account_no` as the Pipelines Key. The rate for the distributor plus its downstream services is

$$[DatabaseTPS]\ 493\ TPS = 1/\sum(1/38{,}000,\ 1/500)$$

The following table shows the results for *DatabaseTPS* when we add more pipelines. The performance improvements are based on the *DatabaseTPS* of 493 TPS.

Performance Improvements from Pipelining

Number of Pipelines	*DatabaseTPS*	Performance Improvement
3	1480	3.0X
5	2467	5.0X
10	4935	9.9X

These estimates are in the ballpark to meet our requirements for the database tier. Even though ten pipelines handle only about one-third of the target requirement, the design does accommodate our needs. We have nested this segment below another layer of pipelines (Pipeline Distributor D); therefore, adding pipelines for Distributor D will multiply the rate of the database tier.

Validate Transaction: Distributor D

As our next step, we examined the processing rate for the service flow from Pipeline Distributor D through to and including the database tier. Distributor D also distributes transactions using `account_no` as the Pipeline Key, but it supports a broader range of values than Distributor E. Using the *DatabaseTPS* at ten pipelines (4935) as our fourth value in the formula, the rate for this flow is

$$[\text{Distributor D ServiceFlowTPS}]\ 1477\ \text{TPS} =$$
$$1/\textstyle\sum(1/89{,}000,\ 1/3800,\ 1/5000,\ 1/4935)$$

The following table shows the results for *ServiceFlowTPS* when we add more pipelines. The performance improvements are based on the *DatabaseTPS* of 493 TPS.

Performance Improvements from Pipelining

Number of Pipelines	*ServiceFlowTPS*	Performance Improvement
3	4431	8.9X
5	7385	14.8X
10	14,770	29.5X

These estimates are reasonable, because a top-tier distributor, Pipeline Distributor C, feeds this service flow.

Validate Transaction: Distributor C

For our next analysis, we incorporated Distributor C into the rate estimate. This distributor uses `branch_id` as the Pipeline Key. Using the Distributor D

ServiceFlowTPS at five pipelines (7385) as our second value in the formula, the rate for this flow is

[Distributor C ServiceFlowTPS] 20,509 TPS = (1/∑(1/92,000, 1/7385)) * 3

The calculation shows that by using three pipelines for Distributor C, we can comfortably achieve the 24-month target (16,500 TPS).

Authorize Transaction: Distributor B

Next, we analyzed the Authorize Transaction service, which feeds all downstream services. This service has its own distributor, Distributor B, and it must support enough volume to accommodate the 24-month target. At this point in the service flow, order of processing is not required, so we decided to use a high-performance Round-Robin Routing Pattern. All the distributors after this point use the Content-Based Routing Pattern and will enforce order of processing, which ensures that each bank account can be updated by only a single transaction at any given time.

The rate for Distributor B plus Authorize Transaction is

[AuthorizeTransactionTPS] 4323 TPS = 1/∑(1/110,000, 1/4500)

We estimated that five pipelines can achieve the 24-month target:

[AuthorizeTransactionTPS] 21,615 TPS = (1/∑(1/110,000, 1/4500)) * 5

Service Flow

Finally, we predicted the rate for the entire service flow. Using the Distributor C *ServiceFlowTPS* (20,509) and the *AuthorizeTransactionTPS* at five pipelines (21,615) as our values for the formula, the rate for the flow is

[ServiceFlowTPS] 10,524 TPS = 1/∑(1/20,509, 1/21,615)

The performance rate for the entire flow is inadequate to meet the expected demand. By adding more pipelines to Distributors B and C, we can accommodate the load. First, we increased Distributor C to five pipelines:

[Distributor C ServiceFlowTPS] 34,182 TPS = (1/∑(1/92,000, 1/7385)) * 5

We also increased Distributor B to ten pipelines:

[AuthorizeTransactionTPS] 43,231 TPS = (1/∑(1/110,000, 1/4500)) * 10

The final calculation shows the expected performance for the entire flow, with all pipelines in place:

[ServiceFlowTPS] 19,088 TPS $= 1/\sum(1/43{,}231, 1/34{,}182)$

By doing the preceding validation, we determined that our Pipelines Design will function as required. We can also adjust the actual performance during and after deployment, if business volume or any other factor affects demand deposit processing.

Summary

In SPOC Step 3, you design your pipelines implementation and predict how it will perform. When you finish this step, you're ready to actually create your pipeline sets, which we'll cover in the next chapter. We'll also describe the development tasks, such as creating and modifying service components, that accompany implementation.

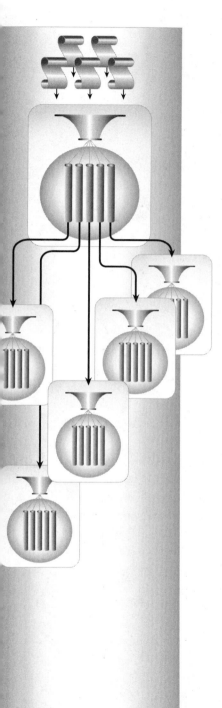

## CHAPTER TWELVE

SPOC Step 4: Pipelines Implementation

SPOC Step 4, Pipelines Implementation, is the development and testing phase of your project. Any SPOC step can be overlaid by another methodology, but this step is the most likely one to be combined with your existing standardized procedures.

Step 4 is broken out into several sub-steps. The report overview for this step, as seen in the next section, shows the overall process and the sequence of the sub-steps.

Step 4: Pipelines Implementation

In this step we cover the technical implementation of the pipelines architecture, which includes all development and testing.

The following cycle diagram outlines the sub-steps for this phase of SPOC:

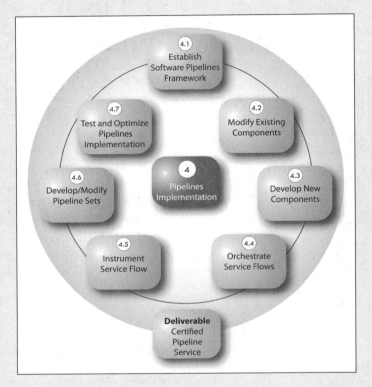

In addition to the usual tasks found in other development methodologies and life cycles, this phase of SPOC contains tasks that are specific to a pipelines implementation:

- Establish the Software Pipelines Framework.
- Package existing components as services. Modify any components that require revision.
- Develop any new components that are needed for each service flow.
- Orchestrate the components into a service flow.
- Instrument the services and the service flow to allow monitoring of performance.
- Develop and test the pipelines implementation.
- Optimize the service components and pipelines as required.

The final output of the Pipelines Implementation step is one or more Certified Pipeline Services—the actual running pipeline service(s), fully tested and ready to deploy.

In the following sections we'll go into the details for each sub-step.

Step 4.1: Establish Software Pipelines Framework

Setting up your framework can be an intricate process, involving many other stakeholders, and it will certainly overlap other frameworks and applications throughout your organization. In this section we'd like to give you some guidelines for selecting or developing your framework components.

In addition to any development or testing frameworks you might want to use, you'll also need a service-oriented development framework. Software Pipelines uses a service-oriented approach; it extends the definition of *service* beyond that of a simple Web service. Virtually any software component in your pipelines implementation—invoked by any protocol—can and should be considered a "service." Therefore, you'll need a service-oriented framework to support this aspect of your project.

You'll also need a Pipelines Framework. In the Pipelines Examples section of the book, we'll present our reference Pipelines Framework, which illustrates what this type of framework should do and, more importantly, how to use it. The Pipelines Framework is the element that provides the base distributor used for creating Pipeline Distributors; therefore, we recommend that you use our reference framework as the foundation for your own implementation. If you do, you'll find it's a simple matter to configure your pipeline sets (which you'll do in the current phase, in Step 4.6).

It's impossible to list or mention all the frameworks and architectures available, so we'll just give you the key points to keep in mind when you assemble your suite:

- You can purchase, assemble, or develop a service-oriented development and operations framework, or use a combination of these methods.
- Vendors optimize their products for handling specific problems. Check out the possibilities and get the one that matches your own situation.

- We recommend assembling a framework tailored to fit your requirements. There's no reason you shouldn't. You can pick and choose from many publicly and commercially available components, such as messaging infrastructures, service hosting capabilities, management frameworks, and policy frameworks.
- Decide which languages and platforms you'll support, and make sure your framework components are compatible with your choices.

The following section from the SPOC report shows the PBCOR results for this sub-step.

Step 4.1: Establish Software Pipelines Framework

Our team evaluated many commercial and open-source frameworks as possible candidates for supporting our service-oriented application development and Software Pipelines implementation.[1] The following approach is compatible with our Java-based applications:

---

[1] We don't endorse any particular product, and we mention products only for the purpose of illustrating examples. This is the case for all PBCOR examples. Your organization should make its own evaluations and choose products that fit its own requirements.

Service-oriented framework: We selected the Spring Framework for the following characteristics:

- It is lightweight.
- It is a proven, well-supported product. We have used this framework in other applications, so our developers have the skills to use it, and we know it works well.
- It integrates well with the Software Pipelines architecture.
- It provides full support for POJOs, which simplifies our messaging requirements.
- It is easily extensible for supporting new and customized protocols.

Software Pipelines Framework: We will develop our own Software Pipelines Framework by extending the reference implementation from www.softwarepipelines.org. Our decision is based on the following reasons:

- It makes it easy to develop and deploy custom Pipeline Distributors.
- It is compatible with Spring.
- It reduces the effort to enhance pipelines in the future.
- It keeps the Pipelines Framework under our own control, and we can enhance or improve it as we go forward

Testing framework: To perform application unit testing, we selected the JUnit testing framework. Our decision is based on the following reasons:

- It is a proven, widely used testing framework.
- We have used JUnit in other applications, so our developers have the skills to use it, and we know it works well.

Performance testing: We selected Apache JMeter as our primary performance-testing tool for the following reasons:

- It is a widely used, well-supported testing tool.
- It makes it easy to perform load tests of our pipelines implementation.

Step 4.2: Modify Existing Components

SPOC Step 4 includes the development and implementation of all the components, both new and existing, for your pipeline service model. Whenever possible, we strongly recommend that you reuse your existing components and code, which might include

- Large, outdated monolithic programs, with all functionality embedded into a single large module
- More modern object-oriented components
- Code in various languages

You can use the workflow in this section to decide which components to reuse in a given service flow and to determine how to package or otherwise incorporate the components into the flow. After the workflow, we'll present the SPOC report with the PBCOR results for this sub-step.

Map Components to Service Flow

Review your service flow, concentrating on the functionality of each service. Evaluate your existing components, then map the functionality of each existing component to an individual service in the flow.

Include monolithic programs and complex objects as candidates for reuse. To determine if any portion of a program or object matches a service, compare code segments to service functionality.

Evaluate Components

When you have a match between a component and a service, take a closer look at the component. Decide if it makes sense to incorporate it, based on the following criteria:

- How well the functionality fits the service and the service flow
- Your ability to support the language or component going forward
- The amount of effort it will take to incorporate the component into the service

Determine How to Incorporate Components

If a component looks like a good fit for a particular service, decide how you'll incorporate it into the flow. Very often you can simply wrap the component as a "service" in your new application model. This is particularly true for components written in the same language you're using for the model. To wrap the component, do the following:

- Define the message type for the service.
- Wrap the existing component in your service class hierarchy.
- Modify the component as required to use the service message instead of its current parameter mechanism. In some cases it's very feasible to wrap the entire component, then perform all message handling (inbound and outbound) in the service wrapper itself.

When your component is not in the same language as your model, you can still use it. Cross-platform tools make it possible to incorporate components written in many languages (such as mainframe procedures written in COBOL) into nearly any environment. You can use Web services or other remoting technologies to invoke disparate components across the network, and there are even products that allow you to perform local native invocations.

If you're reusing a monolithic program, unbundle it. Slice it up and package the code segments that support your service model.

After you have thoroughly investigated the component, if it looks too hard to use it for the service flow, you haven't wasted your time. It's important to fully understand its functionality. After all, you picked it out as a possible candidate, so it must have something to do with your flow. These chunks of "old code" can provide a wealth of information about your organization's operations. Studying them can save you a lot of time on your current project.

Prepare Component Table

Now that you've identified the components and how you're going to incorporate them, prepare a table showing how they map to the functionality of your services. You'll use the mapping in your development requirements and schedule. Table 12.1 shows how to lay out the map.

Develop Components

Proceed with the actual modification/development of the components. Use your organization's standard development process to accomplish this step, but make sure you first define/develop each message type for the service flow, then develop the components that use the messages. As in any solid development process, be sure to create and run unit tests for each component.

Table 12.1 Component to Service Map

Component	Maps to Service(s)	Implementation Method	Requirements
YourOldCobolProc	Service A Service B	Unbundle the procedural code, then redevelop the functionality.	Preserve all key business rules.
JavaDoSomethingClass	Service C	Wrap the class in a service inheritance structure.	Use the component as is. Handle the message input/output in the service wrapper.
DoSomething.NETClass	Service D	Wrap the class in a service inheritance structure.	Requires a Microsoft .NET connection software service interface to the local invocation framework.

Step 4.2: Modify Existing Components

4.2
Modify Existing Components

We evaluated the existing components in demand deposit and identified the ones to reuse in our new service flow and pipelines implementation.

The following table shows each component with the service to which it maps, along with the method we will use to incorporate each one:

Component to Service Map

Component	Maps to Service(s)	Implementation Method	Requirements
`Transaction. authorize`	Authorize Transaction	Wrap the existing Java code in a service.	For optimal performance, modify the class so it directly handles the service message.
`Account. checkBalance`	Validate Transaction	Wrap the existing method as a service.	Leave the method logic intact. We must incorporate its message handling, because it is part of the Validate Transaction service.
`Account.debit`	Debit Account	Wrap the existing code as a service.	The Database Sharding Distributor will add scalability for this component.
`DCS. AuthorizeTrans`	Authorize Transaction	Replace with an extension of the Java-based Authorize Transaction service, which allows us to use the debit card number.	Study the existing C++ code to ensure we include all functionality.

Our development team will modify these components, then package them into the JUnit framework for testing.

Step 4.3: Develop New Components

In this step you'll actually develop the new components required for your service flow. Use your organization's standard development process to do this.

Determining the components you need to develop is obvious; simply go through your service flow and identify the remaining components to be constructed. When you're ready to start coding, you should first define/develop each message type for the flow, then develop the components that use the messages.

Include unit tests for each component. We highly recommend using a test framework; it continually evaluates how well each component performs, and you can catch performance issues quickly, before you deploy anything to production.

Unit tests are even more crucial for Software Pipelines, but they're also relatively easy to implement. You're developing each component as a stand-alone service, which uses messages for input/output, so it's a very straightforward process to run the component from your test framework.

The following section from the SPOC report shows the PBCOR results for this sub-step.

Step 4.3: Develop New Components

4.3
Develop New
Components

In the first phase of our pipelines implementation, we can use existing components for most of the services. However, we need to develop the messaging components, and we need unit tests for the service flows. The following table shows the list of components and tests:

New Components and Unit Tests

Component	Description
`AccountTrans` message	Single message type required for both service flows in the first phase
`AuthorizeTrans` unit test	Unit test for Authorize Transaction
`ValidateTrans` unit test	Unit test for Validate Transaction
`DebitAccount` unit test	Unit test for the Debit Account transaction

These components must pass all unit tests before we run any integration tests.

Step 4.4: Orchestrate Service Flows

You can envision any business application as a flow of transactions moving through a set of service components. Each component performs some type of processing on the transaction, then passes it along to the next component. That is the elegance of a service-oriented environment, in which this vision becomes the reality. Your job in this step is to bring the vision to life by orchestrating your components into working service flows.

Orchestration is the arrangement of parts into a single, coordinated, working system, which you can then manage as a whole entity, much the way a conductor manages a symphony orchestra. However, it's somewhat easier to orchestrate a service flow than a symphony orchestra. There are many tools you can use (both commercial and open-source), including BPEL (Business Process Execution Language) engines, SCA (Service Component Architecture), the Spring Framework, and the least complicated of all—simply invoking components one to the next in your application code.

For simplicity's sake we'll use this last method (service invocation from code) for our examples, but we recommend you use an orchestration tool; it's more elegant and flexible. Vendors are continually improving this type of software, so it's relatively easy to use one of these tools to orchestrate a flow, then apply pipelines to improve the flow's performance.

Such tools represent the future of service-oriented development. As we see it, the next milestone is to add high-performance deployment capabilities to one of these tools and combine it with Software Pipelines architecture.

The following section from the SPOC report shows the PBCOR results for this sub-step. We're using simple object invocations for the PBCOR examples, but, as we already mentioned, you might want to use a BPEL designer or some other orchestration mechanism.

Step 4.4: Orchestrate Service Flows

In this section we present the orchestrated service flows for each phase in our demand deposit application.

We selected a simple design tool to illustrate the orchestration. Actual execution of components in the service flows will be performed in code, using the Spring Framework and our Pipelines Framework.

ATM Stand-alone Service

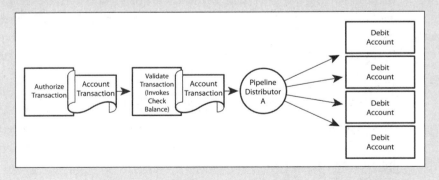

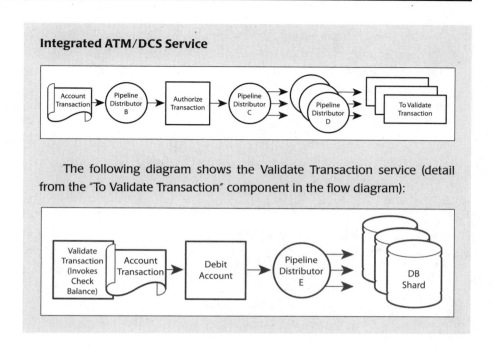

Integrated ATM/DCS Service

The following diagram shows the Validate Transaction service (detail from the "To Validate Transaction" component in the flow diagram):

Step 4.5: Instrument Service Flow

Achieving high performance is one of the main reasons to use pipelines architecture. However, to make this happen, you must measure your components and your service flows. Without valid metrics, you can't plan a pipelines implementation, and you can't optimize or maintain it.

Therefore, you must build instrumentation into *every* component and *every* service flow as an integral part of each element. Later, in the Pipelines Examples section of the book, we'll show you how to use the utility `Instrumentor` class to build this type of instrumentation. The ideal tool would provide these metrics in near-real time to a management console, from which you could control the entire pipelines environment, but we haven't yet seen a tool at this level; that's part of the future vision for Software Pipelines.

If you've adequately instrumented your components and service flows, you can feed the results to any logging mechanism. Set up your testing framework to constantly evaluate the metrics during unit tests while you're in development, and keep using the same mechanism in your production environment. You can use the metrics to identify current bottlenecks and predict new ones. You can also view trends of transaction rates and processing times—vital information your IT operations team will want to see. The feedback from these metrics also drives the iterative SPOC process, in which you incorporate current results into future designs and optimizations.

There's one more role played by your instrumentation metrics: You can use the results to demonstrate the value and scalability you've achieved with your pipelines implementation. Present the metrics in your deliverables reports to management, and you'll get more support for future pipelines projects.

Step 4.6: Develop/Modify Pipeline Sets

The final components you'll develop in the SPOC methodology are the pipeline sets that run in your Pipeline Distributors. If this is your initial implementation, you'll configure pipeline sets for the first time. If you're optimizing an existing implementation, you can modify the configurations you already have.

You will configure pipeline sets for each service, then use a Pipeline Distributor to implement the sets. In Figure 12.1 you can see a high-level overview of the architecture.

The architecture uses the following workflow:

- Various connectors send service requests into the Pipeline Distributor.
- The Pipeline Distributor examines the service request, then routes it to the appropriate Pipelines Router.
- There is one Pipelines Router for each configured service. Each router uses a specified type of distribution logic, such as round-robin or content-based. Using its distribution logic to determine which pipeline to use, the router places the request on the appropriate pipeline.
- The pipeline invokes the actual service instance, which processes the request.

In our reference Pipelines Framework, we use a simple XML document (the Pipelines Configuration file), which defines the key pipelines components, including the Pipeline Distributors. When you use the reference framework, it's easy to implement the architecture:

- Develop your services.
- Create the Pipelines Configuration file. This document defines your pipeline sets and allows you to modify them when required—all without changing the actual service implementations.
- The configuration file tells the Pipeline Distributor what to do.
- The Pipeline Distributor handles the rest of the process.

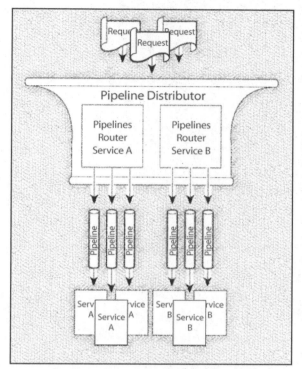

Figure 12.1 Pipeline Distributor and pipeline sets

There are many ways you can specify the Pipelines Configuration for an application. To keep our examples easy to understand, we designed a specialized XML format, but it's totally acceptable to extend other standard XML specifications, such as the Web Services Description Language (WSDL), to support pipelines. Don't let the "Web" stop you if you aren't using Web services; WSDL supports extensions you can adapt to *any* type of service invocation or protocol. Its authors designed custom bindings and other extensible features into the standard for this very purpose. However, a WSDL document is pretty complex, so we developed a simplified configuration document that won't get in the way while we explain the pipelines concept. Our format is valid and totally workable; you can use it for your own project, or pick another format that fits the standards in your organization.

To show you how the Pipelines Configuration file works, we've created an example for the proverbial "Hello Pipelines" service, using our XML format:

```xml
<?xml version="1.0" encoding="UTF-8"?>

<pipelines-config xmlns="http://www.softwarepipelines.
org"
  xmlns:xsi="http://www.w3.org/2001/XMLSchema-instance"
  xsi:schemaLocation="http://www.softwarepipelines.org/
schema/pipelines-config.xsd">

  <pipelines-distributor name="localDistributor"
pattern="push">

    <!-- Local Connector -->
    <pipelines-connector name="localConnector"
type="local"/>

    <!-- Socket Connector -->
    <pipelines-connector name="socketConnector"
type="socket"
      host="localhost" port="8095"/>

    <!-- helloPipelinesService with four alphabetical
ranges -->
    <pipeline-service name="helloPipelinesService" one-
way="true"
      class-name="org.softwarepipelines.framework.
service.HelloPipelineService">

      <pipelines-router
        class-name= "org.softwarepipelines.framework.
router.ContentBasedRouterImpl"
        enforce-sequence="true"/>

      <message type="org.softwarepipelines.framework.
message.HelloMessage"
        pipeline-key="name" />

      <pipeline name="p_athrug" type="local">
        <string-expr match="[a-gA-G].*"/>
      </pipeline>
      <pipeline name="p_hthrum" type="local">
        <string-expr match="[h-mH-M].*"/>
      </pipeline>
      <pipeline name="p_nthrur" type="local">
        <string-expr match="[n-rN-R].*"/>
      </pipeline>
      <pipeline name="p_sthruz" type="local">
        <string-expr match="[s-zS-Z].*"/>
      </pipeline>

    </pipeline-service>

  </pipelines-distributor>

</pipelines-config>
```

Let's go over the elements in the XML document:

- **`<pipelines-config>`**: Root element of the document. Contains definitions for all components in the pipelines application.
- **`<pipelines-distributor>`**: Defines one Pipeline Distributor. Each configuration file can have one or more Pipeline Distributors. The Pipeline Distributor contains definitions for all the pipelines elements belonging to that distributor.
- **`<pipelines-connector>`**: Defines one connector. Each Pipeline Distributor has one or more connectors, which listen for services. Each connector uses a specific protocol. Our example defines two connectors: one for local method invocation, and another one for socket-based connections.
- **`<pipeline-service>`**: Defines one service. Each Pipeline Distributor can host one or more services. Each service is supported by a single implementation class, which performs the actual functionality of the service.
- **`<pipelines-router>`**: Defines the Pipelines Router, the heart of the pipelines architecture and the element that decides where to route messages and service invocations. The router contains distribution logic. When it receives a request, it examines it, uses its logic to select the matching pipeline, and sends the request to the pipeline.

  We've included several types of standard Pipelines Routers in the reference Pipelines Framework, but the router code is fully extensible—you can define your own routers with virtually any type of distribution logic.
- **`<message>`**: Defines one message type. Each pipelines service receives a single message type, which is defined by this element.
- **`<pipeline>`**: Defines one pipeline. Each service can have one or more pipelines. The pipeline's child element `<string-expr/>` contains the expression used to match service requests to the matching pipeline.

  In our example configuration document we use a content-based router, which uses regular expression syntax to make its routing decisions. The `<string-expr/>` for each of our pipelines defines a specific range for the name in the `HelloMessage`. For example, "Hello Albert" is routed to the `p_athrug` (*A* through *G*) pipeline, and "Hello Sam" is routed to the `p_sthruz` (*S* through *Z*) pipeline.

The following section from the SPOC report shows the PBCOR results for this sub-step. We'll show just a fragment of the pipeline sets for the PBCOR application. You can see the entire definition in the Pipelines Examples section of the book.

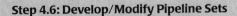

Step 4.6: Develop/Modify Pipeline Sets

We have completed our analysis and design for the demand deposit applications. Based on our design, we have developed the required pipeline sets, which are defined in the following Pipelines Configuration document.

```
<?xml version="1.0" encoding="UTF-8"?>

<pipelines-config xmlns="http://www.
softwarepipelines.org"
  xmlns:xsi="http://www.w3.org/2001/XMLSchema-
instance"
  xsi:schemaLocation="http://www.softwarepipelines.
org/schema/pipelines-config.xsd">

  <pipelines-distributor name="distributorA"
pattern="push">

    <!-- Local Connector -->
    <pipelines-connector name="localConnector"
type="local"/>

    <!-- debitAccountService using ranges by bank
branchID. -->
    <pipeline-service name="debitAccountService"
one-way="false"\
      class-name="com.pbcor.service.
DebitAccountService">

      <pipelines-router
        class-name= "org.softwarepipelines.
framework.router.ContentBasedRouterImpl"
        enforce-sequence="true"/>
```

```xml
      <message type="com.pbcor.message.
AccountTransMessage"
        pipeline-key="branchID" />

      <pipeline name="p_b0000-b0080" type="local">
        <range-expr from="0000" to="0080"/>
      </pipeline>
      <pipeline name="p_b0081-b0160" type="local">
        <range-expr from="0081" to="0160"/>
      </pipeline>
      <pipeline name="p_b0161-b0240" type="local">
        <range-expr from="0161" to="0240"/>
      </pipeline>
      <pipeline name="p_b0241-b0320" type="local">
        <range-expr from="0241" to="0320"/>
      </pipeline>
      <pipeline name="p_b0321-b0400" type="local">
        <range-expr from="00321" to="0400"/>
      </pipeline>

        ...

      <pipeline name="p_b0721-b0800" type="local">
        <range-expr from="0721" to="0800"/>
      </pipeline>

   </pipeline-service>

  </pipelines-distributor>

  <pipelines-distributor name="distributorB"
pattern="push">

    <!-- Socket Connector -->
    <pipelines-connector name="socketConnector"
type="socket"
      host="localhost" port="8095"/>

    <!-- authorizeTransService using round-robin
routing. -->
    <pipeline-service name="authorizeTransService"
one-way="false"
      class-name="com.pbcor.service.
AuthorizeTransService">

      <pipelines-router
        class-name="org.softwarepipelines.framework.
router.RoundRobinRouterImpl" />

      <message type="com.pbcor.message.
AccountTransMessage" />
```

```
        <pipeline name="p_1" type="local" />
        <pipeline name="p_2" type="local" />
        <pipeline name="p_3" type="local" />
        <pipeline name="p_4" type="local" />
        <pipeline name="p_5" type="local" />

    </pipeline-service>

  </pipelines-distributor>

  <pipelines-distributor name="distributorC"
pattern="push">

    <!-- Local Connector -->
    <pipelines-connector name="localConnector"
type="local"/>

    <!-- Socket Connector -->
    <pipelines-connector name="socketConnector"
type="socket"
      host="localhost" port="8090" />

    <!-- accountTransService using relay pipelines.
-->
    <pipeline-service name="accountTransService"
one-way="false"
      class-name="com.pbcor.service.
accountTransService">

    <pipelines-router
      class-name= "org.softwarepipelines.
framework.router.ContentBasedRouterImpl"
      enforce-sequence="true"/>

    <message type="com.pbcor.message.
AccountTransMessage"
      pipeline-key="branchID" />

    <pipeline name="p_b0000-b0300" type="relay"
send-to="distributorD-1" connector="relayLocalConn">
      <range-expr from="0000" to="0300"/>
    </pipeline>
    <pipeline name="p_b0301-b0600" type="relay"
send-to="distributorD-2" connector="relayLocalConn">
      <range-expr from="0301" to="0600"/>
    </pipeline>
    <pipeline name="p_b0601-b0800" type="relay"
send-to="distributorD-3" connector="relayLocalConn">
      <range-expr from="0601" to="0800"/>
    </pipeline>
```

```
      </pipeline-service>

   </pipelines-distributor>

   <pipelines-distributor name="distributorD"
pattern="push">

      <!-- Socket Connector -->
      <pipelines-connector name="socketConnector"
type="socket"
         host="server1" port="8090" />

      <!-- accountTransService accepting relay
pipelines. -->
      <pipeline-service name="accountTransService"
one-way="false"
         class-name="com.pbcor.service.
accountTransService">

         <pipelines-router
            class-name= "org.softwarepipelines.
framework.router.ContentBasedRouterImpl"
            enforce-sequence="true"/>

         <message type="com.pbcor.message.
AccountTransMessage"
            pipeline-key="branchID" />

         <pipeline name="p_b0000-b0100" type="local">
            <range-expr from="0000" to="0100"/>
         </pipeline>
         <pipeline name="p_b0101-b0200" type="local">
            <range-expr from="0101" to="0200"/>
         </pipeline>
         <pipeline name="p_b0201-b0300" type="local">
            <range-expr from="0201" to="0300"/>
         </pipeline>
         <pipeline name="p_b0301-b0400" type="local">
            <range-expr from="0301" to="0400"/>
         </pipeline>

         ...

         <pipeline name="p_b0701-b0800" type="local">
            <range-expr from="0701" to="0800"/>
         </pipeline>

      </pipeline-service>

   </pipelines-distributor>
```

```
  <pipelines-distributor name="distributorE"
pattern="push">

    <!-- Socket Connector -->
    <pipelines-connector name="ShardDBConnector"
type="local" />

    <!-- shardAccountTransService accepting database
transactions. -->
    <pipeline-service
name="shardAccountTransService" one-way="false"
      class-name="com.pbcor.service.
shardAccountDBService">

      <pipelines-router
        class-name= "org.softwarepipelines.
framework.router.shardDBRouterImpl"
        enforce-sequence="true"/>

      <message type="com.pbcor.message.
AccountTransMessage"
        pipeline-key="accountID" />

      <pipeline name="p_a00000000-a00100000"
type="local">
        <range-expr from="00000000" to="00100000"/>
      </pipeline>
      <pipeline name="p_a00100001-a00200000"
type="local">
        <range-expr from="00100001" to="00200000"/>
      </pipeline>
      ...
      <pipeline name="p_a09900001-a10000000"
type="local">
        <range-expr from="09900001" to="10000000"/>
      </pipeline>

    </pipeline-service>

  </pipelines-distributor>

</pipelines-config>
```

Step 4.7: Test and Optimize Pipelines Implementation

It's standard practice, and part of SPOC, to run unit tests throughout the development phase of your project. As we already mentioned, you should develop and run unit test cases for each service component in your service flow; this ensures that your application is functionally correct. And now that we've gotten to the last phase in Step 4, it's time to do the integration testing, where you tie your services together with Pipeline Distributors.

Testing your pipelines implementation is much like testing any other application, with one important caveat: You must have an adequate amount of test hardware for simulating pipelines scalability. Integration testing helps you find out if your implementation is scalable, and it shows whether it is performing as expected. When you've determined that application performance is up to par and that the services are functionally correct, you'll be ready to deploy.

This is one of the SPOC steps in which you can overlay the SPOC methodology onto your own tools and methodology. We used Apache JMeter (open-source) to run performance testing and evaluation on our examples for this book, but there are many other tools available, both commercial and open-source.

Use the following workflow as a rough guide for this step:

- Set up your QA environment.

    Include the minimum number of servers necessary to prove the ultimate scalability required for your application. A good rule of thumb for judging the size of your test environment is to count all the Pipeline Distributors that send transactions over the network. You'll probably need a multiple of this number for the final production environment, but you need only one for each unique remote distributor in your QA environment.

    Include enough "client" service request generators in the QA environment. You'll be using these to simulate adequate load on pipelines and services. It's very easy to underestimate the hardware required to generate a simulated load, and this requirement can vary for each type of application.
- Run your integration tests for each service you intend to deploy. While you test, continuously monitor each service to check scalability.
- Test the overall functionality to make sure it is correct.
- Using your QA results, extrapolate the scalability you expect to achieve in the full production environment.
- Modify or adjust your Pipelines Configuration as required to ensure you can meet the production load.

Your pipelines implementation is now complete and ready for deployment.

The following section from the SPOC report shows PBCOR's signed-off certification. The document certifies that the team completed the testing, and that the implementation is ready for production use.

Step 4.7: Test and Optimize Pipelines Implementation

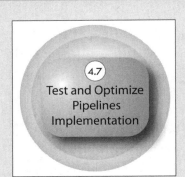

Quality Assurance Certificate

This document certifies that the PBCOR demand deposit pipelines implementation is ready for production deployment. The application has gone through all standard PBCOR application testing procedures and has also been run through an extensive set of performance tests. Application performance is acceptable and will meet the production requirements going forward. The application has also been reviewed and accepted by the business unit that it supports.

Approved by:

Mary Pipewright

Mary Pipewright
QA Manager

Piper Campbell

Piper Campbell
CIO

Don Quicken

Don Quicken
SVP Demand Deposit Accounts

Summary

SPOC Step 4 is a big milestone. After doing your all your calculations, research, and design, you get the opportunity to apply all of it and create the actual elements of your pipelines project—the service components, the Pipeline Distributors, and the pipeline sets. At the end, you pull all the pieces together and run the application in its entirety. When you finish this step, you've got a tested implementation in place, ready to go into production.

In the next chapter you'll learn about Pipelines Deployment, the last phase of SPOC.

## CHAPTER THIRTEEN

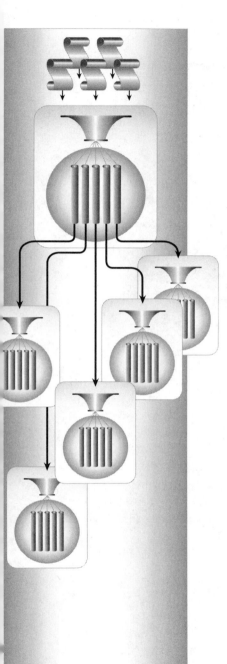

SPOC Step 5: Pipelines Deployment

In SPOC Step 5, Pipelines Deployment, you'll deploy your pipelines implementation to the production environment. This step conforms to other methodologies more than any other step, so we won't provide as much detail for it. However, we do want to stress that deployment is a critical step and should not be brushed off. You should employ all the proven practices your organization already uses for its other applications.

Step 5 is broken out into several sub-steps. The report overview for this step, as seen in the next section, shows the overall process and the sequence of the sub-steps.

Step 5: Pipelines Deployment
This is the final section of the SPOC report, in which we present our production deployment plans and results. The pipelines application is now fully developed and tested and is ready for production use.

The following cycle diagram outlines the sub-steps for this phase of SPOC:

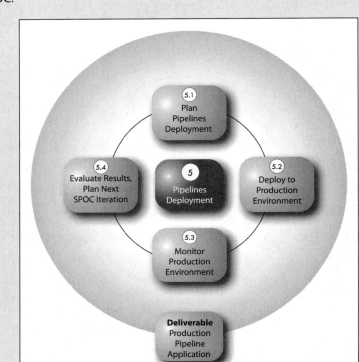

The final output of the Pipelines Deployment step is the Production Pipeline Application—the deployed pipelined service(s), now successfully handling the required transaction volume.

In the following sections we'll go into the details for each sub-step.

Step 5.1: Plan Pipelines Deployment

Effective, comprehensive, careful planning is the key to a successful production deployment. This phase requires tight coordination of many resources: IT and development personnel, stakeholders, hardware, software, network, facilities, and the business community who will use the application. Proper planning is even more important when you're deploying a pipelines application, because of the distributed nature of the architecture.

Consider the following items when you develop your plan:

- **Hardware and facilities requirements:** You must fully define all hardware requirements, including servers, network, and facilities.
- **Disaster recovery:** Using a scalable architecture, such as Software Pipelines, to achieve the strategic goals for which it is best suited pretty much guarantees your application is mission-critical. Therefore, you must plan appropriate offsite disaster recovery.
- **Software deployment:** Define the process for releasing your application to production. This is usually done as the final QA stage, when you verify all the base functionality.
- **User training:** If your application requires retraining of internal users, you must allocate resources and budget for this task. Your implementation will fail if users can't easily and quickly learn the new version.
- **Monitoring:** You must monitor and manage a pipelines application—not only to keep it up and running in a healthy state, but also to enable you to optimize it in future iterations of SPOC.
- **Human capital:** Perhaps nothing is more important to any successful production deployment than people. Their expertise, dedication, and hard work will make it happen. Make sure you have enough staff for the initial stages of deployment, and just as importantly, make sure each individual on the team is adequately trained for the role he or she will perform.

At the end of this step you should have a very complete project plan, and all members of your team should fully understand it.

Step 5.2: Deploy to Production Environment

The statement "Deploy to production environment" seems straightforward and simple, but any experienced developer or project manager knows that deployment can be fatal to a software project if you mishandle it or don't do it correctly. When you're deploying a pipelines application, the distributed environment adds extra complexity, so proper execution is crucial to your success.

We can't describe every action for this step (again, you should use your organization's standardized procedures), but we can list the things that matter the most for a successful pipelines deployment:

- **Deployment coordination:** This is where the project manager truly shines, in coordinating the people, hardware, software, and all project deliverables into a smooth end result. You should hold regular, short, frequent meetings, and make sure your key team members are available when needed.
- **Hardware procurement:** Distributed systems require a large number of components. Start buying them early so you can give your vendors and procurement team adequate lead time for delivery.
- **Software deployment:** Failing to deploy software to production *correctly* and *completely* is quite possibly the number-one reason for deployment problems. Freeze your code after testing, and practice on QA servers before you go live. Remember that hundreds of components must work together in a pipelines application, so it's mandatory to use a consistent methodology and approach.
- **Smoke testing:** It's always a good idea to run a brief set of final tests on the environment before you "pull the switch." It's best to do this during off-hours, right before the application goes live.
- **Standby support:** Your team must allocate time to monitor and correct your application, if needed. Unfortunately, this usually happens after normal business hours. If you've done all the previous steps well, this shouldn't be an undue burden—but be prepared to act quickly if the situation warrants it.

    Your long-term plan should include close monitoring of the application and a solid support staff for end users and customers.

At this point you should have a live pipelines implementation, the payoff for the entire process. However, SPOC does not stop at this point. It was intentionally designed to keep working throughout the life of your application.

Step 5.3: Monitor Production Environment

When your application is up and running, monitoring becomes the most important ingredient for success. We've mentioned this before, but we can't overstate it: When you build a pipelines application, you must monitor how it runs. Otherwise, you won't get the expected result from using the architecture. The ideal situation is to monitor components at all levels, from low-level hardware to functional software.

In SPOC Step 4 you build monitor elements into your system as you develop it, then use them to measure performance while you test. At this point you can use the monitor infrastructure on a daily basis to ensure the health of your application. The metrics show exactly how the pipelines environment is performing.

You'll be able to rapidly identify bottlenecks and inefficiencies when they happen, and you can adjust pipelines elements and components accordingly.

Monitoring is not only intended for current use. It's also the mechanism by which you get the data for the next and last step in SPOC, Step 5.4, in which you use the results of your implementation to make future enhancements and performance improvements.

As of this date there are no "pipelines" tools, but you can adapt many of the available monitoring tools for the task. Figure 13.1 shows an example user interface for a Pipelines Monitor, showing the type of information such a tool might present. IT operations professionals could use it to monitor and control the pipelines infrastructure.

Step 5.4: Evaluate Results, Plan Next SPOC Iteration

SPOC methodology is truly a *cycle*; optimizing your application's performance is a job that is never done. The results of your production operation are incredibly valuable, because they point out areas that require further improvement. You can also learn which parts of the system are meeting or exceeding their capacity requirements—information that is just as important going forward as the identification of problem areas.

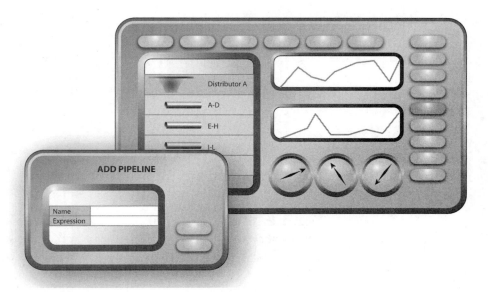

Figure 13.1 Pipelines Monitor user interface

It is also just as important to evaluate the business results, to validate that your application did indeed meet the strategic objectives you set at the beginning of the process. A summary report showing the accomplished scalability, ROI, and other business value is a great asset for getting further support from senior management.

After you evaluate the pipelines results in your production environment, you can start planning your next SPOC iteration. Use your production results to plan future enhancements, make further performance improvements, and meet strategic business requirements (see Figure 13.2).

As you complete the current cycle and start on the next, you'll see that follow-on SPOC iterations are much easier than the first time through, because your Pipelines Framework and base application are in place. You can concentrate on increasing the level of productivity and results for your organization, and that's where the real power of the architecture is fully realized.

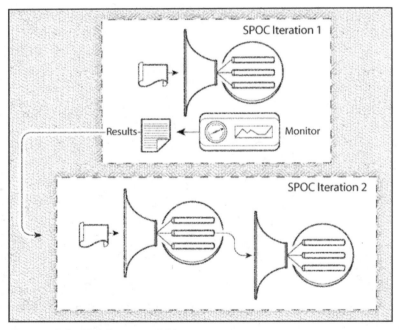

Figure 13.2 SPOC, next cycle

Summary

Software Pipelines Optimization Cycle is fundamentally a simple methodology, but there are a lot of steps and a lot of details to think about. It is important that you employ SPOC as a tool, using the portions that fit your particular application requirements and the specific issues you're facing. It's completely valid to use an isolated segment of SPOC if it helps sort out a particular issue, so use your judgment and apply SPOC to obtain meaningful results for *your* organization.

Pipelines Examples

This section of the book contains the Pipelines Examples. We developed these examples to show you exactly how the Software Pipelines technology works, and to demonstrate as many of the pipelines concepts as possible. Our purposes are to give you a broad understanding of the many ways you can use the concepts in real-world applications and to enable you to implement pipelines in your own applications.

We built the examples using the Pipelines Patterns and our reference Pipelines Framework. Each example includes a flow design, a design walk-through, sample source code, and test results. Some examples include results charts. We planned the examples in a gradient, so that each one builds on the previous one to gradually increase your understanding. Each chapter is fairly self-explanatory and stands on its own; however, we do recommend that you at least study the first three chapters, because they set the stage for the rest of the examples. The complete source code for the Pipelines Framework and all examples is available at www.softwarepipelines.org.

If you are technically minded, you might want to study each example and its source code in detail. You can also read these chapters just to understand how to apply pipelines from a higher-level viewpoint. If you're already planning a pipelines implementation, you can study Chapters 14 through 16 for the basic information, then scan the rest of the examples for patterns that fit into your plans.

We've arranged the examples in the following sequence:

- The first set of examples (which includes most of the examples chapters) illustrates the Pipelines Patterns. We start out with the traditional "Hello Software Pipelines" example, the foundation from which we build all the other examples. This basic example shows you how to create a working, but very simple, pipelines service in just a few minutes. We build on this first example chapter by chapter until we've demonstrated each primary Pipelines Pattern.

- After the examples, we cover the reference Pipelines Framework in Chapter 21. This chapter provides a high-level overview of the framework we use throughout the book, so you can gain a better understanding of how all the pieces fit together and how pipelines function internally. We've provided this chapter for those with an interest in the underlying implementation of a Pipelines Framework. You can use the concepts to work with our framework, to extend it, or to develop your own Pipelines Framework. You can also incorporate the concepts into other frameworks and environments.

In the framework chapter we also discuss the *Instrumentor* class, the component we use to measure performance and view results in our examples.

- In Chapter 22, the final chapter of this section, we show how we implemented the PBCOR project we used for the SPOC methodology chapters. The purpose of this final example is to give you a better understanding of how to use Software Pipelines in a real-world business application. PBCOR is purely fictitious, but the example does parallel fairly realistic banking concepts (again, we're not banking experts by any means, so please attribute any inaccuracies you might find to our creative license).

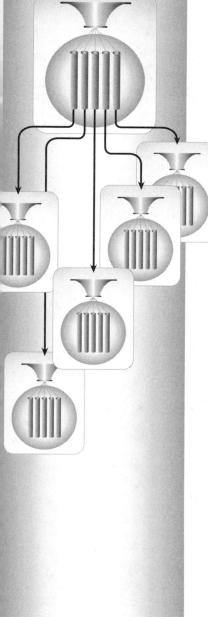

## CHAPTER FOURTEEN

Hello Software Pipelines

The key component in a pipeline service is the service itself. Therefore, for our first example we'll walk through the steps for creating a pipelines service using our reference Pipelines Framework. We'll use the *HelloPipelines-Service*, a variation on the traditional "Hello World" theme.

Figure 14.1 shows the service flow for *HelloPipelinesService*. It has a fairly trivial flow, but it will help explain how the pipelines service operates and what it does.

The service implements the Push One-Way Pattern. *HelloPipelinesClient* sends a *HelloMessage* to *HelloPipelinesService*, then *HelloPipelinesService* simply outputs a message, based on the *HelloMessage* content, to the console or log. Table 14.1 shows the (very simple) distributor configurations for the service.

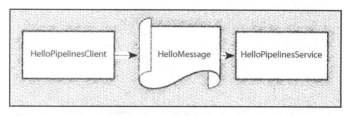

Figure 14.1 Service flow for Hello Software Pipelines

Table 14.1 Distributor Configurations

HelloPipelinesService	Pattern Options
Service Invocation Pattern	Push
Message Exchange Pattern	One-Way
Pipeline Routing Pattern	Round-Robin
	One pipeline
Distributor Pattern	Single Distributor
Distributor Connector Pattern	Local Method Invocation

Define the Message

Before you can build a service, you must define the message type it is intended to receive. The following code is the *HelloMessage* class, which will be generated by the client and consumed by the service:

```java
public class HelloMessage extends AbstractMessage {

  public String name;

  public HelloMessage() {
  }

  public String getName() {
    return name;
  }

  public void setName(String name) {
    this.name = name;
  }

  public String toString() {

    return super.toString() + "\tName: " + this.
getName();
  }

}
```

This message is a simple JavaBean, with a single `String` member, the `name` field. It has the appropriate getters and setters that you would expect from any JavaBean example.

Build the Service

Next, let's look at the service class, *HelloService*:

```
package org.softwarepipelines.examples.hello.ch14;

import org.apache.log4j.Logger;

import org.softwarepipelines.config.service.
PipelineServiceConfig;
import org.softwarepipelines.examples.hello.
HelloMessage;
import org.softwarepipelines.framework.exception.
PipelineException;
import org.softwarepipelines.framework.message.
AbstractMessage;
import org.softwarepipelines.framework.service.
PipelineServiceBase;

public class HelloPipelinesService extends
PipelineServiceBase {
  private static final Logger LOG = Logger.
getLogger(HelloPipelinesService.class);
  private static final int SLEEP_TIME = 50;
  private static final int SLEEP_CYCLES = 10;

  /**
   * Default constructor
   */
  public HelloPipelinesService() {
  }

  /**
   * Constructor used by the framework to pass in the
   * PipelineServiceConfig instance.
   */
  public HelloPipelinesService(final
PipelineServiceConfig config) {
    super(config);
  }

  /**
   * Write the 'Hello' message contents out to the log.
   */
  public synchronized void
processMessage(AbstractMessage msg)
    throws PipelineException {

    /* Cast the HelloMessage.*/
    HelloMessage helloMessage = (HelloMessage)msg;
```

```
    /* Consume some CPU.*/
    eatCpu();

    /* Write the message to the log.*/
    LOG.info("Hello " + helloMessage.getName() + " from
SoftwarePipelines, in " + SLEEP_TIME + " ms!");
  }

 /**
  * Consume some CPU time to simulate processor work.
  */
 private void eatCpu() {
    for (int i = 0; i < SLEEP_CYCLES; i++) {
      try {
        Thread.sleep(SLEEP_TIME/SLEEP_CYCLES);
      } catch (InterruptedException ie) {
        LOG.warn("Interrupted while sleeping for " +
SLEEP_TIME
        + " ms to eat cpu", ie);
      }
    }
  }

}
```

The `processMessage()` method in this service performs the main work:

- The Pipelines Framework creates an instance of the service (it can create many instances, depending on how you configure the pipelines) and passes in the `msg` parameter.
- The `msg` parameter is provided as an *AbstractMessage* type, so the method downcasts it to the *HelloMessage* type.
- Next, `processMessage()` calls `eatCpu()`, a utility method you'll see in many of the examples. This is a simulation process used only for purposes of demonstration. It simulates the CPU processing that would occur in a more realistic business service class, and it enables you to work with multiple pipelines and see the effects of scaling as you go through the examples. To create the simulation, `eatCpu()` simply performs a loop and sleeps for a specified duration and number of iterations. Your actual production services don't need this method.

Each pipeline service extends the *PipelineServiceBase* class, the parent class that enables the framework to support pluggable service components. We'd like to point out some details about the *HelloPipelinesService* constructor, which is required by each implementation of the *PipelineService-Base* class:

```
/**
 * Constructor used by the framework to pass in the
 * PipelineServiceConfig instance.
 */
public HelloPipelinesService(final
PipelineServiceConfig config) {
   super(config);
}
```

The *HelloPipelinesService* constructor takes a single parameter, an instance of *PipelineServiceConfig*, which is provided by the Pipelines Framework. *PipelineServiceConfig* contains all the information needed to run the service, configure pipelines, and more. It loads data from the Pipelines Configuration XML document, which we'll cover next.

Configure the Distributors

After defining the message and building the service, the two components that do the actual work, the next step is to configure the Pipeline Distributor(s) by using the Pipelines Configuration document. The following code (from the single-pipeline-config.xml file) is the configuration document for the current example:

```
<?xml version="1.0" encoding="UTF-8"?>

<pipelines-config xmlns="http://www.softwarepipelines.
org"
  xmlns:xsi="http://www.w3.org/2001/XMLSchema-instance"
  xsi:schemaLocation="http://www.softwarepipelines.
org http://www.softwarepipelines.org/schema/pipelines-
config.xsd">

  <instrumentor log-interval="2000"/>

  <pipelines-distributor name="localDistributor"
pattern="push">

    <!-- Local Connector -->
    <pipelines-connector name="localConnector"
type="local"/>

    <!-- The first example consists of a helloService
with a single pipeline. -->
    <pipeline-service name="helloService" one-way="true"
      class-name="org.softwarepipelines.examples.hello.
HelloPipelinesService">
```

```
        <pipelines-router
            class-name="org.softwarepipelines.framework.
router.RoundRobinRouterImpl"
            enforce-sequence="false"/>

        <message
            type="org.softwarepipelines.examples.hello.
HelloMessage" />

        <pipeline name="p_1" type="local"/>

    </pipeline-service>

  </pipelines-distributor>

</pipelines-config>
```

This config document specifies only one pipeline, which we're using to demonstrate how to get a service running. You can use this configuration to get this first example running, and later we'll show you how to increase the number of pipelines without modifying any of your service or client code.

Let's look at the elements in the Pipelines Configuration document:

- **<pipelines-config>:** Root element of the document.
- **<instrumentor>:** Defines the configuration for the *Instrumentor* class, the monitoring tool. We'll discuss the *Instrumentor* in more detail in Chapter 21, when we walk through the reference Pipelines Framework.
- **<pipelines-distributor>:** Defines one Pipeline Distributor. The config document contains one <pipelines-distributor> for each named distributor in your application, and each distributor operates from its named portion in the file.

    Clients reference a distributor by its name. The example document contains one distributor named *localDistributor*.

    You can define many distributors and services in a single pipelines config document, which enables you to use a single configuration for your entire application. This is not mandatory, but it's easier to use a single document to manage all the distributors and services throughout your environment. In a very complex system you can break the Pipelines Configuration into several files, each for one group of distributors.

Each <pipeline-distributor> has the following child elements:

- **<pipelines-connector>:** Defines a specific connector to the distributor on which it can listen for and receive messages. You can configure and support many types of connectors, and a single distributor can support multiple connectors.

The example document defines a single local connector, `localConnector`, which the client uses to directly invoke the distributor's service method.

- **<pipeline-service>:** Defines one service supported by the distributor. Each distributor can support many individual services. Each service is identified by its `name`.

The example document defines a service named `helloService`, a one-way service (meaning it does not generate a response) that uses the `HelloPipelinesService` service implementation class.

The <pipeline-service> element has the following child elements:

- **<pipelines-router>:** The Pipelines Router is the core component that evaluates incoming messages and distributes them to individual pipelines for processing. Optionally, you can define the router to also evaluate the message content. There is only one <pipelines-router> for each service definition.

In the example document, the <pipelines-router> uses the `RoundRobinRouterImpl` implementation, one of the standard Pipelines Routers included with the reference Pipelines Framework. `RoundRobinRouterImpl` performs the simplest type of routing, round-robin. It takes each incoming service invocation and message, then distributes the service calls across a number of pipelines in sequence.

We designed the reference Pipelines Framework as a fully extensible framework. Our examples utilize two default router implementations, but you can plug in your own custom adaptations for more complex requirements.

- **<message>:** Defines the message type the service will use. In the example document, the message is `HelloMessage`.
- **<pipeline>:** Defines one pipeline. You can define multiple pipelines, but the initial example uses only one. Each pipeline has a `name` and a `type`; the example document has a `local` pipeline named `p_1`. We'll talk about the other types of pipelines in later examples.

You won't see any scalability with this single example pipeline. The pipeline is fed by a round-robin router that invokes services one after another, all using the same pipeline. However, in later examples we'll show you how simple and convenient it is to add more pipelines and increase scalability.

Create the Client

When you've defined the message, the service, and the Pipelines Configuration, the service is ready to run. The last step is to create a pipelines client that will run the service. This example uses a very simple client, which runs from the main method of the class:

```java
package org.softwarepipelines.examples.hello.ch14;

import java.io.File;
import java.io.IOException;

import org.softwarepipelines.config.
PipelinesMasterConfig;
import org.softwarepipelines.config.exception.
ConfigException;
import org.softwarepipelines.examples.hello.
HelloMessage;
import org.softwarepipelines.framework.connector.
PipelinesConnector;
import org.softwarepipelines.framework.distributor.
PipelinesDistributorBase;
import org.softwarepipelines.framework.exception.
PipelineException;
import org.softwarepipelines.framework.util.
PipelinesHelper;

/**
 * This client is the client for the
HelloPipelinesService. It invokes the service
 * via the local connector of the distributor.
 */
public class HelloPipelinesClient {

  /**
   * Usage: HelloPipelinesClient [pipelinesConfig
filename] [distributorName]
   * @param args
   * @throws IOException
   * @throws ConfigException
   * @throws PipelineException
   */
  public static void main(String[] args) throws
IOException, ConfigException, PipelineException{

    /* Get the parameters.*/
    if(args.length != 3) {
      throw new PipelineException("Usage:
HelloPipelinesClient [pipelinesConfig filename]
[distributorName] [connectorName]");
    }
```

```
    String pipelinesConfigFilename = args[0];
    String distributorName = args[1];
    String connectorName = args[2];

    /* Load the Pipelines Configuration.*/
    PipelinesMasterConfig masterConfig
= new PipelinesMasterConfig(new
File(pipelinesConfigFilename));

    /* Get a reference to the distributor by name, and
start it.*/
    PipelinesDistributorBase distributor =
PipelinesHelper.getDistributorByName(distributorName,
masterConfig);
    distributor.start();

    /* Get a reference to the connector.*/
    PipelinesConnector connector = PipelinesHelper.
getConnectorByName(distributorName, connectorName,
masterConfig);

    /* Build the HelloMessage instance, including
'serviceName' and 'name'.*/
    HelloMessage msg = new HelloMessage();
    msg.setServiceName("helloService");
    msg.setName("Cory");

    /* Invoke the service on the distributor, via the
connector.*/
    connector.send(msg);

    /* Clean up by shutting down the connector and the
distributor.*/
    connector.shutdown();
    distributor.shutdown();
  }

}
```

This client requires only a few steps to invoke the service:

• **Load the Pipelines Configuration:** The client gets the location and name of the Pipelines Configuration document by loading a *Pipelines-MasterConfig* instance.

In this example the client loads the Pipelines Configuration directly from a disk file, single-pipeline-config.xml. In a production application you should cache these config objects for improved performance. You can also store them in a database or a JNDI repository.

- **Get a distributor reference:** The client gets a reference to the appropriate distributor, using the `name` of the distributor as defined in the Pipelines Configuration document.

    In this example the client loads *localDistributor* from the *masterConfig* object, then starts the distributor running. Most of our examples load and start the distributor from within the client code. You'd usually do this as a separate process, with clients connecting over the network. Even with local connectors, you can get the distributor reference statically; clients that need to use the direct method invocation (such as the client in the current example) can easily obtain a reference.

- **Get a pipelines connector:** To connect to the distributor, the client gets a connector instance by `name`. The client can obtain any of the connectors defined in the Pipelines Configuration.

    In this example the client gets a `local` connector, which means it will use direct method invocation on the server, as opposed to a network protocol.

- **Build the service message:** Before the client can invoke the service, it must create a message instance of the type the service is expecting, which in this example is *HelloMessage*. Each message requires the `serviceName`, along with any other fields or data needed by the specific message implementation. In the example, the other required field is the `name` to which the service says "hello."

- **Invoke the service:** Now the client can run the service. This example uses the `send()` method, because it's a one-way service that doesn't return a response message.

- **Cleanup:** In this example, for demonstration purposes, the client cleans up by shutting down the connector and distributor.

    In a real application you start and stop the distributor outside the scope of the client, but for this first example, you just want to run the service one time and end the entire process. If you don't shut down the distributor, the example process will just keep running, because the distributor is intended to operate continuously.

Run the Service

Now you're ready to run the service. You can do this from the Java command-line interface, or by using the Apache Ant `build.xml` script provided with the examples. Use the following command to invoke the Ant script:

```
ant run-hello-single-pipeline
```

As you can see, you're passing in the `config.file` and `distributor.name` parameters. Make sure you run the example directly from the example directory.

When you run the service, you should see the following output on your console:

```
run-hello-single-pipeline:
[java] [INFO] HelloPipelinesService: - Hello Cory from
SoftwarePipelines, in 50 ms!
```

Summary

Congratulations; you have successfully run your first Software Pipelines service! Of course, all it does is run a single instance of a single service on a single pipeline—hardly the result you're after. But now you understand the basics of how to build a pipelines service.

In the next chapter we'll show you how to control the scaling of your service, with complete transparency to your client and service code.

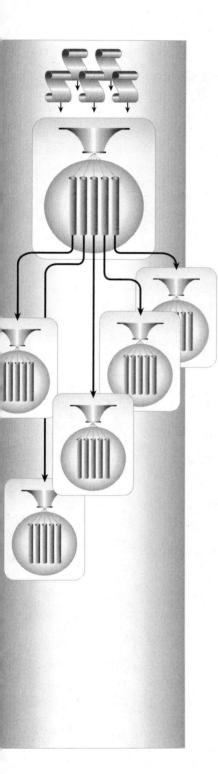

## CHAPTER FIFTEEN

Scaling Hello Software Pipelines

Gaining the ability to scale your services is probably the main reason to use Software Pipelines. We'll show you how quickly and easily you can do this by showing you how to scale the Hello Software Pipelines example.

Scale the Service

All you have to do to scale Hello Software Pipelines is modify the Pipelines Configuration document. The configuration already has a round-robin Pipelines Router, but now you'll set it up to feed multiple pipelines, each one running the Hello Software Pipelines example. Figure 15.1 shows the new service flow.

The new service flow has a Pipeline Distributor, with multiple pipelines running multiple instances of the service. You can see the updated distributor configurations in Table 15.1.

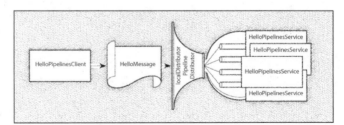

Figure 15.1 New service flow for Hello Software Pipelines

Table 15.1 Distributor Configurations

`HelloPipelinesService`	Pattern Options
Service Invocation Pattern	Push
Message Exchange Pattern	One-Way
Pipeline Routing Pattern	Round-Robin
	Four pipelines
Distributor Pattern	Single Distributor
Distributor Connector Pattern	Local Method Invocation

The only difference in the options is the number of pipelines; all other configuration options are the same. By increasing the number of pipelines to four, we expect to see performance increase 4X.

We updated the Pipelines Configuration document by adding four pipelines. The following code (from the `hello-4-rr-pipelines-config.xml` file) shows the new configuration document:

```
<?xml version="1.0" encoding="UTF-8"?>

<pipelines-config xmlns="http://www.softwarepipelines.
org"
  xmlns:xsi="http://www.w3.org/2001/XMLSchema-instance"
  xsi:schemaLocation="http://www.softwarepipelines.
org http://www.softwarepipelines.org/schema/pipelines-
config.xsd">

  <instrumentor log-interval="2000"/>

  <pipelines-distributor name="localDistributor"
pattern="push">

    <!-- Local Connector -->
    <pipelines-connector name="localConnector"
type="local"/>

    <!-- The example consists of a helloService with
four round-robin pipelines. -->
    <pipeline-service name="helloService" one-way="true"
      class-name="org.softwarepipelines.examples.hello.
HelloPipelinesService">

      <pipelines-router
        class-name="org.softwarepipelines.framework.
```

```
router.RoundRobinRouterImpl"
        enforce-sequence="false"/>

    <message
        type="org.softwarepipelines.examples.hello.
HelloMessage" />

    <pipeline name="p_1" type="local"/>
    <pipeline name="p_2" type="local"/>
    <pipeline name="p_3" type="local"/>
    <pipeline name="p_4" type="local"/>

  </pipeline-service>

 </pipelines-distributor>

</pipelines-config>
```

That's all there is to it. All you need to do now is deploy the updated configuration. When you run the service again, it automatically runs with four pipelines.

Develop a Scalable Test Client

Now that you've scaled the service, you'll probably notice that the client is insufficient for the job. One hard lesson we've learned in scaling software systems is that you need a test client that can simulate sufficient load. There are many tools (commercial and open-source) you can use for this. However, Software Pipelines is a new architecture, and it has some special requirements. It all goes back to the first Pipelines Law: Input equals output. Simply stated, we need to supply enough input to feed our pipelines test. Furthermore, the client should be able to increase the load and report on results. It's obvious the simple main-method client from the previous chapter doesn't meet our criteria.

To accomplish this purpose, you can build another client using the open-source scalability-testing tool JPerf.[1] JPerf is a simple performance and scalability test harness for Java. It is modeled on the well-known JUnit framework but is designed solely for the needs of performance testing.

JPerf can measure both performance and scalability of the test code from the client side. It starts with a single thread and gradually adds new threads, up to the configured maximum. Each thread creates a separate instance of the test class, then repeatedly calls the test method for the specified time period. The frame-

---

[1]   For more information about JPerf, visit the Web site at www.jperf.org.

work measures the number of iterations, which you can use to determine overall throughput.

In addition, you can use the *Instrumentor* components from our reference Pipelines Framework to measure the service from the service side. We'll show its output for the current example later in this chapter.

To write tests with JPerf, you simply implement the PerfTest interface:

```
/**
 * Each performance test must implement this interface.
 */
public interface PerfTest {

  /**
   * The setUp method is invoked once for each test
instance.
   */
  public void setUp() throws Exception;

  /**
   * The test method is invoked repeatedly during the
configurable
   * test period.*/
   */
  public void test() throws Exception;

  /**
   * The tearDown method is called once at the end of
the
   * entire test.
   */
  public void tearDown() throws Exception; }
```

It's very easy to run JPerf tests. When we ran the current example, we simply used the `main()` method of the test client. The following code snippet shows how to run a JPerf test:

```
PerfTestRunner r = new PerfTestRunner();
r.setMaxClient( 25 );
r.setTestPeriod( 1000 );
r.run(MyPerfTest.class);
```

The test starts with one thread, then ramps up to the number of threads specified in the `setMaxClient()` call. Each thread runs for the specified test period before the framework increments the number of active threads.

The following code shows the new scalable test client, *HelloPipelines PerfTest*, which we developed using JPerf:

```
package org.softwarepipelines.examples.hello.ch15;

import java.io.File;
import java.io.IOException;

import org.jperf.PerfTest;
import org.jperf.PerfTestRunner;
import org.softwarepipelines.config.
PipelinesMasterConfig;
import org.softwarepipelines.config.exception.
ConfigException;
import org.softwarepipelines.examples.hello.
HelloMessage;
import org.softwarepipelines.framework.connector.
PipelinesConnector;
import org.softwarepipelines.framework.distributor.
PipelinesDistributorBase;
import org.softwarepipelines.framework.exception.
PipelineException;
import org.softwarepipelines.framework.util.
PipelinesHelper;

public class HelloPipelinesPerfTest implements PerfTest
{

  /* Master Pipelines Config */
  private static PipelinesMasterConfig masterConfig;

  /* Singleton static distributor instance used by all
the threads.*/
  private static PipelinesDistributorBase distributor;

  /* Connector instance which each thread will
instantiate separately.*/
  private PipelinesConnector connector;
  private static String connectorName;

  /**
   * Set up the test.
   */
  public void setUp() throws Exception {
    /* Check out a connector instance.*/
    connector = PipelinesHelper.
getConnectorByName(distributor.getConfig().getName(),
connectorName, masterConfig);
  }

  /**
   * Tear down the test, performing any cleanup.
   */
  public void tearDown() throws Exception {
    connector.shutdown();
  }
```

```
   /**
    * Run the service test.
    */
  public void test() throws Exception {
    /* Build the HelloMessage instance, including
'serviceName' and 'name'.*/
    HelloMessage msg = new HelloMessage();
    msg.setServiceName("helloService");
    msg.setName("Cory");

    /* Invoke the service on the distributor, via the
connector.*/
    connector.send(msg);
  }

  /**
   * Main method for starting the test.
   * @param args
   * @throws IOException
   * @throws ConfigException
   * @throws PipelineException
   */
  public static void main(String[] args) throws
IOException, ConfigException, PipelineException {
    String pipelinesConfigFilename, distributorName;

    /* Get the parameters.*/
    if(args.length != 3) {
      throw new PipelineException("Usage:
HelloPipelinesClient [pipelinesConfig filename]
[distributorName] [connectorName]");
    }
    pipelinesConfigFilename = args[0];
    distributorName = args[1];
    connectorName = args[2];

    /* Load the Pipelines Configuration.*/
    masterConfig = new PipelinesMasterConfig(new
File(pipelinesConfigFilename));

    /* Get and start a singleton distributor instance by
name. */
    distributor = PipelinesHelper.getDistributorByName
(distributorName, masterConfig);
    distributor.start();

    /* Set up the PerfTest runner for 6 threads, 4
seconds between threads.*/
    PerfTestRunner r = new PerfTestRunner();
    r.setMaxClient(6);
    r.setTestPeriod(4000);
```

```
    /* Specify the results output file.*/
    r.setResultFile(new File("results/test/
HelloPipelinesPerfTest-results.xml"));

    /* Run the test.*/
    r.run(HelloPipelinesPerfTest.class);

    /* Shut down the distributor.*/
    distributor.shutdown();
  }

}
```

The new client is primarily a reorganization of `HelloPipelinesClient`. The important differences are the following.

- To make sure each running instance of the test uses its own connector, the `localConnector` is obtained and released inside the `setUp()` and `tearDown()` methods.
- The `main()` method creates the static distributor instance, starts the distributor, creates an instance of the test class, configures the test, and runs the test.
- The JPerf framework automatically calls the `test()` method iteratively, and `test()` does the work of the test.

Run the Service

Now you're ready to run the test. To establish a base benchmark, run it first using the `hello-single-pipelines-config.xml` configuration. The first test will run six threads, which it increments every four seconds. Use the following Ant command to run the test:

```
ant run-jperf-hello-single-pipeline
```

The following partial output is from the baseline test:

```
run-jperf-hello-single-pipeline:
  [java] [INFO] JPerf is testing org.softwarepipelines.
examples.hello.ch15.HelloPipelinesPerfTest
  [java] [INFO] Instrumentor: - org.softwarepipelines.
framework.router.PipelinesRouterBase:p_1 = 37.0(18.5
TPS)
  [java] [INFO] Instrumentor: - org.softwarepipelines.
framework.router.PipelinesRouterBase:p_1 = 39.0(19.5
TPS)
```

```
   [java] [INFO]     1 threads: 25 tps, 715,384 mem.
   [java] [INFO] Instrumentor: - org.softwarepipelines.
framework.router.PipelinesRouterBase:p_1 = 40.0(20.0
TPS)
   [java] [INFO] Instrumentor: - org.softwarepipelines.
framework.router.PipelinesRouterBase:p_1 = 40.0(20.0
TPS)
   [java] [INFO]     2 threads: 20 tps, 587,712 mem.
   [java] [INFO] Instrumentor: - org.softwarepipelines.
framework.router.PipelinesRouterBase:p_1 = 40.0(20.0
TPS)
   [java] [INFO] Instrumentor: - org.softwarepipelines.
framework.router.PipelinesRouterBase:p_1 = 40.0(20.0
TPS)
   [java] [INFO]     3 threads: 20 tps, 983,720 mem.
   [java] [INFO] Instrumentor: - org.softwarepipelines.
framework.router.PipelinesRouterBase:p_1 = 40.0(20.0
TPS)
   [java] [INFO] Instrumentor: - org.softwarepipelines.
framework.router.PipelinesRouterBase:p_1 = 40.0(20.0
TPS)
   [java] [INFO]     4 threads: 20 tps, 874,096 mem.
   [java] [INFO] Instrumentor: - org.softwarepipelines.
framework.router.PipelinesRouterBase:p_1 = 40.0(20.0
TPS)
   [java] [INFO] Instrumentor: - org.softwarepipelines.
framework.router.PipelinesRouterBase:p_1 = 40.0(20.0
TPS)
   [java] [INFO]     5 threads: 20 tps, 757,920 mem.
   [java] [INFO] Instrumentor: - org.softwarepipelines.
framework.router.PipelinesRouterBase:p_1 = 39.0(19.5
TPS)
   [java] [INFO] Instrumentor: - org.softwarepipelines.
framework.router.PipelinesRouterBase:p_1 = 40.0(20.0
TPS)
   [java] [INFO]     6 threads: 20 tps, 650,256 mem.
...
```

The JPerf output shows how many transactions the service completes on each pipeline throughout the test. Since there's only one pipeline, even as the thread count increases, you can't scale up to more than 20 TPS.

We'll be using JPerf output for the rest of the pipelines examples, so we'll go over how to read it. First, let's take a look at the values from the *Instrumentor*. The reference Pipelines Framework contains an *Instrumentor* class, which monitors the performance of each individual service. In the following output sample, *p_1* is the name of the pipeline, 37.0 is the total number of transactions processed by the test thread's run, and 18.5 is the average TPS handled by the service:

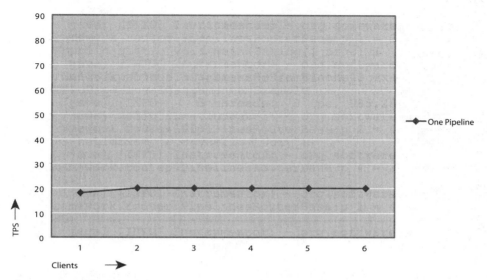

Figure 15.2 JPerf output

```
[java] [INFO] Instrumentor: - org.softwarepipelines.
framework.router.PipelinesRouterBase:p_1 = 37.0(18.5
TPS)
```

At the end of each test cycle for a given number of threads, JPerf outputs the TPS processed from the test client:

```
[java] [INFO]    1 threads: 25 tps, 715,384 mem.
```

These values can vary somewhat from the *Instrumentor* values, because the Pipelines Framework performs buffering within the framework. This final output does provide an overall view of the performance from the client side, but in general, the *Instrumentor* output is the most important.

In Figure 15.2 you can see a chart of the results, using the file output that JPerf produces.

Now run the new example so you can see how it scales using four pipelines. Use the following Ant command to run the test:

```
ant run-jperf-hello-4-rr-pipelines
```

The following partial output is from the new test run:

```
run-jperf-hello-4-rr-pipelines:
  [java] [INFO] JPerf is testing org.softwarepipelines.
examples.hello.ch15.HelloPipelinesPerfTest
...
  [java] [INFO] Instrumentor: - org.softwarepipelines.
framework.router.PipelinesRouterBase:p_2 = 40.0(20.0
TPS)
  [java] [INFO] Instrumentor: - org.softwarepipelines.
framework.router.PipelinesRouterBase:p_4 = 40.0(20.0
TPS)
  [java] [INFO] Instrumentor: - org.softwarepipelines.
framework.router.PipelinesRouterBase:p_1 = 40.0(20.0
TPS)
  [java] [INFO] Instrumentor: - org.softwarepipelines.
framework.router.PipelinesRouterBase:p_3 = 40.0(20.0
TPS)
  [java] [INFO] Instrumentor: - org.softwarepipelines.
framework.router.PipelinesRouterBase:p_2 = 40.0(20.0
TPS)
  [java] [INFO] Instrumentor: - org.softwarepipelines.
framework.router.PipelinesRouterBase:p_4 = 40.0(20.0
TPS)
  [java] [INFO] Instrumentor: - org.softwarepipelines.
framework.router.PipelinesRouterBase:p_1 = 40.0(20.0
TPS)
  [java] [INFO] Instrumentor: - org.softwarepipelines.
framework.router.PipelinesRouterBase:p_3 = 40.0(20.0
TPS)
  [java] [INFO]    2 threads: 79 tps, 597,096 mem.
  [java] [INFO] Instrumentor: - org.softwarepipelines.
framework.router.PipelinesRouterBase:p_2 = 40.0(20.0
TPS)
  [java] [INFO] Instrumentor: - org.softwarepipelines.
framework.router.PipelinesRouterBase:p_4 = 40.0(20.0
TPS)
  [java] [INFO] Instrumentor: - org.softwarepipelines.
framework.router.PipelinesRouterBase:p_1 = 40.0(20.0
TPS)
  [java] [INFO] Instrumentor: - org.softwarepipelines.
framework.router.PipelinesRouterBase:p_3 = 40.0(20.0
TPS)
  [java] [INFO] Instrumentor: - org.softwarepipelines.
framework.router.PipelinesRouterBase:p_2 = 40.0(20.0
TPS)
  [java] [INFO] Instrumentor: - org.softwarepipelines.
framework.router.PipelinesRouterBase:p_4 = 40.0(20.0
TPS)
  [java] [INFO] Instrumentor: - org.softwarepipelines.
framework.router.PipelinesRouterBase:p_1 = 40.0(20.0
TPS)
  [java] [INFO] Instrumentor: - org.softwarepipelines.
framework.router.PipelinesRouterBase:p_3 = 40.0(20.0
TPS)
```

```
[java] [INFO]    3 threads: 79 tps, 1,070,064 mem.
[java] [INFO] Instrumentor: - org.softwarepipelines.
framework.router.PipelinesRouterBase:p_2 = 39.0(19.5
TPS)
[java] [INFO] Instrumentor: - org.softwarepipelines.
framework.router.PipelinesRouterBase:p_4 = 39.0(19.5
TPS)
[java] [INFO] Instrumentor: - org.softwarepipelines.
framework.router.PipelinesRouterBase:p_1 = 39.0(19.5
TPS)
[java] [INFO] Instrumentor: - org.softwarepipelines.
framework.router.PipelinesRouterBase:p_3 = 39.0(19.5
TPS)
[java] [INFO] Instrumentor: - org.softwarepipelines.
framework.router.PipelinesRouterBase:p_2 = 40.0(20.0
TPS)
[java] [INFO] Instrumentor: - org.softwarepipelines.
framework.router.PipelinesRouterBase:p_4 = 40.0(20.0
TPS)
[java] [INFO] Instrumentor: - org.softwarepipelines.
framework.router.PipelinesRouterBase:p_1 = 40.0(20.0
TPS)
[java] [INFO] Instrumentor: - org.softwarepipelines.
framework.router.PipelinesRouterBase:p_3 = 40.0(20.0
TPS)
...
[java] [INFO] Instrumentor: - org.softwarepipelines.
framework.router.PipelinesRouterBase:p_2 = 40.0(20.0
TPS)
[java] [INFO] Instrumentor: - org.softwarepipelines.
framework.router.PipelinesRouterBase:p_4 = 40.0(20.0
TPS)
[java] [INFO] Instrumentor: - org.softwarepipelines.
framework.router.PipelinesRouterBase:p_1 = 40.0(20.0
TPS)
[java] [INFO] Instrumentor: - org.softwarepipelines.
framework.router.PipelinesRouterBase:p_3 = 40.0(20.0
TPS)
[java] [INFO] Instrumentor: - org.softwarepipelines.
framework.router.PipelinesRouterBase:p_2 = 40.0(20.0
TPS)
[java] [INFO] Instrumentor: - org.softwarepipelines.
framework.router.PipelinesRouterBase:p_4 = 40.0(20.0
TPS)
[java] [INFO] Instrumentor: - org.softwarepipelines.
framework.router.PipelinesRouterBase:p_1 = 40.0(20.0
TPS)
[java] [INFO] Instrumentor: - org.softwarepipelines.
framework.router.PipelinesRouterBase:p_3 = 40.0(20.0
TPS)
[java] [INFO]    6 threads: 80 tps, 1,033,512 mem.
```

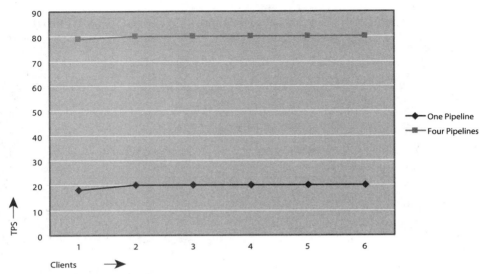

Figure 15.3 Four pipelines compared to one pipeline

In Figure 15.3 the chart shows how four pipelines compare to one pipeline.

The scalability works perfectly. Each pipeline produces approximately 20 TPS, and the total test run generates 80 TPS when using all four pipelines.

Summary

In this example you learned more about the basic mechanism of pipelines. Without modifying the client or service code, you can change your Pipelines Configuration and improve performance by many times.

In the next chapter we'll show you how to use content-based routing—so you can take advantage of parallel processing, while still preserving sequential transaction order.

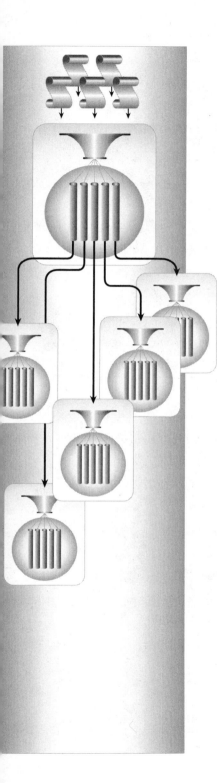

## CHAPTER SIXTEEN

Additional Pipelines Router Configurations

Content-Based Router

In our first examples we showed you how to use the Pipeline Distributor for simple, *unordered* round-robin scalability. Although this is useful, one of the key benefits of Software Pipelines is the ability to handle *sequential* transactions in a parallel framework. This capability is a key requirement for many business applications, and it's often the preferred mechanism for implementing a pipelines system. To accomplish this, you must use a content-based router, which uses a Pipeline Key to route transactions to a particular pipeline.

The Pipeline Key can be any value in the service message that is evaluated by the content-based router. In the Hello Software Pipelines service, there is only one field in the message, name. You can use that for the Pipeline Key and create a set of pipelines that use an expression based on the first letter of each name. Figure 16.1 shows the revised service flow.

You can see the distributor configurations, revised for content-based routing, in Table 16.1.

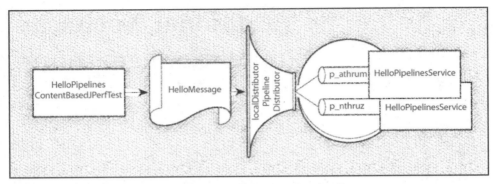

Figure 16.1 Revised service flow for Hello Software Pipelines

To implement this set of pipelines, all you need to do is modify the Pipelines Configuration document to use the content-based router provided with the reference Pipelines Framework. The following code shows the new configuration from the `hello-2-cb-pipelines-config.xml` file:

```
<?xml version="1.0" encoding="UTF-8"?>

<pipelines-config xmlns="http://www.softwarepipelines.
org"
   xmlns:xsi="http://www.w3.org/2001/XMLSchema-instance"
   xsi:schemaLocation="http://www.softwarepipelines.
org http://www.softwarepipelines.org/schema/pipelines-
config.xsd">

   <instrumentor log-interval="2000"/>
```

Table 16.1 Distributor Configurations

HelloPipelinesService	Pattern Options
Service Invocation Pattern	Push
Message Exchange Pattern	One-Way
Pipeline Routing Pattern	Content-Based
Pipelines	p_athrum
	p_nthruz
Distributor Pattern	Single Distributor
Distributor Connector Pattern	Local Method Invocation

```
    <pipelines-distributor name="localDistributor"
pattern="push">

    <!-- Local Connector -->
    <pipelines-connector name="localConnector"
type="local"/>

    <!-- Configure the service with 2 content-based
pipelines. -->
    <pipeline-service name="helloService" one-way="true"
      class-name="org.softwarepipelines.examples.hello.
HelloPipelinesService">

      <pipelines-router
        class-name="org.softwarepipelines.framework.
router.ContentBasedRouterImpl"
        enforce-sequence="true"/>

      <message
        type="org.softwarepipelines.examples.hello.
HelloMessage"
        pipeline-key="name" />

      <pipeline name="p_athrum" type="local">
        <string-expr match="[a-mA-M].*"/>
      </pipeline>

      <pipeline name="p_nthruz" type="local">
        <string-expr match="[n-zN-Z].*"/>
      </pipeline>

    </pipeline-service>

  </pipelines-distributor>

</pipelines-config>
```

The important modifications to the Pipelines Configuration are as follows:

- In <pipelines-router>, set class-name to the *ContentBased RouterImpl*, the router that supports content-based routing. *Content BasedRouterImpl* supports routing by regular expression or by an integer range, such as customer ID values.
- In <pipelines-router>, set enforce-sequence to true.
- In <message>, add pipeline-key and set it to name, the field in *HelloMessage*.
- Define the pipelines. Each one uses a regular expression match based on the first letter of the name value. The configuration has two pipelines, each one covering half the alphabet.

The service is now ready to run, but before you run it, change the client so it provides a range of name values when it calls the service. The following code shows the relevant portions of the new client, *HelloPipelinesContentBasedJ PerfTest*:

```
package org.softwarepipelines.examples.hello.ch16;

import java.io.File;
import java.io.IOException;
import java.util.Random;

import org.jperf.PerfTest;
import org.jperf.PerfTestRunner;
import org.softwarepipelines.config.
PipelinesMasterConfig;
import org.softwarepipelines.config.exception.
ConfigException;
import org.softwarepipelines.examples.hello.
HelloMessage;
import org.softwarepipelines.framework.connector.
PipelinesConnector;
import org.softwarepipelines.framework.distributor.
PipelinesDistributorBase;
import org.softwarepipelines.framework.exception.
PipelineException;
import org.softwarepipelines.framework.util.
PipelinesHelper;

public class HelloPipelinesContentBasedPerfTest
implements PerfTest {

  /* Pipelines Master Config */
  private static PipelinesMasterConfig masterConfig;

  /* Singleton static distributor instance used by all
the threads.*/
  private static PipelinesDistributorBase distributor;

  /* Connector instance which each thread will
instantiate separately.*/
  private PipelinesConnector connector;
  private static String connectorName;

  /* Define an array of names throughout the alphabet.*/
  String[] names = {"Abbey", "Barbara", "Colin",
      "Devyn", "Edward", "Fred", "George",
      "Harry", "Isabel", "John", "Karl", "Larry",
      "Monty", "Nancy", "Oprah", "Patrick",
      "Quinn", "Roger", "Sam", "Tyler",
      "Ursula", "Victor", "Wayne",
      "Xavier", "Yolanda", "Zeb"};
```

```
    /* Random number generator*/
    Random random = new Random();

    /**
     * Set up the test.
     */
    public void setUp() throws Exception {
        /* Check out a local connector instance.*/
        connector = PipelinesHelper.
getConnectorByName(distributor.getConfig().getName(),
connectorName, masterConfig);
    }

    /**
     * Tear down the test, performing any cleanup.
     */
    public void tearDown() throws Exception {
        /* Shut the connector down.*/
        connector.shutdown();
    }

    /**
     * Run the service test.
     */
    public void test() throws Exception {
        /* Build the HelloMessage instance, including
'serviceName' and 'name'.*/
        HelloMessage msg = new HelloMessage();
        msg.setServiceName("helloService");

        /* Set the name to a random value from the array.*/
        msg.setName(names[random.nextInt(26)]);

        /* Invoke the service on the distributor, via the
connector.*/
        connector.send(msg);
    }

    /**
     * Main method for starting the test.
     * @param args
     * @throws IOException
     * @throws ConfigException
     * @throws PipelineException
     */
    public static void main(String[] args) throws
IOException, ConfigException, PipelineException {
        String pipelinesConfigFilename, distributorName;
```

```
   /* Get the parameters.*/
   if(args.length != 3) {
     throw new PipelineException("Usage:
HelloPipelinesClient [pipelinesConfig filename]
[distributorName] [connectorName]");
   }

   pipelinesConfigFilename = args[0];
   distributorName = args[1];
   connectorName = args[2];

   /* Load the Pipelines Configuration.*/
   masterConfig = new PipelinesMasterConfig(new
File(pipelinesConfigFilename));

   /* Get a reference to the distributor by name.*/
   distributor = PipelinesHelper.getDistributorByName
(distributorName, masterConfig);
   distributor.start();

   /* Set up the PerfTest runner for 6 threads, 4
seconds between threads.*/
   PerfTestRunner r = new PerfTestRunner();
   r.setMaxClient(6);
   r.setTestPeriod(4000);

   /* Specify the results output file.*/
   r.setResultFile(new File("results/test/HelloPipeline
sContentBasedPerfTest-results.xml"));

   /* Run the test.*/
   r.run(HelloPipelinesContentBasedPerfTest.class);

   /* Shut down the distributor.*/
   distributor.shutdown();
 }

}
```

The important modifications to the client are as follows:

- Use a class member variable to add an array of names, one for each letter of the alphabet. The client uses these when it calls *helloService*.
- Use a class member variable to add an instance of the Java random number generator.
- Modify the test() method to select a random name from the array to send to the service.

To run the test, use the following Ant command:

```
ant run-jperf-hello-2-cb-pipelines
```

The following output is from the test run:

```
run-jperf-hello-2-cb-pipelines:
    [java] [INFO] JPerf is testing org.softwarepipelines.
examples.hello.ch16.HelloPipelinesContentBasedPerfTest
    [java] [INFO] Instrumentor: - org.softwarepipelines.
framework.router.PipelinesRouterBase:p_nthruz =
36.0(18.0 TPS)
    [java] [INFO] Instrumentor: - org.softwarepipelines.
framework.router.PipelinesRouterBase:p_athrum =
36.0(18.0 TPS)
    [java] [INFO] Instrumentor: - org.softwarepipelines.
framework.router.PipelinesRouterBase:p_nthruz =
40.0(20.0 TPS)
    [java] [INFO] Instrumentor: - org.softwarepipelines.
framework.router.PipelinesRouterBase:p_athrum =
40.0(20.0 TPS)
    [java] [INFO]     1 threads: 48 tps, 846,864 mem.
    [java] [INFO] Instrumentor: - org.softwarepipelines.
framework.router.PipelinesRouterBase:p_nthruz =
40.0(20.0 TPS)
    [java] [INFO] Instrumentor: - org.softwarepipelines.
framework.router.PipelinesRouterBase:p_athrum =
32.0(16.0 TPS)
    [java] [INFO] Instrumentor: - org.softwarepipelines.
framework.router.PipelinesRouterBase:p_nthruz =
40.0(20.0 TPS)
    [java] [INFO] Instrumentor: - org.softwarepipelines.
framework.router.PipelinesRouterBase:p_athrum =
33.0(16.5 TPS)
    [java] [INFO]     2 threads: 34 tps, 589,456 mem.
    [java] [INFO] Instrumentor: - org.softwarepipelines.
framework.router.PipelinesRouterBase:p_nthruz =
40.0(20.0 TPS)
    [java] [INFO] Instrumentor: - org.softwarepipelines.
framework.router.PipelinesRouterBase:p_athrum =
40.0(20.0 TPS)
    [java] [INFO] Instrumentor: - org.softwarepipelines.
framework.router.PipelinesRouterBase:p_nthruz =
40.0(20.0 TPS)
    [java] [INFO] Instrumentor: - org.softwarepipelines.
framework.router.PipelinesRouterBase:p_athrum =
40.0(20.0 TPS)
    [java] [INFO]     3 threads: 39 tps, 964,904 mem.
    [java] [INFO] Instrumentor: - org.softwarepipelines.
framework.router.PipelinesRouterBase:p_nthruz =
40.0(20.0 TPS)
```

```
   [java] [INFO] Instrumentor: - org.softwarepipelines.
framework.router.PipelinesRouterBase:p_athrum =
40.0(20.0 TPS)
   [java] [INFO] Instrumentor: - org.softwarepipelines.
framework.router.PipelinesRouterBase:p_nthruz =
39.0(19.5 TPS)
   [java] [INFO] Instrumentor: - org.softwarepipelines.
framework.router.PipelinesRouterBase:p_athrum =
39.0(19.5 TPS)
   [java] [INFO]    4 threads: 44 tps, 923,144 mem.
   [java] [INFO] Instrumentor: - org.softwarepipelines.
framework.router.PipelinesRouterBase:p_nthruz =
40.0(20.0 TPS)
   [java] [INFO] Instrumentor: - org.softwarepipelines.
framework.router.PipelinesRouterBase:p_athrum =
40.0(20.0 TPS)
   [java] [INFO] Instrumentor: - org.softwarepipelines.
framework.router.PipelinesRouterBase:p_nthruz =
40.0(20.0 TPS)
   [java] [INFO] Instrumentor: - org.softwarepipelines.
framework.router.PipelinesRouterBase:p_athrum =
40.0(20.0 TPS)
   [java] [INFO]    5 threads: 39 tps, 779,976 mem.
   [java] [INFO] Instrumentor: - org.softwarepipelines.
framework.router.PipelinesRouterBase:p_nthruz =
40.0(20.0 TPS)
   [java] [INFO] Instrumentor: - org.softwarepipelines.
framework.router.PipelinesRouterBase:p_athrum =
40.0(20.0 TPS)
   [java] [INFO] Instrumentor: - org.softwarepipelines.
framework.router.PipelinesRouterBase:p_nthruz =
40.0(20.0 TPS)
   [java] [INFO] Instrumentor: - org.softwarepipelines.
framework.router.PipelinesRouterBase:p_athrum =
40.0(20.0 TPS)
[java] [INFO]    6 threads: 40 tps, 675,672 mem.
```

In Figure 16.2 you can see a chart of the results. The performance is approximately 2X the baseline (we're using one pipeline as the baseline), which is exactly what you'd expect.

Now, to check out how easy it is to add more pipelines, modify the Pipelines Configuration to define four content-based pipelines. The following code shows the revised configuration from the `hello-4-cb-pipelines-config.xml` file:

```
<?xml version="1.0" encoding="UTF-8"?>

<pipelines-config xmlns="http://www.softwarepipelines.
org"
```

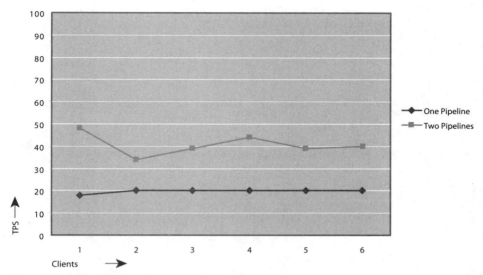

Figure 16.2 Output results

```
xmlns:xsi="http://www.w3.org/2001/XMLSchema-instance"
xsi:schemaLocation="http://www.softwarepipelines.
org http://www.softwarepipelines.org/schema/pipelines-
config.xsd">

<instrumentor log-interval="2000"/>

<pipelines-distributor name="localDistributor"
pattern="push">

    <!-- Local Connector -->
    <pipelines-connector name="localConnector"
type="local"/>

    <!-- Configure the service with 4 content-based
pipelines. -->
    <pipeline-service name="helloService" one-way="true"
      class-name="org.softwarepipelines.examples.hello.
HelloPipelinesService">

        <pipelines-router
          class-name="org.softwarepipelines.framework.
router.ContentBasedRouterImpl"
          enforce-sequence="true"/>

        <message
          type="org.softwarepipelines.examples.hello.
HelloMessage"
```

```
                   pipeline-key="name" />

          <pipeline name="p_athrug" type="local">
            <string-expr match="[a-gA-G].*"/>
          </pipeline>

          <pipeline name="p_hthrum" type="local">
            <string-expr match="[h-mH-M].*"/>
          </pipeline>

          <pipeline name="p_nthrus" type="local">
            <string-expr match="[n-sN-S].*"/>
          </pipeline>

          <pipeline name="p_tthruz" type="local">
            <string-expr match="[t-zT-Z].*"/>
          </pipeline>

        </pipeline-service>

      </pipelines-distributor>

    </pipelines-config>
```

To run the test, use the following Ant command:

```
ant run-jperf-hello-4-cb-pipelines
```

The following output is from the test run:

```
run-jperf-hello-4-cb-pipelines:
   [java] [INFO] JPerf is testing org.softwarepipelines.
examples.hello.ch16.HelloPipelinesContentBasedPerfTest
   [java] [INFO] Instrumentor: - org.softwarepipelines.
framework.router.PipelinesRouterBase:p_tthruz =
36.0(18.0 TPS)
   [java] [INFO] Instrumentor: - org.softwarepipelines.
framework.router.PipelinesRouterBase:p_athrug =
36.0(18.0 TPS)
   [java] [INFO] Instrumentor: - org.softwarepipelines.
framework.router.PipelinesRouterBase:p_nthrus =
36.0(18.0 TPS)
   [java] [INFO] Instrumentor: - org.softwarepipelines.
framework.router.PipelinesRouterBase:p_hthrum =
36.0(18.0 TPS)
   [java] [INFO] Instrumentor: - org.softwarepipelines.
framework.router.PipelinesRouterBase:p_tthruz =
37.0(18.5 TPS)
   [java] [INFO] Instrumentor: - org.softwarepipelines.
framework.router.PipelinesRouterBase:p_athrug =
37.0(18.5 TPS)
```

```
[java] [INFO] Instrumentor: - org.softwarepipelines.
framework.router.PipelinesRouterBase:p_nthrus =
32.0(16.0 TPS)
[java] [INFO] Instrumentor: - org.softwarepipelines.
framework.router.PipelinesRouterBase:p_hthrum =
36.0(18.0 TPS)
[java] [INFO]     1 threads: 88 tps, 820,832 mem.
[java] [INFO] Instrumentor: - org.softwarepipelines.
framework.router.PipelinesRouterBase:p_tthruz =
40.0(20.0 TPS)
[java] [INFO] Instrumentor: - org.softwarepipelines.
framework.router.PipelinesRouterBase:p_athrug =
40.0(20.0 TPS)
[java] [INFO] Instrumentor: - org.softwarepipelines.
framework.router.PipelinesRouterBase:p_nthrus =
29.0(14.5 TPS)
[java] [INFO] Instrumentor: - org.softwarepipelines.
framework.router.PipelinesRouterBase:p_hthrum =
37.0(18.5 TPS)
[java] [INFO] Instrumentor: - org.softwarepipelines.
framework.router.PipelinesRouterBase:p_tthruz =
40.0(20.0 TPS)
[java] [INFO] Instrumentor: - org.softwarepipelines.
framework.router.PipelinesRouterBase:p_athrug =
39.0(19.5 TPS)
[java] [INFO] Instrumentor: - org.softwarepipelines.
framework.router.PipelinesRouterBase:p_nthrus =
30.0(15.0 TPS)
[java] [INFO] Instrumentor: - org.softwarepipelines.
framework.router.PipelinesRouterBase:p_hthrum =
25.0(12.5 TPS)
[java] [INFO]     2 threads: 66 tps, 805,056 mem.
[java] [INFO] Instrumentor: - org.softwarepipelines.
framework.router.PipelinesRouterBase:p_tthruz =
39.0(19.5 TPS)
[java] [INFO] Instrumentor: - org.softwarepipelines.
framework.router.PipelinesRouterBase:p_athrug =
40.0(20.0 TPS)
[java] [INFO] Instrumentor: - org.softwarepipelines.
framework.router.PipelinesRouterBase:p_nthrus =
29.0(14.5 TPS)
[java] [INFO] Instrumentor: - org.softwarepipelines.
framework.router.PipelinesRouterBase:p_hthrum =
36.0(18.0 TPS)
[java] [INFO] Instrumentor: - org.softwarepipelines.
framework.router.PipelinesRouterBase:p_tthruz =
40.0(20.0 TPS)
[java] [INFO] Instrumentor: - org.softwarepipelines.
framework.router.PipelinesRouterBase:p_athrug =
40.0(20.0 TPS)
[java] [INFO] Instrumentor: - org.softwarepipelines.
```

```
framework.router.PipelinesRouterBase:p_nthrus =
32.0(16.0 TPS)
    [java] [INFO] Instrumentor: - org.softwarepipelines.
framework.router.PipelinesRouterBase:p_hthrum =
30.0(15.0 TPS)
    [java] [INFO]    3 threads: 71 tps, 920,960 mem.
    [java] [INFO] Instrumentor: - org.softwarepipelines.
framework.router.PipelinesRouterBase:p_tthruz =
40.0(20.0 TPS)
    [java] [INFO] Instrumentor: - org.softwarepipelines.
framework.router.PipelinesRouterBase:p_athrug =
40.0(20.0 TPS)
    [java] [INFO] Instrumentor: - org.softwarepipelines.
framework.router.PipelinesRouterBase:p_nthrus =
30.0(15.0 TPS)
    [java] [INFO] Instrumentor: - org.softwarepipelines.
framework.router.PipelinesRouterBase:p_hthrum =
30.0(15.0 TPS)
    [java] [INFO] Instrumentor: - org.softwarepipelines.
framework.router.PipelinesRouterBase:p_tthruz =
40.0(20.0 TPS)
    [java] [INFO] Instrumentor: - org.softwarepipelines.
framework.router.PipelinesRouterBase:p_athrug =
40.0(20.0 TPS)
    [java] [INFO] Instrumentor: - org.softwarepipelines.
framework.router.PipelinesRouterBase:p_nthrus =
29.0(14.5 TPS)
    [java] [INFO] Instrumentor: - org.softwarepipelines.
framework.router.PipelinesRouterBase:p_hthrum =
39.0(19.5 TPS)
    [java] [INFO]    4 threads: 74 tps, 1,088,888 mem.
    [java] [INFO] Instrumentor: - org.softwarepipelines.
framework.router.PipelinesRouterBase:p_tthruz =
39.0(19.5 TPS)
    [java] [INFO] Instrumentor: - org.softwarepipelines.
framework.router.PipelinesRouterBase:p_athrug =
39.0(19.5 TPS)
    [java] [INFO] Instrumentor: - org.softwarepipelines.
framework.router.PipelinesRouterBase:p_nthrus =
31.0(15.5 TPS)
    [java] [INFO] Instrumentor: - org.softwarepipelines.
framework.router.PipelinesRouterBase:p_hthrum =
38.0(19.0 TPS)
    [java] [INFO] Instrumentor: - org.softwarepipelines.
framework.router.PipelinesRouterBase:p_tthruz =
40.0(20.0 TPS)
    [java] [INFO] Instrumentor: - org.softwarepipelines.
framework.router.PipelinesRouterBase:p_athrug =
40.0(20.0 TPS)
    [java] [INFO] Instrumentor: - org.softwarepipelines.
framework.router.PipelinesRouterBase:p_nthrus =
39.0(19.5 TPS)
    [java] [INFO] Instrumentor: - org.softwarepipelines.
```

```
framework.router.PipelinesRouterBase:p_hthrum =
40.0(20.0 TPS)
   [java] [INFO]    5 threads: 78 tps, 836,424 mem.
   [java] [INFO] Instrumentor: - org.softwarepipelines.
framework.router.PipelinesRouterBase:p_tthruz =
40.0(20.0 TPS)
   [java] [INFO] Instrumentor: - org.softwarepipelines.
framework.router.PipelinesRouterBase:p_athrug =
40.0(20.0 TPS)
   [java] [INFO] Instrumentor: - org.softwarepipelines.
framework.router.PipelinesRouterBase:p_nthrus =
34.0(17.0 TPS)
   [java] [INFO] Instrumentor: - org.softwarepipelines.
framework.router.PipelinesRouterBase:p_hthrum =
24.0(12.0 TPS)
   [java] [INFO] Instrumentor: - org.softwarepipelines.
framework.router.PipelinesRouterBase:p_tthruz =
40.0(20.0 TPS)
   [java] [INFO] Instrumentor: - org.softwarepipelines.
framework.router.PipelinesRouterBase:p_athrug =
40.0(20.0 TPS)
   [java] [INFO] Instrumentor: - org.softwarepipelines.
framework.router.PipelinesRouterBase:p_nthrus =
34.0(17.0 TPS)
   [java] [INFO] Instrumentor: - org.softwarepipelines.
framework.router.PipelinesRouterBase:p_hthrum =
30.0(15.0 TPS)
   [java] [INFO]    6 threads: 72 tps, 983,640 mem.
```

When we ran this test ourselves, we realized on average about 70 to 80 TPS. Because the client uses a randomly generated value, the TPS varies from 80, but the scaling is still very impressive.

In Figure 16.3 you can see a chart of the results. The performance is approximately 4X the baseline.

Custom Pipelines Router

In our examples up to this point, it's been easy to configure a service with multiple pipelines by using either round-robin or content-based routing with expressions or numeric ranges. But how do you handle a situation that requires more complex routing decisions? The answer is a custom Pipelines Router.

The reference Pipelines Framework is designed so you can implement any router logic your application requires, which allows you to perform complex evaluations on your message object. Let's extend our example so that we now require a custom router:

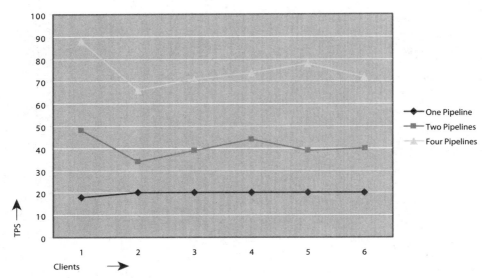

Figure 16.3 Output results

- Change the name values to first and last name, such as "Cory Isaacson."
- Create a custom Pipelines Router that routes messages based on the last name portion of the string.

These requirements are easy to implement. Build a custom router that parses the first/last name, then performs a regular expression match on the last name. You can see the distributor configurations, revised for custom routing, in Table 16.2.

The following code is the *CustomContentBasedRouterImpl*:

```
package org.softwarepipelines.examples.hello.ch16;

import org.apache.log4j.Logger;
import org.softwarepipelines.config.router.
PipelinesRouterConfig;
import org.softwarepipelines.framework.distributor.
PipelinesDistributorBase;
import org.softwarepipelines.framework.exception.
PipelineException;
import org.softwarepipelines.framework.message.
AbstractMessage;
import org.softwarepipelines.framework.pipeline.
Pipeline;
import org.softwarepipelines.framework.pipeline.
PipelineImpl;
```

Table 16.2 Distributor Configurations

HelloPipelinesService	Pattern Options
Service Invocation Pattern	Push
Message Exchange Pattern	One-Way
Pipeline Routing Pattern	Custom: CustomContentBasedRouter
Pipelines	p_athrum
	p_nthruz
	p_nthruz
	p_nthruz
Distributor Pattern	Single Distributor
Distributor Connector Pattern	Local Method Invocation

```
import org.softwarepipelines.framework.router.
PipelinesRouterBase;

public class CustomContentBasedRouterImpl extends
PipelinesRouterBase {
  private final static Logger LOG = Logger.getLogger(
CustomContentBasedRouterImpl.class );

  public CustomContentBasedRouterImpl(){
  }

  /**
   * Constructor to set pipelines configuration.
   * @param config
   * @param dist
   * @throws PipelineException
   */
  public CustomContentBasedRouterImpl
(final PipelinesRouterConfig config, final
PipelinesDistributorBase dist) throws PipelineException
{
    super(config, dist);
  }

  /**
   * Route the service request to the appropriate
pipeline. In this case,
   * parse the first/last name values, and route based
on the last name.
```

```
    */
    public void route(final AbstractMessage msg) throws
PipelineException {
        /* Get the Pipeline Key value, the full name.*/
        String keyVal = (String) getPipelineKey(msg);

        /* Parse out the last name.*/
        String lastName = keyVal.substring(keyVal.indexOf('
') + 1, keyVal.length());
        LOG.debug("Parsed last name '" + lastName + "' from
full name '" + keyVal + "'");

        /* Match the last name to a pipeline.*/
        PipelineImpl plImpl;
        for (Pipeline pipeline : this.getPipelines()) {
            plImpl = (PipelineImpl) pipeline;
            if (plImpl.getConfig().getMatch().
matcher(lastName).matches()) {
                LOG.debug("Invoking service for message with
last name " + lastName + " in pipeline " + plImpl.
getConfig().getName() +
                    " with match pattern " + plImpl.getConfig().
getMatch().pattern());
                plImpl.invokeService(msg);
                return;

            }
        }

        /* If we get to this point, no matching pipeline was
found, so throw an error.*/
        throw new PipelineException("No pipeline regexp
matched last name " + lastName +
            "!\nPipelines: " + config.getServiceConfig().
getPipelines());
    }
}
```

The router implementation works as follows:

- Each Pipelines Router implementation extends the *PipelinesRouter-Base*, which is an abstract class.
- You must implement the route() method, which makes the routing decisions. The service message is passed into the router, which can use its routing logic to evaluate any aspect of the message. In our example the name is first parsed into the first and last name values, then evaluated.
- After evaluating the name, the route() method loops through each of the pipelines to determine which pipeline matches the last name value. It does

this by using the `java.util.regex.Pattern` class, which creates a `Pattern` object from the match expression in the Pipelines Configuration.

- When a match is found, the router calls the `invokeService()` method on the pipeline instance.
- The service performs its task(s).

After you build the custom router, plug it into the Pipelines Configuration. The following code shows the new configuration from the `hello-4-custom-pipelines-config.xml` file:

```xml
<?xml version="1.0" encoding="UTF-8"?>

<pipelines-config xmlns="http://www.softwarepipelines.
org"
  xmlns:xsi="http://www.w3.org/2001/XMLSchema-instance"
  xsi:schemaLocation="http://www.softwarepipelines.
org http://www.softwarepipelines.org/schema/pipelines-
config.xsd">

  <instrumentor log-interval="2000"/>

  <pipelines-distributor name="localDistributor"
pattern="push">

    <!-- Local Connector -->
    <pipelines-connector name="localConnector"
type="local"/>

    <!-- Configure 4 pipelines using a custom router to
parse the last name value. -->
    <pipeline-service name="helloService" one-way="true"
      class-name="org.softwarepipelines.examples.hello.
HelloPipelinesService">

      <pipelines-router
        class-name="org.softwarepipelines.examples.
hello.ch16.CustomContentBasedRouterImpl"
        enforce-sequence="true"/>

      <message
        type="org.softwarepipelines.examples.hello.
HelloMessage"
        pipeline-key="name" />

      <pipeline name="p_athrug" type="local">
        <string-expr match="[a-gA-G].*"/>
      </pipeline>

      <pipeline name="p_hthrum" type="local">
        <string-expr match="[h-mH-M].*"/>
      </pipeline>
```

```
    <pipeline name="p_nthrus" type="local">
      <string-expr match="[n-sN-S].*"/>
    </pipeline>

    <pipeline name="p_tthruz" type="local">
      <string-expr match="[t-zT-Z].*"/>
    </pipeline>

  </pipeline-service>

 </pipelines-distributor>

</pipelines-config>
```

You'll need to modify the test client to include last name values. The following code shows the new *HelloPipelinesLastNameContentBased PerfTest* class, with the relevant modified snippet:

```
package org.softwarepipelines.examples.hello.ch16;

...

public class HelloPipelinesLastNameContentBasedPerfTest
implements PerfTest {

...

  /* Define an array of names throughout the alphabet;
   * load the letters a-g with twice as many last names
   * to demonstrate uneven pipeline demand.
   */
  String[] names = {"John Adams", "Abigail Adams", "Ali
Belle",
    "Michael Bolton", "Johnny Carson", "Samantha
Cascadia",
    "Doris Day", "Rodney Dangerfield", "Helen Ewing",
    "John Edwards", "Benjamin Franklin", "Wilma
Flintstone",
    "Andy Grove", "Bonnie Grealey", "Colin Holm",
    "Cory Isaacson", "Thomas Jefferson", "Tom Kite",
    "Lisa Leslie", "George Mican", "Paul Newman",
    "Paddy O'Brien", "Claire Peterson", "Joel
Quenneville",
    "Aaron Rodgers", "Joan Smith", "Jim Thompson",
    "Mary Underwood", "Zach Victorino", "John Wayne",
    "Bradley Xavier", "Steve Yzerman", "Marc Zebediah"};

...


...
}
```

Notice there are more last names that start with *A* through *G* than start with other letters. This is intentional, so that the client generates an uneven flow for the pipelines.

Now run the service using the Ant command

```
ant run-jperf-hello-4-custom-pipelines
```

The following output is from the test run:

```
run-jperf-hello-4-custom-pipelines:
    [java] [INFO] JPerf is testing org.
softwarepipelines.examples.hello.ch16.
HelloPipelinesLastNameContentBasedPerfTest
    [java] [INFO] Instrumentor: - org.softwarepipelines.
framework.router.PipelinesRouterBase:p_tthruz =
35.0(17.5 TPS)
    [java] [INFO] Instrumentor: - org.softwarepipelines.
framework.router.PipelinesRouterBase:p_athrug =
36.0(18.0 TPS)
    [java] [INFO] Instrumentor: - org.softwarepipelines.
framework.router.PipelinesRouterBase:p_nthrus =
36.0(18.0 TPS)
    [java] [INFO] Instrumentor: - org.softwarepipelines.
framework.router.PipelinesRouterBase:p_hthrum =
30.0(15.0 TPS)
    [java] [INFO] Instrumentor: - org.softwarepipelines.
framework.router.PipelinesRouterBase:p_tthruz = 12.0(6.0
TPS)
    [java] [INFO] Instrumentor: - org.softwarepipelines.
framework.router.PipelinesRouterBase:p_athrug =
40.0(20.0 TPS)
    [java] [INFO] Instrumentor: - org.softwarepipelines.
framework.router.PipelinesRouterBase:p_nthrus =
25.0(12.5 TPS)
    [java] [INFO] Instrumentor: - org.softwarepipelines.
framework.router.PipelinesRouterBase:p_hthrum =
20.0(10.0 TPS)
    [java] [INFO]     1 threads: 66 tps, 999,496 mem.
    [java] [INFO] Instrumentor: - org.softwarepipelines.
framework.router.PipelinesRouterBase:p_tthruz =
20.0(10.0 TPS)
    [java] [INFO] Instrumentor: - org.softwarepipelines.
framework.router.PipelinesRouterBase:p_athrug =
40.0(20.0 TPS)
    [java] [INFO] Instrumentor: - org.softwarepipelines.
framework.router.PipelinesRouterBase:p_nthrus = 18.0(9.0
TPS)
    [java] [INFO] Instrumentor: - org.softwarepipelines.
framework.router.PipelinesRouterBase:p_hthrum = 11.0(5.5
TPS)
```

```
[java] [INFO] Instrumentor: - org.softwarepipelines.
framework.router.PipelinesRouterBase:p_tthruz =
27.0(13.5 TPS)
    [java] [INFO] Instrumentor: - org.softwarepipelines.
framework.router.PipelinesRouterBase:p_athrug =
40.0(20.0 TPS)
    [java] [INFO] Instrumentor: - org.softwarepipelines.
framework.router.PipelinesRouterBase:p_nthrus =
21.0(10.5 TPS)
    [java] [INFO] Instrumentor: - org.softwarepipelines.
framework.router.PipelinesRouterBase:p_hthrum = 19.0(9.5
TPS)
    [java] [INFO]    2 threads: 48 tps, 658,256 mem.
    [java] [INFO] Instrumentor: - org.softwarepipelines.
framework.router.PipelinesRouterBase:p_tthruz =
27.0(13.5 TPS)
    [java] [INFO] Instrumentor: - org.softwarepipelines.
framework.router.PipelinesRouterBase:p_athrug =
39.0(19.5 TPS)
    [java] [INFO] Instrumentor: - org.softwarepipelines.
framework.router.PipelinesRouterBase:p_nthrus = 18.0(9.0
TPS)
    [java] [INFO] Instrumentor: - org.softwarepipelines.
framework.router.PipelinesRouterBase:p_hthrum =
23.0(11.5 TPS)
    [java] [INFO] Instrumentor: - org.softwarepipelines.
framework.router.PipelinesRouterBase:p_tthruz = 14.0(7.0
TPS)
    [java] [INFO] Instrumentor: - org.softwarepipelines.
framework.router.PipelinesRouterBase:p_athrug =
40.0(20.0 TPS)
    [java] [INFO] Instrumentor: - org.softwarepipelines.
framework.router.PipelinesRouterBase:p_nthrus = 8.0(4.0
TPS)
    [java] [INFO] Instrumentor: - org.softwarepipelines.
framework.router.PipelinesRouterBase:p_hthrum = 13.0(6.5
TPS)
    [java] [INFO]    3 threads: 46 tps, 814,744 mem.
    [java] [INFO] Instrumentor: - org.softwarepipelines.
framework.router.PipelinesRouterBase:p_tthruz =
25.0(12.5 TPS)
    [java] [INFO] Instrumentor: - org.softwarepipelines.
framework.router.PipelinesRouterBase:p_athrug =
39.0(19.5 TPS)
    [java] [INFO] Instrumentor: - org.softwarepipelines.
framework.router.PipelinesRouterBase:p_nthrus =
25.0(12.5 TPS)
    [java] [INFO] Instrumentor: - org.softwarepipelines.
framework.router.PipelinesRouterBase:p_hthrum = 13.0(6.5
TPS)
    [java] [INFO] Instrumentor: - org.softwarepipelines.
framework.router.PipelinesRouterBase:p_tthruz =
25.0(12.5 TPS)
```

```
[java] [INFO] Instrumentor: - org.softwarepipelines.
framework.router.PipelinesRouterBase:p_athrug =
40.0(20.0 TPS)
[java] [INFO] Instrumentor: - org.softwarepipelines.
framework.router.PipelinesRouterBase:p_nthrus = 13.0(6.5
TPS)
[java] [INFO] Instrumentor: - org.softwarepipelines.
framework.router.PipelinesRouterBase:p_hthrum = 14.0(7.0
TPS)
[java] [INFO]    4 threads: 47 tps, 1,009,912 mem.
[java] [INFO] Instrumentor: - org.softwarepipelines.
framework.router.PipelinesRouterBase:p_tthruz =
24.0(12.0 TPS)
[java] [INFO] Instrumentor: - org.softwarepipelines.
framework.router.PipelinesRouterBase:p_athrug =
40.0(20.0 TPS)
[java] [INFO] Instrumentor: - org.softwarepipelines.
framework.router.PipelinesRouterBase:p_nthrus =
29.0(14.5 TPS)
[java] [INFO] Instrumentor: - org.softwarepipelines.
framework.router.PipelinesRouterBase:p_hthrum =
22.0(11.0 TPS)
[java] [INFO] Instrumentor: - org.softwarepipelines.
framework.router.PipelinesRouterBase:p_tthruz =
21.0(10.5 TPS)
[java] [INFO] Instrumentor: - org.softwarepipelines.
framework.router.PipelinesRouterBase:p_athrug =
40.0(20.0 TPS)
[java] [INFO] Instrumentor: - org.softwarepipelines.
framework.router.PipelinesRouterBase:p_nthrus =
21.0(10.5 TPS)
[java] [INFO] Instrumentor: - org.softwarepipelines.
framework.router.PipelinesRouterBase:p_hthrum = 19.0(9.5
TPS)
[java] [INFO]    5 threads: 53 tps, 845,400 mem.
[java] [INFO] Instrumentor: - org.softwarepipelines.
framework.router.PipelinesRouterBase:p_tthruz = 12.0(6.0
TPS)
[java] [INFO] Instrumentor: - org.softwarepipelines.
framework.router.PipelinesRouterBase:p_athrug =
40.0(20.0 TPS)
[java] [INFO] Instrumentor: - org.softwarepipelines.
framework.router.PipelinesRouterBase:p_nthrus = 17.0(8.5
TPS)
[java] [INFO] Instrumentor: - org.softwarepipelines.
framework.router.PipelinesRouterBase:p_hthrum = 18.0(9.0
TPS)
[java] [INFO] Instrumentor: - org.softwarepipelines.
framework.router.PipelinesRouterBase:p_tthruz =
20.0(10.0 TPS)
[java] [INFO] Instrumentor: - org.softwarepipelines.
framework.router.PipelinesRouterBase:p_athrug =
40.0(20.0 TPS)
```

```
    [java] [INFO] Instrumentor: - org.softwarepipelines.
framework.router.PipelinesRouterBase:p_nthrus =
23.0(11.5 TPS)
    [java] [INFO] Instrumentor: - org.softwarepipelines.
framework.router.PipelinesRouterBase:p_hthrum = 13.0(6.5
TPS)
    [java] [INFO]    6 threads: 46 tps, 1,028,104 mem.
```

What is interesting in this test run is that pipelines handling the *A* to *G* range performed more transactions than others, because the content of the input transaction is not evenly distributed. In a real application this is a very likely occurrence—it would be impractical to dictate to your users or other applications what types of transactions to send, how often, and in what volume (although it would be nice . . .).

Fortunately, the solution is easy enough to fix. Just reconfigure the Pipelines Configuration to add more pipelines for the busier portions of the alphabet. This reduces the granularity of each pipeline and its load, preserves sequential processing, and handles the performance bottleneck.

Many industries, such as securities trading, often have uneven processing loads. In some cases there are indicators ahead of time. For example, when a particular company releases some big news, everyone expects heavy volume of trading of the associated security. When you've got the luxury of prediction, it's easy to tune your pipelines to accommodate the load before you get hit.

Most of the time, fluctuations happen without notice, but it's still useful to have pipelines architecture in these situations, because you can reconfigure pipelines on the fly. In the future, the ultimate solution could be Dynamic Pipelines—pipelines that automatically evaluate loads and reconfigure themselves. We'll tell you more about Dynamic Pipelines and other ideas in the final chapter, when we talk about the future of Software Pipelines.

The following code shows the revised Pipelines Configuration, with a total of five pipelines. We divided the *A* to *G* range into two pipelines to better accommodate the load:

```
<?xml version="1.0" encoding="UTF-8"?>

<pipelines-config xmlns="http://www.softwarepipelines.
org"
   xmlns:xsi="http://www.w3.org/2001/XMLSchema-instance"
```

```
    xsi:schemaLocation="http://www.softwarepipelines.
org http://www.softwarepipelines.org/schema/pipelines-
config.xsd">

  <instrumentor log-interval="2000"/>

  <pipelines-distributor name="localDistributor"
pattern="push">

    <!-- Local Connector -->
    <pipelines-connector name="localConnector"
type="local"/>

    <!-- Configure 5 pipelines using a custom router to
parse the last name value. -->
    <pipeline-service name="helloService" one-way="true"
      class-name="org.softwarepipelines.examples.hello.
HelloPipelinesService">

      <pipelines-router
        class-name="org.softwarepipelines.examples.
hello.ch16.CustomContentBasedRouterImpl"
        enforce-sequence="true"/>

      <message
        type="org.softwarepipelines.examples.hello.
HelloMessage"
        pipeline-key="name" />

      <pipeline name="p_athrud" type="local">
        <string-expr match="[a-dA-D].*"/>
      </pipeline>

      <pipeline name="p_ethrug" type="local">
        <string-expr match="[e-gE-G].*"/>
      </pipeline>

      <pipeline name="p_hthrum" type="local">
        <string-expr match="[h-mH-M].*"/>
      </pipeline>

      <pipeline name="p_nthrus" type="local">
        <string-expr match="[n-sN-S].*"/>
      </pipeline>

      <pipeline name="p_tthruz" type="local">
        <string-expr match="[t-zT-Z].*"/>
      </pipeline>

    </pipeline-service>

  </pipelines-distributor>

</pipelines-config>
```

You can run this example using the Ant command

```
ant run-jperf-hello-5-custom-pipelines
```

The following output is from the test run:

```
run-jperf-hello-5-custom-pipelines:
   [java] [INFO] JPerf is testing org.
softwarepipelines.examples.hello.ch16.
HelloPipelinesLastNameContentBasedPerfTest
   [java] [INFO] Instrumentor: - org.softwarepipelines.
framework.router.PipelinesRouterBase:p_tthruz =
37.0(18.5 TPS)
   [java] [INFO] Instrumentor: - org.softwarepipelines.
framework.router.PipelinesRouterBase:p_nthrus =
36.0(18.0 TPS)
   [java] [INFO] Instrumentor: - org.softwarepipelines.
framework.router.PipelinesRouterBase:p_ethrug =
37.0(18.5 TPS)
   [java] [INFO] Instrumentor: - org.softwarepipelines.
framework.router.PipelinesRouterBase:p_athrud =
37.0(18.5 TPS)
   [java] [INFO] Instrumentor: - org.softwarepipelines.
framework.router.PipelinesRouterBase:p_hthrum =
34.0(17.0 TPS)
   [java] [INFO] Instrumentor: - org.softwarepipelines.
framework.router.PipelinesRouterBase:p_tthruz =
30.0(15.0 TPS)
   [java] [INFO] Instrumentor: - org.softwarepipelines.
framework.router.PipelinesRouterBase:p_nthrus =
28.0(14.0 TPS)
   [java] [INFO] Instrumentor: - org.softwarepipelines.
framework.router.PipelinesRouterBase:p_ethrug =
39.0(19.5 TPS)
   [java] [INFO] Instrumentor: - org.softwarepipelines.
framework.router.PipelinesRouterBase:p_athrud =
39.0(19.5 TPS)
   [java] [INFO] Instrumentor: - org.softwarepipelines.
framework.router.PipelinesRouterBase:p_hthrum =
27.0(13.5 TPS)
   [java] [INFO]    1 threads: 101 tps, 931,744 mem.
   [java] [INFO] Instrumentor: - org.softwarepipelines.
framework.router.PipelinesRouterBase:p_tthruz =
31.0(15.5 TPS)
   [java] [INFO] Instrumentor: - org.softwarepipelines.
framework.router.PipelinesRouterBase:p_nthrus =
39.0(19.5 TPS)
   [java] [INFO] Instrumentor: - org.softwarepipelines.
framework.router.PipelinesRouterBase:p_ethrug =
35.0(17.5 TPS)
```

```
    [java] [INFO] Instrumentor: - org.softwarepipelines.
framework.router.PipelinesRouterBase:p_athrud =
40.0(20.0 TPS)
    [java] [INFO] Instrumentor: - org.softwarepipelines.
framework.router.PipelinesRouterBase:p_hthrum =
40.0(20.0 TPS)
    [java] [INFO] Instrumentor: - org.softwarepipelines.
framework.router.PipelinesRouterBase:p_tthruz =
26.0(13.0 TPS)
    [java] [INFO] Instrumentor: - org.softwarepipelines.
framework.router.PipelinesRouterBase:p_nthrus =
27.0(13.5 TPS)
    [java] [INFO] Instrumentor: - org.softwarepipelines.
framework.router.PipelinesRouterBase:p_ethrug =
32.0(16.0 TPS)
    [java] [INFO] Instrumentor: - org.softwarepipelines.
framework.router.PipelinesRouterBase:p_athrud =
40.0(20.0 TPS)
    [java] [INFO] Instrumentor: - org.softwarepipelines.
framework.router.PipelinesRouterBase:p_hthrum =
20.0(10.0 TPS)
    [java] [INFO]     2 threads: 80 tps, 907,088 mem.
    [java] [INFO] Instrumentor: - org.softwarepipelines.
framework.router.PipelinesRouterBase:p_tthruz =
34.0(17.0 TPS)
    [java] [INFO] Instrumentor: - org.softwarepipelines.
framework.router.PipelinesRouterBase:p_nthrus =
36.0(18.0 TPS)
    [java] [INFO] Instrumentor: - org.softwarepipelines.
framework.router.PipelinesRouterBase:p_ethrug =
34.0(17.0 TPS)
    [java] [INFO] Instrumentor: - org.softwarepipelines.
framework.router.PipelinesRouterBase:p_athrud =
40.0(20.0 TPS)
    [java] [INFO] Instrumentor: - org.softwarepipelines.
framework.router.PipelinesRouterBase:p_hthrum =
32.0(16.0 TPS)
    [java] [INFO] Instrumentor: - org.softwarepipelines.
framework.router.PipelinesRouterBase:p_tthruz =
31.0(15.5 TPS)
    [java] [INFO] Instrumentor: - org.softwarepipelines.
framework.router.PipelinesRouterBase:p_nthrus =
38.0(19.0 TPS)
    [java] [INFO] Instrumentor: - org.softwarepipelines.
framework.router.PipelinesRouterBase:p_ethrug =
28.0(14.0 TPS)
    [java] [INFO] Instrumentor: - org.softwarepipelines.
framework.router.PipelinesRouterBase:p_athrud =
40.0(20.0 TPS)
    [java] [INFO] Instrumentor: - org.softwarepipelines.
framework.router.PipelinesRouterBase:p_hthrum =
29.0(14.5 TPS)
```

```
[java] [INFO]    3 threads: 80 tps, 915,832 mem.
[java] [INFO] Instrumentor: - org.softwarepipelines.
framework.router.PipelinesRouterBase:p_tthruz =
33.0(16.5 TPS)
[java] [INFO] Instrumentor: - org.softwarepipelines.
framework.router.PipelinesRouterBase:p_nthrus =
36.0(18.0 TPS)
[java] [INFO] Instrumentor: - org.softwarepipelines.
framework.router.PipelinesRouterBase:p_ethrug =
33.0(16.5 TPS)
[java] [INFO] Instrumentor: - org.softwarepipelines.
framework.router.PipelinesRouterBase:p_athrud =
40.0(20.0 TPS)
[java] [INFO] Instrumentor: - org.softwarepipelines.
framework.router.PipelinesRouterBase:p_hthrum =
35.0(17.5 TPS)
[java] [INFO] Instrumentor: - org.softwarepipelines.
framework.router.PipelinesRouterBase:p_tthruz =
32.0(16.0 TPS)
[java] [INFO] Instrumentor: - org.softwarepipelines.
framework.router.PipelinesRouterBase:p_nthrus =
34.0(17.0 TPS)
[java] [INFO] Instrumentor: - org.softwarepipelines.
framework.router.PipelinesRouterBase:p_ethrug =
26.0(13.0 TPS)
[java] [INFO] Instrumentor: - org.softwarepipelines.
framework.router.PipelinesRouterBase:p_athrud =
40.0(20.0 TPS)
[java] [INFO] Instrumentor: - org.softwarepipelines.
framework.router.PipelinesRouterBase:p_hthrum =
24.0(12.0 TPS)
[java] [INFO]    4 threads: 83 tps, 1,020,200 mem.
[java] [INFO] Instrumentor: - org.softwarepipelines.
framework.router.PipelinesRouterBase:p_tthruz =
39.0(19.5 TPS)
[java] [INFO] Instrumentor: - org.softwarepipelines.
framework.router.PipelinesRouterBase:p_nthrus =
34.0(17.0 TPS)
[java] [INFO] Instrumentor: - org.softwarepipelines.
framework.router.PipelinesRouterBase:p_ethrug =
23.0(11.5 TPS)
[java] [INFO] Instrumentor: - org.softwarepipelines.
framework.router.PipelinesRouterBase:p_athrud =
39.0(19.5 TPS)
[java] [INFO] Instrumentor: - org.softwarepipelines.
framework.router.PipelinesRouterBase:p_hthrum =
29.0(14.5 TPS)
[java] [INFO] Instrumentor: - org.softwarepipelines.
framework.router.PipelinesRouterBase:p_tthruz =
40.0(20.0 TPS)
[java] [INFO] Instrumentor: - org.softwarepipelines.
framework.router.PipelinesRouterBase:p_nthrus =
37.0(18.5 TPS)
```

```
[java] [INFO] Instrumentor: - org.softwarepipelines.
framework.router.PipelinesRouterBase:p_ethrug =
37.0(18.5 TPS)
[java] [INFO] Instrumentor: - org.softwarepipelines.
framework.router.PipelinesRouterBase:p_athrud =
40.0(20.0 TPS)
[java] [INFO] Instrumentor: - org.softwarepipelines.
framework.router.PipelinesRouterBase:p_hthrum =
27.0(13.5 TPS)
[java] [INFO]    5 threads: 89 tps, 778,488 mem.
[java] [INFO] Instrumentor: - org.softwarepipelines.
framework.router.PipelinesRouterBase:p_tthruz =
37.0(18.5 TPS)
[java] [INFO] Instrumentor: - org.softwarepipelines.
framework.router.PipelinesRouterBase:p_nthrus =
37.0(18.5 TPS)
[java] [INFO] Instrumentor: - org.softwarepipelines.
framework.router.PipelinesRouterBase:p_ethrug =
34.0(17.0 TPS)
[java] [INFO] Instrumentor: - org.softwarepipelines.
framework.router.PipelinesRouterBase:p_athrud =
40.0(20.0 TPS)
[java] [INFO] Instrumentor: - org.softwarepipelines.
framework.router.PipelinesRouterBase:p_hthrum =
37.0(18.5 TPS)
[java] [INFO] Instrumentor: - org.softwarepipelines.
framework.router.PipelinesRouterBase:p_tthruz =
37.0(18.5 TPS)
[java] [INFO] Instrumentor: - org.softwarepipelines.
framework.router.PipelinesRouterBase:p_nthrus = 19.0(9.5
TPS)
[java] [INFO] Instrumentor: - org.softwarepipelines.
framework.router.PipelinesRouterBase:p_ethrug =
24.0(12.0 TPS)
[java] [INFO] Instrumentor: - org.softwarepipelines.
framework.router.PipelinesRouterBase:p_athrud =
40.0(20.0 TPS)
[java] [INFO] Instrumentor: - org.softwarepipelines.
framework.router.PipelinesRouterBase:p_hthrum =
34.0(17.0 TPS)
[java] [INFO]    6 threads: 84 tps, 912,864 mem.
```

Because of the random values, the load isn't perfect across the pipelines, but it's much more even than in the earlier example. This new configuration illustrates some of the nice benefits of using pipelines—you can do this type of load balancing, and you can adjust your Pipelines Configuration to keep your processors busier and accommodate an increased load.

Summary

In this example we demonstrated how flexible and easy it is to configure many different kinds of pipelines configurations. It is this flexibility and capability for adapting to a wide variety of business requirements that give Software Pipelines its power and utility.

In the next chapter we'll show you how to increase performance by using Request-Response messaging.

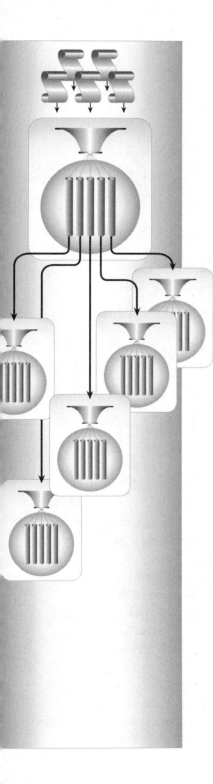

## CHAPTER SEVENTEEN

Getting an Answer from Hello Software Pipelines

In our examples so far, we've only covered one-way transactions. But most applications require a response from a given service. In this chapter we address the issue by upgrading *HelloPipelinesService* to use Request-Response for its Message Exchange Pattern.

Request-Response Messaging

Request-Response messaging is vital to any application, but it has special implications in Software Pipelines architecture, as it does in any distributed computing architecture. Figure 17.1 shows how Request-Response works.

If the application performs Request-Response in a fully synchronous manner, where all points of the service flow wait for the response, it's impossible to realize the full benefits of Software Pipelines. The reason is obvious: Each pipeline, plus the Pipeline Distributor thread that invoked the pipeline, must remain occupied until the response gets all the way back to the client. This greatly reduces the capacity of the Pipeline Distributor and turns it into a bottleneck—a fatal error in this type of architecture.

Furthermore, we've considered an application with only one Pipeline Distributor and one service. Imagine what happens if you have several distributors and services, as in Figure 17.2, all running in a single execution chain. Each element has to wait for a response from its downstream component, then relay the message all the way

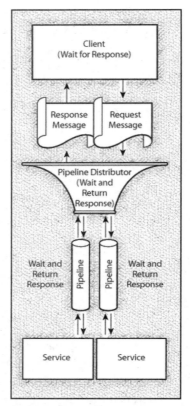

Figure 17.1 Request-Response

back to the originating client. This design is inefficient and complex, and it places a heavy burden on resources. It removes much of the performance benefit you're trying to achieve.

This problem isn't specific to Software Pipelines. Any distributed system might face this challenge. The solution is to use an asynchronous callback mechanism, as shown in Figure 17.3. The client waits for a callback from the service processing tier, which provides the message when it is ready. This method is available in many other distributed architectures, including Web services via the WS-Addressing specification.

An asynchronous callback is really two separate one-way flows. The first flow goes from the client via the distributor to the service, and when the service (which has the address of the client) finishes processing the message, it responds directly to the client. The client still has to wait for a response, but it does this as a sleep

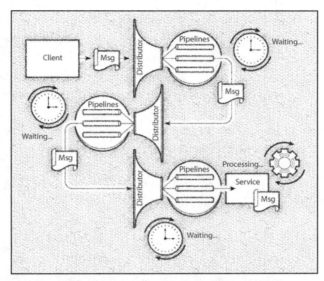

Figure 17.2 Fully synchronous Request-Response

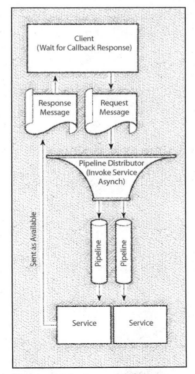

Figure 17.3 Asynchronous callback mechanism

function that doesn't consume CPU, and the client can perform other processing while it waits. More importantly, this design frees the Pipeline Distributor to continue receiving requests, and it frees other downstream services from the burden of waiting for and relaying response messages. In Figure 17.4 you can see a multistep service flow, in which the final service is the only component that must respond to the client.

One issue you might see with this design involves the handling of errors within the service flow. For example, an error can occur in a midflow component, but not in the component that is supposed to return the response. To address this, make sure all components can short-circuit the flow and return to the client in an error condition, as shown in Figure 17.5.

Our reference Pipelines Framework supports asynchronous callbacks for the network-based connectors (socket connector and Web service connector), and we can add support for local connectors in the future.

Keep the following tips in mind when you're building a Request-Response pipelines design:

- Since pipeline services are likely to be arranged in several "hops" using multiple Pipeline Distributors, pipelines, and individual services, it's a good idea

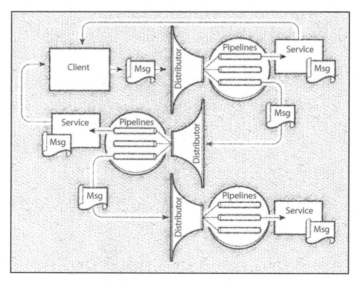

Figure 17.4 Asynchronous callback mechanism in multistep service flow

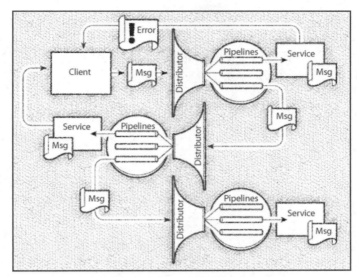

Figure 17.5 Component returns error to client.

to send a response to the client only when all processing is complete, or if an error has occurred.

- Try to avoid chaining responses. To do this, design your service components as stateless components whenever possible.
- Pipelines messaging actually supports only one-way transactions. Request-Response is a simulated behavior that uses the asynchronous callback mechanism.
- Many organizations use a messaging queue to perform the callback mechanism. This requires a distributor that implements a pull-based connector. You must also use response queues or temporary queues, which are monitored by the client. In some cases, pull-based patterns are easier to implement than push-based patterns, but you'll often get a performance penalty—all transactions must travel through a centralized facility for message queuing, which can become a bottleneck. In addition, using a centralized message queue adds an extra step to the flow.

Use Request-Response with Hello Software Pipelines

Figure 17.6 shows the service flow for our Request-Response example. You can see the distributor configurations in Table 17.1.

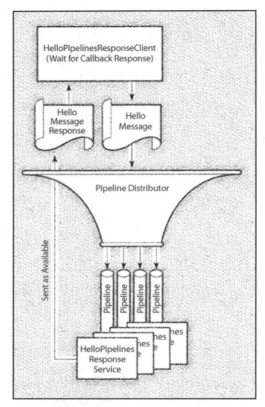

Figure 17.6 New service flow for Hello Software Pipelines

To support the Request-Response Message Exchange Pattern, you'll need to modify the Pipelines Configuration. The following code is from the new `hello-4-pipelines-response-config.xml` file:

```xml
<?xml version="1.0" encoding="UTF-8"?>

<pipelines-config xmlns="http://www.softwarepipelines.
org"
  xmlns:xsi="http://www.w3.org/2001/XMLSchema-instance"
  xsi:schemaLocation="http://www.softwarepipelines.
org http://www.softwarepipelines.org/schema/pipelines-
config.xsd">
```

Table 17.1 Distributor Configurations

HelloPipelinesService	Pattern Options
Service Invocation Pattern	Push
Message Exchange Pattern	Request-Response
Pipeline Routing Pattern	`ContentBasedRouterImpl`
Pipelines	`p_athrum`
	`p_nthruz`
	`p_nthruz`
	`p_nthruz`
Distributor Pattern	Single Distributor
Distributor Connector Pattern	Socket Invocation

```
    <instrumentor log-interval="2000"/>

    <pipelines-distributor name="localDistributor"
pattern="push">

      <!-- Local Connector -->
      <pipelines-connector name="localConnector"
type="local"/>

      <!-- Configure 4 round-robin pipelines, for Request-
Response. -->
      <pipeline-service name="helloService" one-
way="false"
          class-name="org.softwarepipelines.examples.
hello.HelloPipelinesResponseService">

        <pipelines-router
            class-name="org.softwarepipelines.framework.
router.RoundRobinRouterImpl"
            enforce-sequence="false"/>

        <message
          type="org.softwarepipelines.examples.hello.
HelloMessage" />

        <pipeline name="p_1" type="local"/>
        <pipeline name="p_2" type="local"/>
        <pipeline name="p_3" type="local"/>
        <pipeline name="p_4" type="local"/>
```

```
        </pipeline-service>

    </pipelines-distributor>

</pipelines-config>
```

The important specifications in the new Pipelines Configuration are as follows:

- In `<pipeline-service>`, set `class-name` to the *HelloPipelines ResponseService*.
- In `<pipeline-service>`, set `one-way` to `false`. This enables a Request-Response service.

You'll also need to make a minor modification to the service, so it returns a response message. The following code shows the revised service, *HelloPipelinesResponseService*:

```
package org.softwarepipelines.examples.hello;

import org.apache.log4j.Logger;

import org.softwarepipelines.config.service.
PipelineServiceConfig;
import org.softwarepipelines.framework.exception.
PipelineException;
import org.softwarepipelines.framework.message.
AbstractMessage;
import org.softwarepipelines.framework.service.
PipelineServiceBase;

public class HelloPipelinesResponseService extends
PipelineServiceBase {
    private static final Logger LOG = Logger.getLogger
(HelloPipelinesResponseService.class);
    private static final int SLEEP_TIME = 50;
    private static final int SLEEP_CYCLES = 10;

    /**
     * Default constructor
     */
    public HelloPipelinesResponseService() {
    }

    /**
     * Constructor used by the framework to pass in the
     * PipelineServiceConfig instance.
     */
```

```
    public HelloPipelinesResponseService(final
PipelineServiceConfig config) {
        super(config);
    }

    /**
     * Write the 'Hello' message contents out to the
log.
     */
    public synchronized void
processMessage(AbstractMessage msg) throws
PipelineException {
        /* Cast the HelloMessage.*/
         HelloMessage helloMessage = (HelloMessage)msg;

        /* Consume some CPU.*/
        eatCpu();

        /* Write the message to the log.*/
        LOG.debug("Hello " + helloMessage.getName() + "
from SoftwarePipelines, in " + SLEEP_TIME + " ms!");

        /* Send the response. */
        HelloMessage toRet = new HelloMessage();
        toRet.setName("Software Pipelines");
        sendResultMessage(toRet);
    }

    /**
     * Consume some CPU time to simulate processor work.
     */
    private void eatCpu() {
      for (int i = 0; i < SLEEP_CYCLES; i++) {
        try {
          Thread.sleep(SLEEP_TIME/SLEEP_CYCLES);
        } catch (InterruptedException ie) {
          LOG.warn("Interrupted while sleeping for " +
SLEEP_TIME + " ms to eat cpu", ie);
        }
      }
    }
}
```

The service now creates a return message, then calls sendResultMessage().

To run this example, use a simple client that makes a service call from its main() method. This will allow you to see the response output from the client.

The following code shows the new client, *HelloPipelinesResponse Client*:

```
package org.softwarepipelines.examples.hello.ch17;

import java.io.File;
import java.io.IOException;

import org.apache.log4j.Logger;
import org.softwarepipelines.config.
PipelinesMasterConfig;
import org.softwarepipelines.config.exception.
ConfigException;
import org.softwarepipelines.examples.hello.
HelloMessage;
import org.softwarepipelines.framework.connector.
PipelinesConnector;
import org.softwarepipelines.framework.distributor.
PipelinesDistributorBase;
import org.softwarepipelines.framework.exception.
PipelineException;
import org.softwarepipelines.framework.message.
AbstractMessage;
import org.softwarepipelines.framework.util.
PipelinesHelper;

/**
 * This client is the client for the
HelloPipelinesService. It invokes the service
 * via the local connector of the distributor.
 */
public class HelloPipelinesResponseClient {
   final private static Logger LOG = Logger.getLogger
(HelloPipelinesResponseClient.class);

  /**
   * Usage: HelloPipelinesClient [pipelinesConfig
filename] [distributorName]
   * @param args
   * @throws IOException
   * @throws ConfigException
   * @throws PipelineException
   */
  public static void main(String[] args) throws
IOException, ConfigException, PipelineException{

    /* Get the parameters.*/
    if(args.length != 3) {
      throw new PipelineException("Usage:
HelloPipelinesClient [pipelinesConfig filename]
[distributorName] [connectorName]");
    }
```

```
    String pipelinesConfigFilename = args[0];
    String distributorName = args[1];
    String connectorName = args[2];

    /* Load the Pipelines Configuration.*/
    PipelinesMasterConfig masterConfig
= new PipelinesMasterConfig(new
File(pipelinesConfigFilename));

    /* Get the remote destination distributor and start
it. */
    PipelinesDistributorBase distributor =
PipelinesHelper.getDistributorByName(distributorName,
masterConfig);
    distributor.start();

    /* Check out a connector instance from the client
broker.*/
    PipelinesConnector connector = PipelinesHelper.
getConnectorByName(distributorName, connectorName,
masterConfig);

    /* Build the HelloMessage instance, including
'serviceName' and 'name'.*/
    HelloMessage msg = new HelloMessage();
    msg.setServiceName("helloService");
    msg.setName("Cory");

    /* Invoke the service on the distributor, via the
connector.*/
    LOG.info("Sending message: " + msg);
    AbstractMessage resp = connector.
sendAndReceive(msg);

    /* Cast the response to a HelloMessage. */
    HelloMessage helloResp = (HelloMessage) resp;
    LOG.info("Received response from: " + helloResp.
getName());

    /* Clean up by shutting down the singleton
distributor and all message brokers.*/
    connector.shutdown();
    distributor.shutdown();
  }

}
```

The important change in the new client is the call to the `sendAndReceive()` method instead of the `send()` method used in our earlier examples. The `sendAndReceive()` method returns a response message. The client casts the response message to another *HelloMessage* instance, then uses the instance's data to log the response.

The following output is from a single service execution:

```
run-hello-response-pipelines:
   [java] [INFO] HelloPipelinesResponseClient: - Sending
message:
   [java] [Message]
   [java] Destination Service Name:  helloService
   [java] Name:  Cory
   [java] [INFO] HelloPipelinesResponseClient: - Received
response from Software Pipelines
```

The response message is "Received response from Software Pipelines."

To see how the service performs with four pipelines, use the modified test client *HelloPipelinesResponsePerfTest*:

```java
package org.softwarepipelines.examples.hello.ch17;

import java.io.File;
import java.io.IOException;

import org.apache.log4j.Logger;
import org.jperf.PerfTest;
import org.jperf.PerfTestRunner;
import org.softwarepipelines.config.
PipelinesMasterConfig;
import org.softwarepipelines.config.exception.
ConfigException;
import org.softwarepipelines.examples.hello.
HelloMessage;
import org.softwarepipelines.framework.connector.
PipelinesConnector;
import org.softwarepipelines.framework.distributor.
PipelinesDistributorBase;
import org.softwarepipelines.framework.exception.
PipelineException;
import org.softwarepipelines.framework.util.
PipelinesHelper;

public class HelloPipelinesResponsePerfTest implements
PerfTest {
   final private static Logger LOG = Logger.getLogger
(HelloPipelinesResponsePerfTest.class);

   /* Master Pipelines Config */
   private static PipelinesMasterConfig masterConfig;

   /* Message Brokers */
   private static PipelinesDistributorBase distributor;

   /* Connector instance which each thread will
instantiate separately.*/
```

```
   private PipelinesConnector connector;
   private static String connectorName;

   /**
    * Set up the test.
    */
   public void setUp() throws Exception {
     /* Check out a socket connector instance.*/
     connector = PipelinesHelper.
getConnectorByName(distributor.getConfig().getName(),
connectorName, masterConfig);
   }

   /**
    * Tear down the test, performing any cleanup.
    */
   public void tearDown() throws Exception {
     // shut down connector
     connector.shutdown();
   }

   /**
    * Run the service test.
    */
   public void test() throws Exception {
     /* Build the HelloMessage instance, including
'serviceName' and 'name'.*/
     HelloMessage msg = new HelloMessage();
     msg.setServiceName("helloService");
     msg.setName("Cory");
     LOG.debug("Sending message: " + msg);

     /* Invoke the service on the distributor, via the
connector.*/
     HelloMessage resp = (HelloMessage)connector.
sendAndReceive(msg);
     LOG.debug("Received response: " + resp);
   }

   /**
    * Main method for starting the test.
    * @param args
    * @throws IOException
    * @throws ConfigException
    * @throws PipelineException
    */
   public static void main(String[] args) throws
IOException, ConfigException, PipelineException {
     String pipelinesConfigFilename, distributorName;

     /* Get the parameters.*/
     if(args.length != 3) {
```

```
      throw new PipelineException("Usage:
HelloPipelinesClient [pipelinesConfig filename]
[distributorName]");
   }
   pipelinesConfigFilename = args[0];
   distributorName = args[1];
   connectorName = args[2];

   /* Load the Pipelines Configuration.*/
   masterConfig = new PipelinesMasterConfig(new
File(pipelinesConfigFilename));

   /* Set up the destination distributor. */
   distributor = PipelinesHelper.getDistributorByName
(distributorName, masterConfig);
   distributor.start();

   /* Set up the PerfTest runner for 6 threads, 4
seconds between threads.*/
   PerfTestRunner r = new PerfTestRunner();
   r.setMaxClient(6);
   r.setTestPeriod(4000);

   /* Specify the results output file.*/
   r.setResultFile(new File("results/test/
HelloPipelinesResponsePerfTest-results.xml"));

   /* Run the test.*/
   r.run(HelloPipelinesResponsePerfTest.class);

   /* Shut down the brokers and executor threads.*/
   distributor.shutdown();

   }

}
```

The only modification required in the client is to receive the result in the test() method. The class does this by calling sendAndReceive(), which returns a result message.

To run the test, use the following Ant command:

```
ant run-jperf-hello-4-response-pipelines
```

The following output is from the test run:

```
run-jperf-hello-4-response-pipelines:
  [java] [INFO] JPerf is testing org.softwarepipelines.
examples.hello.ch17.HelloPipelinesResponsePerfTest
```

```
[java] [INFO] Instrumentor: - org.softwarepipelines.
framework.router.PipelinesRouterBase:p_2 = 9.0(4.5 TPS)
   [java] [INFO] Instrumentor: - org.softwarepipelines.
framework.router.PipelinesRouterBase:p_4 = 9.0(4.5 TPS)
   [java] [INFO] Instrumentor: - org.softwarepipelines.
framework.router.PipelinesRouterBase:p_1 = 9.0(4.5 TPS)
   [java] [INFO] Instrumentor: - org.softwarepipelines.
framework.router.PipelinesRouterBase:p_3 = 9.0(4.5 TPS)
   [java] [INFO] Instrumentor: - org.softwarepipelines.
framework.router.PipelinesRouterBase:p_2 = 10.0(5.0 TPS)
   [java] [INFO] Instrumentor: - org.softwarepipelines.
framework.router.PipelinesRouterBase:p_4 = 10.0(5.0 TPS)
   [java] [INFO] Instrumentor: - org.softwarepipelines.
framework.router.PipelinesRouterBase:p_1 = 10.0(5.0 TPS)
   [java] [INFO] Instrumentor: - org.softwarepipelines.
framework.router.PipelinesRouterBase:p_3 = 10.0(5.0 TPS)
   [java] [INFO]     1 threads: 20 tps, 755,568 mem.
   [java] [INFO] Instrumentor: - org.softwarepipelines.
framework.router.PipelinesRouterBase:p_2 = 19.0(9.5 TPS)
   [java] [INFO] Instrumentor: - org.softwarepipelines.
framework.router.PipelinesRouterBase:p_4 = 19.0(9.5 TPS)
   [java] [INFO] Instrumentor: - org.softwarepipelines.
framework.router.PipelinesRouterBase:p_1 = 19.0(9.5 TPS)
   [java] [INFO] Instrumentor: - org.softwarepipelines.
framework.router.PipelinesRouterBase:p_3 = 19.0(9.5 TPS)
   [java] [INFO] Instrumentor: - org.softwarepipelines.
framework.router.PipelinesRouterBase:p_2 = 20.0(10.0
TPS)
   [java] [INFO] Instrumentor: - org.softwarepipelines.
framework.router.PipelinesRouterBase:p_4 = 19.0(9.5 TPS)
   [java] [INFO] Instrumentor: - org.softwarepipelines.
framework.router.PipelinesRouterBase:p_1 = 20.0(10.0
TPS)
   [java] [INFO] Instrumentor: - org.softwarepipelines.
framework.router.PipelinesRouterBase:p_3 = 20.0(10.0
TPS)
   [java] [INFO]     2 threads: 40 tps, 540,328 mem.
   [java] [INFO] Instrumentor: - org.softwarepipelines.
framework.router.PipelinesRouterBase:p_2 = 28.0(14.0
TPS)
   [java] [INFO] Instrumentor: - org.softwarepipelines.
framework.router.PipelinesRouterBase:p_4 = 29.0(14.5
TPS)
   [java] [INFO] Instrumentor: - org.softwarepipelines.
framework.router.PipelinesRouterBase:p_1 = 29.0(14.5
TPS)
   [java] [INFO] Instrumentor: - org.softwarepipelines.
framework.router.PipelinesRouterBase:p_3 = 28.0(14.0
TPS)
   [java] [INFO] Instrumentor: - org.softwarepipelines.
framework.router.PipelinesRouterBase:p_2 = 30.0(15.0
TPS)
```

```
    [java] [INFO] Instrumentor: - org.softwarepipelines.
framework.router.PipelinesRouterBase:p_4 = 30.0(15.0
TPS)
    [java] [INFO] Instrumentor: - org.softwarepipelines.
framework.router.PipelinesRouterBase:p_1 = 30.0(15.0
TPS)
    [java] [INFO] Instrumentor: - org.softwarepipelines.
framework.router.PipelinesRouterBase:p_3 = 30.0(15.0
TPS)
    [java] [INFO]    3 threads: 60 tps, 756,024 mem.
    [java] [INFO] Instrumentor: - org.softwarepipelines.
framework.router.PipelinesRouterBase:p_2 = 39.0(19.5
TPS)
    [java] [INFO] Instrumentor: - org.softwarepipelines.
framework.router.PipelinesRouterBase:p_4 = 38.0(19.0
TPS)
    [java] [INFO] Instrumentor: - org.softwarepipelines.
framework.router.PipelinesRouterBase:p_1 = 38.0(19.0
TPS)
    [java] [INFO] Instrumentor: - org.softwarepipelines.
framework.router.PipelinesRouterBase:p_3 = 39.0(19.5
TPS)
    [java] [INFO] Instrumentor: - org.softwarepipelines.
framework.router.PipelinesRouterBase:p_2 = 40.0(20.0
TPS)
    [java] [INFO] Instrumentor: - org.softwarepipelines.
framework.router.PipelinesRouterBase:p_4 = 40.0(20.0
TPS)
    [java] [INFO] Instrumentor: - org.softwarepipelines.
framework.router.PipelinesRouterBase:p_1 = 40.0(20.0
TPS)
    [java] [INFO] Instrumentor: - org.softwarepipelines.
framework.router.PipelinesRouterBase:p_3 = 40.0(20.0
TPS)
    [java] [INFO]    4 threads: 80 tps, 863,704 mem.
    [java] [INFO] Instrumentor: - org.softwarepipelines.
framework.router.PipelinesRouterBase:p_2 = 39.0(19.5
TPS)
    [java] [INFO] Instrumentor: - org.softwarepipelines.
framework.router.PipelinesRouterBase:p_4 = 40.0(20.0
TPS)
    [java] [INFO] Instrumentor: - org.softwarepipelines.
framework.router.PipelinesRouterBase:p_1 = 40.0(20.0
TPS)
    [java] [INFO] Instrumentor: - org.softwarepipelines.
framework.router.PipelinesRouterBase:p_3 = 39.0(19.5
TPS)
    [java] [INFO] Instrumentor: - org.softwarepipelines.
framework.router.PipelinesRouterBase:p_2 = 40.0(20.0
TPS)
    [java] [INFO] Instrumentor: - org.softwarepipelines.
framework.router.PipelinesRouterBase:p_4 = 40.0(20.0
TPS)
```

```
    [java] [INFO] Instrumentor: - org.softwarepipelines.
framework.router.PipelinesRouterBase:p_1 = 39.0(19.5
TPS)
    [java] [INFO] Instrumentor: - org.softwarepipelines.
framework.router.PipelinesRouterBase:p_3 = 40.0(20.0
TPS)
    [java] [INFO]    5 threads: 79 tps, 985,280 mem.
    [java] [INFO] Instrumentor: - org.softwarepipelines.
framework.router.PipelinesRouterBase:p_2 = 40.0(20.0
TPS)
    [java] [INFO] Instrumentor: - org.softwarepipelines.
framework.router.PipelinesRouterBase:p_4 = 39.0(19.5
TPS)
    [java] [INFO] Instrumentor: - org.softwarepipelines.
framework.router.PipelinesRouterBase:p_1 = 40.0(20.0
TPS)
    [java] [INFO] Instrumentor: - org.softwarepipelines.
framework.router.PipelinesRouterBase:p_3 = 40.0(20.0
TPS)
    [java] [INFO] Instrumentor: - org.softwarepipelines.
framework.router.PipelinesRouterBase:p_2 = 40.0(20.0
TPS)
    [java] [INFO] Instrumentor: - org.softwarepipelines.
framework.router.PipelinesRouterBase:p_4 = 40.0(20.0
TPS)
    [java] [INFO] Instrumentor: - org.softwarepipelines.
framework.router.PipelinesRouterBase:p_1 = 40.0(20.0
TPS)
    [java] [INFO] Instrumentor: - org.softwarepipelines.
framework.router.PipelinesRouterBase:p_3 = 40.0(20.0
TPS)
    [java] [INFO]    6 threads: 80 tps, 623,912 mem.
```

With only minor modifications, the client now receives messages generated by the service. The performance is very consistent with earlier tests, which demonstrates the scalability of pipelines, even when you're using a Request-Response model.

Summary

In this example we showed you how to implement a pipeline service with a response.

In the next chapter you'll learn about connectors. We've used local connectors in our examples up to this point, so we'll look at the other types we support in the reference Pipelines Framework: the socket and Web service connectors.

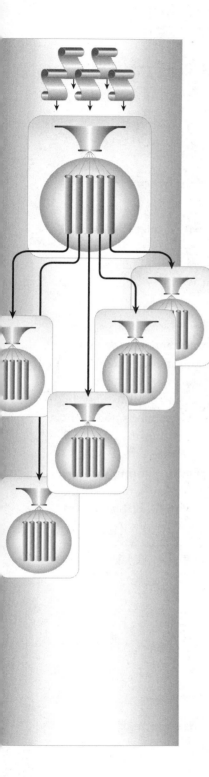

## CHAPTER EIGHTEEN

Additional Distributor Connector Patterns

A vital part of any good service-oriented framework, especially the Software Pipelines framework, is flexible support for connecting to services. So far our examples have all used the local connector; in this next example we'll use the socket and Web service connectors.

Define and Configure a Connector

In the Pipelines Configuration document, you define connectors by adding one or more `<pipelines-connector>` elements to each Pipeline Distributor. The distributor listens on each of its connectors for clients, which connect to the distributor by using the appropriate interface. The following snippet from a sample Pipelines Configuration shows each supported connector type:

```
...
  <!-- Configure the distributor. -->
  <pipelines-distributor
    name="localDistributor"
pattern="push">

    <!-- Define a Local Connector. -->
    <pipelines-connector
      name="localConnector"
type="local"/>

    <pipelines-connector
      name="socketConnector"
type="socket"
```

```
        send-to-host="localhost" send-to-port="8092"
        response-host="localhost" response-port="8093"/>

    <!-- Web Service Connector -->
    <pipelines-connector
      name="wsConnector" type="ws"
      url="http://localhost:8080/Pipelines/services/
PipelinesDistributorEndpointService"/>
...
```

Supported connectors include the following:

- **Local:** Hard-wired to the distributor. Uses a local method call to invoke services.
- **Socket:** Designed for high-performance network invocation of services.
- **WS:** Web service connector type. Supports typical Web service invocation, generally using SOAP.

Of course, there can be many other types of connectors, each for a specific remote procedure or protocol. We'll add more in the future, and you can extend the reference Pipelines Framework to add your own custom connectors.

To maintain flexibility in the framework, the connectors were designed to be interchangeable. A given client can automatically hook up to any distributor by simply using the distributor and connector names. After it connects, the client can invoke any service supported by that distributor, with all of the plumbing details completely masked from the client—*and* from the service.

Let's take a look at the code for configuring a connector, starting with the new client for our first connector example. You can use this client, which uses the `main()` method for a single service invocation, with any of the available connectors:

```
package org.softwarepipelines.examples.hello.ch18;

import java.io.File;
import java.io.IOException;

import org.softwarepipelines.config.
PipelinesMasterConfig;
import org.softwarepipelines.config.exception.
ConfigException;
import org.softwarepipelines.examples.hello.
HelloMessage;
import org.softwarepipelines.framework.connector.
PipelinesConnector;
import org.softwarepipelines.framework.distributor.
PipelinesDistributorBase;
```

```
import org.softwarepipelines.framework.exception.
PipelineException;
import org.softwarepipelines.framework.util.
PipelinesHelper;

/**
 * This client is the client for the
HelloPipelinesService. It invokes the service
 * via the local connector of the distributor.
 */
public class HelloPipelinesClient {

  /**
   * Usage: HelloPipelinesClient [pipelinesConfig
filename] [distributorName]
   * @param args
   * @throws IOException
   * @throws ConfigException
   * @throws PipelineException
   */
  public static void main(String[] args) throws
IOException, ConfigException, PipelineException{

    /* Get the parameters.*/
    if(args.length != 3) {
      throw new PipelineException("Usage:
HelloPipelinesClient [pipelinesConfig filename]
[distributorName] [connectorName]");
    }
    String pipelinesConfigFilename = args[0];
    String distributorName = args[1];
    String connectorName = args[2];

    /* Load the Pipelines Configuration.*/
    PipelinesMasterConfig masterConfig
= new PipelinesMasterConfig(new
File(pipelinesConfigFilename));

    /* Get a reference to the distributor by name, and
start it.*/
    PipelinesDistributorBase distributor =
PipelinesHelper.getDistributorByName(distributorName,
masterConfig);
    distributor.start();

    /* Get a reference to the connector.*/
    PipelinesConnector connector = PipelinesHelper.
getConnectorByName(distributorName, connectorName,
masterConfig);

    /* Build the HelloMessage instance, including
'serviceName' and 'name'.*/
    HelloMessage msg = new HelloMessage();
```

```
    msg.setServiceName("helloService");
    msg.setName("Cory");

    /* Invoke the service on the distributor, via the
connector.*/
    connector.send(msg);

    /* Clean up by shutting down the connector and the
distributor.*/
    connector.shutdown();
    distributor.shutdown();
  }

}
```

To obtain the connector, pass in the name of the distributor, the name of the connector, and the object reference for the Pipelines Configuration. The client loads and starts the distributor (as you've seen in earlier examples), then uses the following code snippet to load the connector:

```
/* Get a reference to the connector.*/
PipelinesConnector connector = PipelinesHelper.getConnec
torByName(distributorName, connectorName, masterConfig);
```

Socket Connector

To use a specific type of connector, just define it in the Pipelines Configuration. Our first connector example uses a socket connector, which you can see in the new hello-4-pipelines-socket-config.xml file:

```
<?xml version="1.0" encoding="UTF-8"?>

<pipelines-config xmlns="http://www.softwarepipelines.
org"
  xmlns:xsi="http://www.w3.org/2001/XMLSchema-instance"
  xsi:schemaLocation="http://www.softwarepipelines.
org http://www.softwarepipelines.org/schema/pipelines-
config.xsd">

  <instrumentor log-interval="2000"/>

  <pipelines-distributor name="remoteDistributor"
pattern="push">

    <!-- Socket Connector -->
    <pipelines-connector name="socketConnector"
```

```
type="socket"
       send-to-host="localhost" send-to-port="8092"
       response-host="localhost" response-port="8093"/>

    <!-- The example consists of a helloService with
four round-robin pipelines. -->
    <pipeline-service
      name="helloService" one-way="false"
      class-name="org.softwarepipelines.examples.hello.
HelloPipelinesService">

      <pipelines-router
        class-name="org.softwarepipelines.framework.
router.RoundRobinRouterImpl"
        enforce-sequence="false"/>

      <message
        type="org.softwarepipelines.examples.hello.
HelloMessage" />

      <pipeline name="p_1" type="local"/>
      <pipeline name="p_2" type="local"/>
      <pipeline name="p_3" type="local"/>
      <pipeline name="p_4" type="local"/>

    </pipeline-service>

  </pipelines-distributor>

</pipelines-config>
```

Look over the `<pipelines-connector>` element. The following attributes support its connection functions:

- **send-to-host:** Host that runs the distributor, which in turn hosts the service.
- **send-to-port:** Host port on which the distributor is listening.
- **response-port:** When you're using the Request-Response Message Exchange Pattern, this is the port to which services respond.

When you define the socket connector in the Pipelines Configuration, the client can automatically reference it and communicate with the remote distributor and service across the network. You can run this example with the following Ant command:

```
ant run-hello-socket-pipelines
```

In the output you'll see the standard *HelloPipelinesService* content:

```
[DEBUG] HelloPipelinesService: - Hello Cory from
SoftwarePipelines, in 50 ms!
```

Web Service Connector

For our next connector example, let's use a Web service. You can configure a Web service as seamlessly as a socket connection, because the Pipelines Configuration controls the definition. In fact, you can use exactly the same client code you used for the socket example. You only need to modify the Pipelines Configuration.

> Due to the flexibility of connector configurations, it's easy to fit Software Pipelines into other commonly used frameworks. To prove this, we used the Spring Framework for Web service support when we developed our Web service connector.
>
> You can use Spring to configure your Pipeline Distributor, Pipelines Router, message, and service components. Doing this makes it very easy to manage all of your pipelines components. The details are beyond the scope of this book; however, if you're familiar with Spring, or if you'd like to use another framework, it's fairly easy to determine how to use a separate framework with Software Pipelines.

The new `hello-4-pipelines-spring-ws-config.xml` file shows how to use a Web service connector:

```xml
<?xml version="1.0" encoding="UTF-8"?>

<pipelines-config xmlns="http://www.softwarepipelines.
org"
    xmlns:xsi="http://www.w3.org/2001/XMLSchema-instance"
    xsi:schemaLocation="http://www.softwarepipelines.
org http://www.softwarepipelines.org/schema/pipelines-
config.xsd">

    <instrumentor log-interval="2000"/>

    <pipelines-distributor name="springWsDistributor"
pattern="push">
```

```
<!-- Define a Web Service Connector. -->
<pipelines-connector
  name="wsConnector"
  type="ws" url="http://localhost:8080/Pipelines/
services/PipelinesDistributorEndpointService"/>

<!-- The example consists of a helloService with
four round-robin pipelines. -->
<pipeline-service
  name="helloService" one-way="true"
  class-name="org.softwarepipelines.examples.hello.
HelloPipelinesService">

    <pipelines-router
      class-name="org.softwarepipelines.framework.
router.RoundRobinRouterImpl"
      enforce-sequence="false"/>

    <message
      type="org.softwarepipelines.examples.hello.
HelloMessage" />

    <pipeline name="p_1" type="local"/>
    <pipeline name="p_2" type="local"/>
    <pipeline name="p_3" type="local"/>
    <pipeline name="p_4" type="local"/>

  </pipeline-service>

 </pipelines-distributor>

</pipelines-config>
```

The `<pipelines-connector>` element now has the following attributes, which define the Web service:

- **type:** Type of connector. Set it to `ws` for supporting a pipelines Web service.
- **url:** URL of the Web service. In the reference Pipelines Framework `url` is alwayssettohttp://[hostname]:[port]/Pipelines/services/PipelinesDistributor EndpointService.

You can use the Web service to process any pipelines service by name, and to accept any pipelines message as a parameter. You can also implement a Web service connector to include multiple type/operation-specific Web service endpoints in a distributor, and thus support compile-time type checking.

To deploy the Web service example, you must run it in an application server such as Apache Tomcat. The software that accompanies this book contains all of the Tomcat deployment files you'll need for setting this up.

Use the following Ant command to run the Web service example:

```
ant run-hello-spring-ws-pipelines
```

The output from the service invocation is generated by log4j and is output to the application server log file. If you're using Tomcat, the log file is `catalina.out` or `tomcat.out`.

The following fragment is from a test run of the client performing a single invoke of the service (your output might be different; it depends on how you configured logging for the application server). We're showing only the relevant portion of the output:

```
[INFO] HelloPipelinesService: - Hello Cory from
SoftwarePipelines, in 50 ms!
```

There you have it—you can now run the same service, via a distributor, using two very different connector types, but with complete transparency.

Summary

In this example we showed you how easy it is to use different kinds of pipelines connectors, providing a great deal of flexibility in your deployment.

In the next chapter we'll go into a more advanced subject, the Multi-tier Distributor Pattern.

## CHAPTER NINETEEN

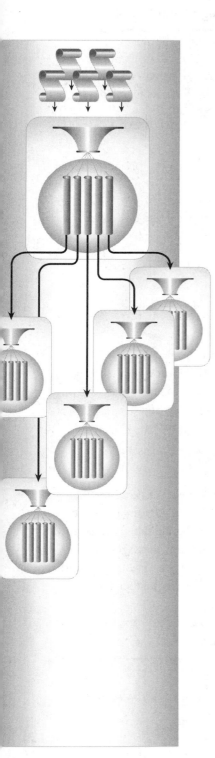

Using a Multi-Tier Distributor

For many applications, especially ones with complex service flows and process-intensive services, you'll need a Multi-Tier Distributor Pattern. When you use this pattern, one distributor routes requests to one or more remote distributors on different servers in the network, and you can distribute processing far more effectively than you can within the confines of a single machine. You can use a Multi-Tier Distributor for many types of services, including high-volume transactions, calculation-intensive applications, and long-running batch processes.

Over the next few years we expect to see vendors pack more processing cores into a single multi-core CPU. When they reach levels of 16, 32, and 64 cores per chip (and beyond), it might be very desirable to use the Multi-Tier Distributor configuration *within* a single server, as well as across the network.

The use of such a high number of cores approaches supercomputing levels of scalability, and we predict you'll be able to take advantage of this by purchasing high-end commodity hardware. The Multi-Tier Distributor Pattern will be a good design

choice for these systems. You'll get access to enormously increased processing power, and at the same time you'll enjoy the normal benefits you'd expect from using Software Pipelines.

Configure the Multi-Tier Distributors

To show the concept of the Multi-Tier Distributor, we'll use one local and
two remote distributors to invoke the *HelloPipelinesResponseService*.
You can see the new service flow in Figure 19.1.

The flow follows this sequence:

1. *HelloPipelinesResponseClient* sends the
   HelloMessage to the *relayDistributor*. To the client, this
   looks just like any other service call.

2. The *relayDistributor* uses pipeline routing to relay
   HelloMessage to the appropriate downstream distributor—
   either *invokeDistributor1* or *invokeDistributor2*—in
   the second tier. Both downstream distributors can run on any
   server.

3. When one of the second-tier distributors receives *HelloMessage*,
   it invokes *HelloPipelinesResponseService*.

The configurations for each distributor appear in Tables 19.1 through 19.3.

Our scheme uses the first-tier distributor, *relayDistributor*, to route
transactions onto two pipelines, each covering half of the alphabet. These are
relay pipelines; they don't invoke any services—they forward messages to other
distributors. Each of the second-tier distributors, *invokeDistributor1* and
invokeDistributor2, has two pipelines, which they use to further subdivide
the transactions by alphabetical range.

The new Pipelines Configuration file `hello-two-tier-config.xml`
shows how to set up the Multi-Tier Distributor scheme:

```
<?xml version="1.0" encoding="UTF-8"?>

<pipelines-config xmlns="http://www.softwarepipelines.
org"
  xmlns:xsi="http://www.w3.org/2001/XMLSchema-instance"
```

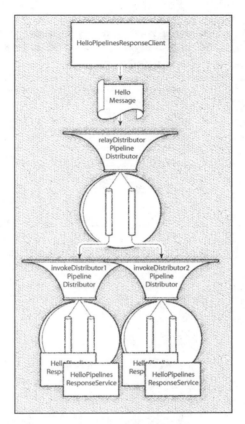

Figure 19.1 Multi-Tier Distributor service flow

Table 19.1 Distributor Configurations for `relayDistributor`

HelloPipelinesResponseService relayDistributor	Pattern Options
Service Invocation Pattern	Push
Message Exchange Pattern	Request-Response
Pipeline Routing Pattern	`ContentBasedRouterImpl`
Pipelines	`p_athrum`, relay
	`p_nthruz`, relay
Distributor Pattern	Multi-Tier Distributor
Distributor Connector Pattern	Socket Invocation

Table 19.2 Distributor Configurations for `invokeDistributor1`

HelloPipelinesResponseService *invokeDistributor1*	Pattern Options
Service Invocation Pattern	Push
Message Exchange Pattern	Request-Response
Pipeline Routing Pattern	`ContentBasedRouterImpl`
Pipelines	`p_athrug`
	`p_hthrum`
Distributor Pattern	Multi-Tier Distributor
Distributor Connector Pattern	Socket Invocation

```
xsi:schemaLocation="http://www.softwarepipelines.
org http://www.softwarepipelines.org/schema/pipelines-
config.xsd">

<instrumentor log-interval="2000"/>

<pipelines-distributor name="relayDistributor"
pattern="push">

   <!-- Socket Connector -->
   <pipelines-connector name="socketConnector"
type="socket" send-to-host="localhost" send-to-
port="8094"
      response-host="localhost" response-port="8097"/>
```

Table 19.3 Distributor Configurations for `invokeDistributor2`

HelloPipelinesResponseService *invokeDistributor2*	Pattern Options
Service Invocation Pattern	Push
Message Exchange Pattern	Request-Response
Pipeline Routing Pattern	`ContentBasedRouterImpl`
Pipelines	`p_nthrur`
	`p_sthruz`
Distributor Pattern	Multi-Tier Distributor
Distributor Connector Pattern	Socket Invocation

```
     <!-- Configure the helloService using two relay
pipelines. -->
     <pipeline-service name="helloService" one-
way="false"
        class-name="org.softwarepipelines.examples.hello.
HelloPipelinesResponseService">

     <pipelines-router
        class-name="org.softwarepipelines.framework.
router.ContentBasedRouterImpl" enforce-sequence="true"/>

     <message
        type="org.softwarepipelines.examples.hello.
HelloMessage"
        pipeline-key="name" />

     <pipeline name="p_athrum" type="relay"
        send-to="invokeDistributor1"
connector="socketConnector">
        <string-expr match="[a-mA-M].*"/>
     </pipeline>

     <pipeline name="p_nthruz" type="relay"
        send-to="invokeDistributor2"
connector="socketConnector">
        <string-expr match="[n-zN-Z].*"/>
     </pipeline>

  </pipeline-service>

 </pipelines-distributor>

 <pipelines-distributor name="invokeDistributor1"
pattern="push">

   <!-- Socket Connector -->
   <pipelines-connector name="socketConnector"
type="socket" send-to-host="localhost" send-to-
port="8095"
        response-host="localhost" response-port="8098"/>

   <!-- Configure two pipelines for the distributor
that invokes the service. -->
   <pipeline-service name="helloService" one-
way="false"
        class-name="org.softwarepipelines.examples.hello.
HelloPipelinesResponseService">

     <pipelines-router
        class-name="org.softwarepipelines.framework.
router.ContentBasedRouterImpl" enforce-sequence="true"/>
```

```
    <message
       type="org.softwarepipelines.examples.hello.
HelloMessage"
       pipeline-key="name" />

    <pipeline name="p_athrug" type="local">
       <string-expr match="[a-gA-G].*"/>
    </pipeline>
    <pipeline name="p_hthrum" type="local">
       <string-expr match="[h-mH-M].*"/>
    </pipeline>

  </pipeline-service>

 </pipelines-distributor>

 <pipelines-distributor name="invokeDistributor2"
pattern="push">

 <!-- Socket Connector -->
 <pipelines-connector name="socketConnector"
type="socket" send-to-host="localhost" send-to-
port="8096"
    response-host="localhost" response-port="8099"/>

 <!-- Configure two pipelines for the distributor that
invokes the service. -->
 <pipeline-service name="helloService" one-way="false"
    class-name="org.softwarepipelines.examples.hello.
HelloPipelinesResponseService">

    <pipelines-router
       class-name="org.softwarepipelines.framework.
router.ContentBasedRouterImpl" enforce-sequence="true"/>

    <message
       type="org.softwarepipelines.examples.hello.
HelloMessage"
       pipeline-key="name" />

    <pipeline name="p_nthrur" type="local">
       <string-expr match="[n-rN-R].*"/>
    </pipeline>
    <pipeline name="p_sthruz" type="local">
       <string-expr match="[s-zS-Z].*"/>
    </pipeline>

  </pipeline-service>

 </pipelines-distributor>

</pipelines-config>
```

The important points in this configuration are the following:

- There are three separate `<pipelines-distributor>` elements, *relay-Distributor*, *invokeDistributor1*, and *invokeDistributor2*.
- The pipelines belonging to *relayDistributor* relay messages to one or the other of the `invokeDistributor` instances. The following snippet from the Pipelines Configuration shows how to define this type of pipeline:

```
<pipeline name="p_athrum" type="relay" send-to=
"invokeDistributor1" connector="socketConnector">
```

Set `type` to `relay` instead of `local` (our earlier examples were set to `local`). The `relay` type tells the router to forward the invocation to another distributor.

The `send-to` attribute identifies the distributor to which the pipeline should route its messages.

The `connector` attribute identifies the connector to use on the remote distributor. In this example, set it to `socketConnector`.

- To define the two `invokeDistributor` instances, *invokeDistributor1* and *invokeDistributor2*, use the same configuration as used in earlier examples. These distributors receive messages via socket connectors, and they directly invoke *HelloPipelinesResponseService*.

Create the Client

Let's take a look at the new client for the multi-tier example:

```
package org.softwarepipelines.examples.hello.ch19;

import java.io.File;
import java.io.IOException;

import org.apache.log4j.Logger;
import org.softwarepipelines.config.
PipelinesMasterConfig;
import org.softwarepipelines.config.exception.
ConfigException;
import org.softwarepipelines.examples.hello.
HelloMessage;
import org.softwarepipelines.framework.connector.
PipelinesConnector;
import org.softwarepipelines.framework.distributor.
PipelinesDistributorBase;
import org.softwarepipelines.framework.exception.
PipelineException;
```

```
import org.softwarepipelines.framework.message.
AbstractMessage;
import org.softwarepipelines.framework.util.
PipelinesHelper;

/**
 * This client is the client for the
HelloPipelinesResponseService. It invokes the service
 * via the local connector of the distributor.
 */
public class HelloPipelinesResponseClient {
  final private static Logger LOG = Logger.getLogger(Hel
loPipelinesResponseClient.class);

  /**
   * Usage: HelloPipelinesClient [pipelinesConfig
filename] [distributorName]
   * @param args
   * @throws IOException
   * @throws ConfigException
   * @throws PipelineException
   */
  public static void main(String[] args) throws
IOException, ConfigException, PipelineException{

    /* Get the parameters.*/
    if(args.length != 5) {
      throw new PipelineException("Usage:
HelloPipelinesResponseClient [pipelinesConfig filename]
[distributor1Name] [distributor2Name] [distributor3Name]
[connectorName]");
    }
    String pipelinesConfigFilename = args[0];
    String distributorName1 = args[1];
    String distributorName2 = args[2];
    String distributorName3 = args[3];
    String connectorName = args[4];

    /* Load the Pipelines Configuration.*/
    PipelinesMasterConfig masterConfig
= new PipelinesMasterConfig(new
File(pipelinesConfigFilename));
    System.out.println("distributorName3: " +
distributorName3);

    /* Get the two destination distributors. */
    PipelinesDistributorBase distributor1 =
PipelinesHelper.getDistributorByName(distributorName1,
masterConfig);
    PipelinesDistributorBase distributor2 =
PipelinesHelper.getDistributorByName(distributorName2,
masterConfig);
```

```
        PipelinesDistributorBase distributor3 =
PipelinesHelper.getDistributorByName(distributorName3,
masterConfig);

        /* Start them. */
        distributor1.start();
        distributor2.start();
        distributor3.start();

        /* Check out a socket connector instance from the
client broker.*/
        PipelinesConnector connector = PipelinesHelper.
getConnectorByName(distributorName1, connectorName,
masterConfig);

        /* Build the HelloMessage instance, including
'serviceName' and 'name'.*/
        HelloMessage msg = new HelloMessage();
        msg.setServiceName("helloService");
        msg.setName("Cory");

        /* Invoke the service on the distributor, via the
connector.*/
        LOG.info("Sending message: " + msg);
        AbstractMessage resp = connector.
sendAndReceive(msg);

        /* Cast the response to a HelloMessage. */
        HelloMessage helloResp = (HelloMessage) resp;
        LOG.info("Received response: " + helloResp);

        /* Clean up by shutting down the singleton
distributor and all message brokers.*/
        connector.shutdown();
        distributor1.shutdown();
        distributor2.shutdown();
        distributor3.shutdown();
    }

}
```

The new client has a single `main()` method that does the following:

- It configures, creates, and starts all three distributors.
- It obtains a connector to `distributor1` (the *relayDistributor* defined in the Pipelines Configuration).
- It invokes `sendAndReceive()` on the connector to run a single call to the service.

Run the Service

To run the example, use the following Ant command:

```
ant run-hello-two-tier-pipelines
```

The following debug output shows how the pipelines and service operate:

```
. . .
 [INFO] HelloPipelinesResponseClient: - Sending message:
[Message]
  Destination Service Name:  helloService
  Name:  Cory
. . .
[INFO] HelloPipelinesResponseClient: - Received
response:
[Message]
  Destination Service Name:  helloService
  Name:  Software Pipelines

# relayDistributor pipelines:
[INFO] Instrumentor: - org.softwarepipelines.framework.
router.PipelinesRouterBase:p_athrum = 1.0(0.5 TPS)
[INFO] Instrumentor: - org.softwarepipelines.framework.
router.PipelinesRouterBase:p_nthruz = 0.0(0.0 TPS)

# invokeDistributor1 pipelines:
[INFO] Instrumentor: - org.softwarepipelines.framework.
router.PipelinesRouterBase:p_athrug = 1.0(0.5 TPS)
[INFO] Instrumentor: - org.softwarepipelines.framework.
router.PipelinesRouterBase:p_hthrum = 0.0(0.0 TPS)

# invokeDistributor2 pipelines:
[INFO] Instrumentor: - org.softwarepipelines.framework.
router.PipelinesRouterBase:p_nthrur = 0.0(0.0 TPS)
[INFO] Instrumentor: - org.softwarepipelines.framework.
router.PipelinesRouterBase:p_sthruz = 0.0(0.0 TPS)
. . .
```

From the output you can see that *HelloPipelinesResponseClient* sends a message to *helloService*, then receives the response "Software Pipelines." The output also contains results for each distributor's pipelines (we added identifying comments for readability):

- The *relayDistributor* has two pipelines, *p_athrum* and *p_nthruz*. The first pipeline had one transaction, and the second pipeline had 0 transactions.

- The *invokeDistributor1* has two pipelines, *p_athrug* and *p_hthrum*. The first pipeline received the single relay transaction from the *relayDistributor* pipeline. The second pipeline had 0 transactions, as expected.
- The *invokeDistributor2* has two pipelines. Neither one had any activity, because the transaction content didn't match the evaluation expression for either pipeline.

An interesting aspect to this example is the handling of the response to the client. The Pipelines Framework automatically keeps a reference to the calling client. This functionality is the callback mechanism we described in an earlier example. The Multi-Tier Distributor Pattern reinforces the need for such a function; accordingly, *HelloPipelinesResponseService* sends its response directly back to the client using the callback mechanism. This is far more efficient than relaying the response back through multiple tiers of distributors on the invocation path.

Summary

In this example we covered the basics of configuring the Multi-Tier Distributor Pattern. The example itself is trivial, but it does illustrate how it works, and you can use it as a foundation for a more complex system.

In the next chapter we'll show you how to use pipelines to overcome the final bottleneck in a service flow, your database.

## CHAPTER TWENTY

Database Sharding Distributor

We've used our examples up to this point to show you how to increase scalability. However, the "last mile" is often the final barrier to better performance. According to Pipelines Law, performance is always limited by the capacity of your downstream components. And because there's almost always a database downstream at the end of the line, finding a way to increase its performance is vital for any scalable business application.

There are many valid techniques for improving database performance and scalability. Software Pipelines doesn't replace them or attempt to improve on the existing techniques. Instead, it uses the pipelines concept to address the inherent bottleneck that databases present in most business systems. The basic technology for handling this is called database sharding.

The term *database sharding*, coined by Google engineers, relates to a partitioning concept that's been around for many years. It means breaking large databases up into many smaller ones, then distributing the load across the resulting "shards" (think of broken glass, but in a more planned and organized format).

When you shard a database, you can scale to multiple independent servers—meaning multiple sets of disks, CPUs, and memory—with each server holding a portion of the database. Effectively, then, database sharding provides a "shared nothing" environment. This technique is

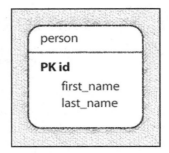

Figure 20.1 `person` **table**

used by many large SaaS vendors, including names we'd all recognize (such as Google, which popularized the concept).

We'll show you how to use database sharding in the example for this chapter. To demonstrate how it works, we'll use a very simple table, the *person* table, which you can see in Figure 20.1.

The *person* table has a numeric id column that has a first_name and a last_name. The goal is to shard the data, based on last_name, and create several databases. Each database has *person* rows for a portion of the alphabet. Figure 20.2 shows the logical schema.

> There are many techniques, available from both commercial and open-source DBMS vendors, for partitioning databases. Your situation might require a higher-level approach, such as database sharding. Because every application situation is unique, you should evaluate the options and choose the technique that best suits your particular requirements.

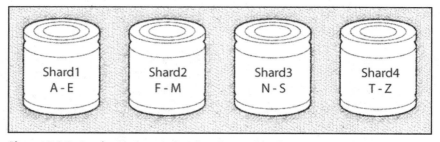

Figure 20.2 Logical schema for database shards

For sharding to work, database rows must come from or go to the correct shard whenever the application reads or writes rows to the database. You can use pipelines to solve this problem in two ways:

- Create a set of content-based pipelines, and connect each service instance to a specific database shard. The application must be aware of the shard scheme; therefore, depending on your application requirements, this might not be a workable method.

  This approach is very similar to earlier examples (just add connections to specific database shards), so we won't use it for the sharding demonstration.

- Use a shard-aware JDBC driver, which makes the shard routing decisions. It automatically interprets the JDBC/SQL calls to determine the correct shard for any given statement or transaction. Sharding is transparent to the application layer, which doesn't have to know anything about the shard scheme.

  We'll use this approach for the current example. Our driver is the dbShards JDBC driver.[1]

We can't cover all aspects of database sharding, but we have isolated some of the important points for successful development. You'll find other issues as you go along, but you should start with this list:

- Handle auto-increment across shards to ensure consistent numeric identifiers.
- Develop a scheme to avoid cross-shard joins. The usual way to do this is by replicating common static tables across all shards.
- Aggregate read-only queries from multiple shards. This supports parallel query processing against each shard. For example, you can use this for data analysis queries.
- Ensure synchronization and reliability of shards. This includes backup, replication, and automated fail-over.

Database Shards Example

In our sharding example there are two distributors: `distributor1`, a simple round-robin distributor that runs the service, and `databaseShard`, which routes transactions by content to the correct database shard. The configurations for `distributor1` appear in Table 20.1.

---

[1] You can get the dbShards JDBC driver from www.dbshards.com.

Table 20.1 Distributor Configurations

HelloPipelinesDatabaseService distributor1	Pattern Options
Service Invocation Pattern	Push
Message Exchange Pattern	Request-Response
Pipeline Routing Pattern	Round-Robin
Pipelines	p_1 (single pipeline for the normal dbShards router)
Distributor Pattern	Single Distributor
Distributor Connector Pattern	Local Method Invocation

The service, which is hosted on *distributor1*, invokes *databaseShard* via the sharding JDBC driver, then *databaseShard* uses the JDBC driver to route transactions into the correct database. The configurations for *database-Shard* appear in Table 20.2.

Table 20.2 Distributor Configurations

HelloPipelinesDatabaseService databaseShard	Pattern Options
Service Invocation Pattern	Push
Message Exchange Pattern	Request-Response (JDBC)
Pipeline Routing Pattern	Content-Based (via sharding JDBC driver)
Pipelines	*shard1* (A–E)
	shard2 (F–M)
	shard3 (N–S)
	shard4 (T–Z)
Distributor Pattern	Single Distributor
Distributor Connector Pattern	JDBC directly from service

Create the Database Shards

The first step in the example is to create the databases. There are four independent databases named *shard1*, *shard2*, *shard3*, and *shard4*—one for each shard. You can create them on the same server, on independent servers, or on any combination of servers.

The following sample SQL shows how to create a shard on a server:

```
# shard 1
create database shard1;

create table person (
id int not null auto_increment,
first_name varchar(25) not null,
last_name varchar(25) not null,
primary key (id))
engine=InnoDB;

ALTER TABLE person AUTO_INCREMENT = 1;
```

You can use the same code (with unique names) to create additional shards. However, for this simple example, you should also alter the AUTO_INCREMENT to prevent the test values from overlapping:

```
# shard 2
create database shard2;

create table person (
id int not null auto_increment,
first_name varchar(25) not null,
last_name varchar(25) not null,
primary key (id))
engine=InnoDB;

ALTER TABLE person AUTO_INCREMENT = 1000000;
```

By setting the start values for AUTO_INCREMENT to prevent overlapping, you'll eliminate collision of id numbers in the test run. Please note, however, that this technique would not be adequate for most real-world business applications.

Build the Service

The next component for the example is the *HelloPipelinesDatabase Service*, the service that receives *HelloMessage* and writes the *person* record to the database:

```
package org.softwarepipelines.examples.hello.ch20;

import java.sql.Connection;
import java.sql.DriverManager;
import java.sql.PreparedStatement;

import org.apache.log4j.Logger;
import org.softwarepipelines.config.service.
PipelineServiceConfig;
import org.softwarepipelines.examples.hello.
HelloMessage;
import org.softwarepipelines.framework.exception.
PipelineException;
import org.softwarepipelines.framework.message.
AbstractMessage;
import org.softwarepipelines.framework.service.
PipelineServiceBase;

/**
 * The HelloPipelinesDatabaseService uses a technique
for partitioning
 * database calls over a number of DBMS databases,
servers, or instances.
 * It utilizes the dbShards JDBC driver to perform
sharding transparently
 * to the application. The service invokes the normal
JDBC methods to
 * INSERT rows into the database, and the driver
"shards" the statements
 * accordingly, based on the shard-config.xml file.
 *
 */
  public class HelloPipelinesDatabaseService extends
PipelineServiceBase {
  final private static Logger LOG = Logger.getLogger(Hel
loPipelinesDatabaseService.class);
  Connection conn = null;
  final String jdbcUrl = "jdbc:dbshards:source/examples/
src/org/softwarepipelines/examples/hello/ch20/conf/";

  /**
   * Required constructor which creates the driver
instance and
   * opens a connection to the sharding JDBC driver.
Note that
   * the actual physical database connections are
managed by
   * the sharding JDBC driver.
   * @param config
   * @throws PipelineException
   */
```

```
   public HelloPipelinesDatabaseService(PipelineServiceCo
nfig config) throws PipelineException {
    super(config);

    /* Initialize the database sharding driver.*/
    try {
      Class.forName( "com.dbshards.jdbc.Driver"
).newInstance();

      /* Open a connection using the driver.*/
      conn = DriverManager.getConnection(jdbcUrl,
"user", "password");
      conn.setAutoCommit(false);
    } catch (Exception e) {
      throw new PipelineException("Error initializing
the database sharding connection!");
    }

  }

  /**
   * Receive the HelloMessage, parse the first and last
name
   * values, and insert the person into the database.
   */
  public void processMessage(AbstractMessage msg) throws
PipelineException {
    /* Cast the incoming message to a HelloMessage. */
    if (!(msg instanceof HelloMessage)) {
      throw new PipelineException("Service " + this.
getName() + " requires " + HelloMessage.class.
getName());
    }
    HelloMessage helloMsg = (HelloMessage) msg;

    /* Parse the first and last names from the full name
in the message. */
    String [] names = helloMsg.getName().split(" ");
    try {
      insertPerson(names[0], names[1]);
    } catch (Exception e) {
      throw new PipelineException("Error inserting
person: " + helloMsg.getName());
    }

    /* Send a confirmation message. */
    helloMsg.setName("Software Pipelines Database");
    sendResultMessage(helloMsg);
  }

  /**
   * Insert the person into the database using the
sharding JDBC driver.
```

```
 * @param firstName
 * @param lastName
 * @throws Exception
 */
private void insertPerson(String firstName, String
lastName) throws Exception {

    PreparedStatement stmt = conn
        .prepareStatement("INSERT INTO person (first_
name, last_name) VALUES (?, ?)");
    stmt.setString(1, firstName);
    stmt.setString(2, lastName);
    int rows = stmt.executeUpdate();

    LOG.debug("updated: " + rows + " row(s)");

    stmt.close();

    conn.commit();
}

public void finalize() {

    try {
      /* Close the database sharding connection.*/
      conn.close();
    } catch (Exception e) {
      // No Exception needed from finalize method.
    }
  }
}
```

We'll briefly describe each method:

- *HelloPipelinesDatabaseService():* Mandatory constructor. In addition to setting the configuration, it also creates an instance of the sharding JDBC driver, and it establishes a virtual connection to the database. In reality, the sharding driver manages the actual physical connection to the correct underlying database shard.

- **processMessage():** Handles the service invocation. It parses out the first/last name values, then invokes the insertPerson() method. It also returns a response to the client.

- **insertPerson():** Uses the sharding driver to perform the actual database INSERT. The driver evaluates the last name value, then performs the INSERT against the correct shard.

The sharding driver uses a configuration document, `shard-config.xml`, to determine the sharding scheme. This is similar to the Pipelines Configuration document that guides a Pipeline Distributor.

- **`finalize()`:** Simply cleans up and closes the JDBC connection to the sharding driver.

As you can see, the actual database sharding is completely transparent to the service itself.

Configure the Distributor

Next, let's look at `hello-1-pipelines-db-shards-config.xml`, the Pipelines Configuration for *distributor1*:

```xml
<?xml version="1.0" encoding="UTF-8"?>

<pipelines-config xmlns="http://www.softwarepipelines.org"
   xmlns:xsi="http://www.w3.org/2001/XMLSchema-instance"
   xsi:schemaLocation="http://www.softwarepipelines.org http://www.softwarepipelines.org/schema/pipelines-config.xsd">

   <instrumentor log-interval="2000"/>

   <pipelines-distributor name="localDistributor" pattern="push">

      <!-- Local Connector -->
      <pipelines-connector name="localConnector" type="local"/>

      <!-- Create a single round-robin pipeline to invoke the database service. -->
      <pipeline-service name="helloService" one-way="false"
         class-name="org.softwarepipelines.examples.hello.ch20.HelloPipelinesDatabaseService">

         <pipelines-router
            class-name="org.softwarepipelines.framework.router.RoundRobinRouterImpl"
            enforce-sequence="false"/>

         <message
            type="org.softwarepipelines.examples.hello.HelloMessage" />
```

```
        <pipeline name="p_1" type="local"/>

      </pipeline-service>

    </pipelines-distributor>

  </pipelines-config>
```

There's nothing special about this configuration example; it simply creates a single round-robin pipeline to drive the service. You can use any combination of pipelines or pipeline pattern with database sharding, because all the shard routing takes place within the service itself.

Configure the Sharding Driver

As we mentioned earlier, the sharding JDBC driver has its own configuration file, `shard-config.xml`:

```xml
<dbshards-config>

  <database
    name="hello" db-platform="MySQL"
    db-version="5.1" driver="com.mysql.jdbc.Driver">

    <table name="person">
      <column name="id" type="int" key="true"/>
      <column name="first_name" type="varchar(50)" />
      <column name="last_name" type="varchar(50)" />
      <shard-strategy type="range" key="last_name">
        <vshard id="1" start="A" end="E" />
        <vshard id="2" start="F" end="M" />
        <vshard id="3" start="N" end="S" />
        <vshard id="4" start="T" end="Z" />
      </shard-strategy>
    </table>

  </database>

  <!-- Mapping of virtual shards to physical shards -->
  <shard-mapping>
    <shard id="1"
      jdbc-url="jdbc:mysql://server1/shard1"
      user="user" password="password" vshards="1"  />
    <shard id="2"
      jdbc-url="jdbc:mysql://server2/shard2"
      user="user" password="password" vshards="2"  />
    <shard id="3"
      jdbc-url="jdbc:mysql://server3/shard3"
      user="user" password="password" vshards="3"  />
```

```
      <shard id="4"
        jdbc-url="jdbc:mysql://server4/shard4"
        user="user" password="password" vshards="4"  />
    </shard-mapping>

</dbshards-config>
```

The important elements are the following:

- **<database>**: Specifies the basic information needed by the sharding driver and the application. The name attribute is the name of the virtual database to which the application "connects" (in reality, the sharding driver connects to the shard databases). The driver attribute specifies the underlying physical DBMS. Our example uses MySQL.
- **<table>**: Defines the table that is going to be sharded by the driver. A <table> can have one or more child <column> elements, and it must have one shard key <column>, which is a <column> with its key attribute set to true.
- **<shard-strategy>**: Analogous to the <pipelines-router> element in a Pipelines Configuration. Specifies the method used to route transactions to the underlying shard databases. In this example the driver uses the range method type against the last_name column value.
- **<vshard>**: Each <shard-strategy> element has one or more child <vshard> elements, which are analogous to the pipelines in a Pipeline Distributor. Each <vshard> defines a virtual shard and contains start and end values for the range expression.

    In our example document, the number of virtual shards and the number of physical shards are the same; however, in most situations it's better to define more virtual shards to allow for future expansion and scalability.
- **<shard-mapping>**: Container for the <shard> elements. Each <shard> defines a physical database shard and contains the shard's actual physical jdbc-url, along with attributes for connection information, such as user and password. The vshards attribute maps the physical shard to the virtual shard(s).

Create the Client

At this point the database sharding service is set up to run. All you need now is the client, *HelloPipelinesDatabaseResponseClient*:

```
package org.softwarepipelines.examples.hello.ch20;

import java.io.File;
import java.io.IOException;

import org.apache.log4j.Logger;
import org.softwarepipelines.config.
PipelinesMasterConfig;
import org.softwarepipelines.config.exception.
ConfigException;
import org.softwarepipelines.examples.hello.
HelloMessage;
import org.softwarepipelines.framework.connector.
PipelinesConnector;
import org.softwarepipelines.framework.distributor.
PipelinesDistributorBase;
import org.softwarepipelines.framework.exception.
PipelineException;
import org.softwarepipelines.framework.message.
AbstractMessage;
import org.softwarepipelines.framework.util.
PipelinesHelper;

/**
 * This client is the client for the
HelloPipelinesService. It invokes the service
 * via the local connector of the distributor.
 */
public class HelloPipelinesDatabaseResponseClient {
  final private static Logger LOG = Logger.getLogger(Hel
loPipelinesDatabaseResponseClient.class);

  /**
   * Usage: HelloPipelinesClient [pipelinesConfig
filename] [distributorName]
   * @param args
   * @throws IOException
   * @throws ConfigException
   * @throws PipelineException
   */
  public static void main(String[] args) throws
IOException, ConfigException, PipelineException{

    /* Get the parameters.*/
    if(args.length != 3) {
      throw new PipelineException("Usage:
HelloPipelinesClient [pipelinesConfig filename]
[distributorName] [connectorName]");
    }
    String pipelinesConfigFilename = args[0];
    String distributorName = args[1];
    String connectorName = args[2];

    /* Load the Pipelines Configuration.*/
```

```
        PipelinesMasterConfig masterConfig = new
PipelinesMasterConfig(
        new File(pipelinesConfigFilename));

        /* Get the remote destination distributor and start
it. */
        PipelinesDistributorBase distributor =
PipelinesHelper.getDistributorByName(distributorName,
masterConfig);
        distributor.start();

        /* Check out a socket connector instance from the
client broker.*/
        PipelinesConnector connector = PipelinesHelper.
getConnectorByName(distributorName, connectorName,
masterConfig);

        /* Build the HelloMessage instance, including
'serviceName' and 'name'.*/
        HelloMessage msg = new HelloMessage();
        msg.setServiceName("helloService");
        msg.setName("Cory Isaacson");

        /* Invoke the service on the distributor, via the
connector.*/
        LOG.info("Sending message: " + msg);
        AbstractMessage resp = connector.
sendAndReceive(msg);

        /* Cast the response to a HelloMessage. */
        HelloMessage helloResp = (HelloMessage) resp;
        LOG.info("Received response: " + helloResp);

        /* Clean up by shutting down the singleton
distributor and all message brokers.*/
        connector.shutdown();
        distributor.shutdown();
    }

}
```

The new client uses a simple `main()` method with a single service execution. There's nothing special at all about this client; in fact, the client itself has no knowledge of the underlying distribution or sharding mechanism.

Run the Service

To run the example, use the following Ant command:

```
ant run-hello-db-shards-pipelines
```

The following debug output is from the test run:

```
run-hello-db-shards-pipelines:
...
# Client invokes the service via the distributor.
   [java] [INFO] HelloPipelinesDatabaseResponseClient: -
Sending message:
   [java] [Message]
   [java] Destination Service Name:  helloService
   [java] Name:  Cory Isaacson
# Connector is invoked.
   [java] [DEBUG] LocalPipelinesConnector: - Sending and
receiving response for message:
   [java] [Message]
   [java] Destination Service Name:  helloService
   [java] Name:  Cory Isaacson
   [java] [DEBUG] PushPatternDistributor: - Distributing
message:
   [java] [Message]
   [java] Destination Service Name:  helloService
   [java] Name:  Cory Isaacson
# Router routes the message.
   [java] [DEBUG] RoundRobinRouterImpl: - Round robin
invoking service for message in pipeline p_1
# Message is placed on the pipeline.
   [java] [DEBUG] PipelineImpl: - Pipeline p_1 now has 1
messages in queue
...
# The service is invoked.
...
# Sharding driver uses a resolver to evaluate the SQL
statement.
   [java] [DEBUG] DefaultShardResolver: - executing
INSERT INTO person (first_name, last_name) VALUES (?, ?)
against shard(s) 2

# A connection to shard #2 is created.
   [java] [DEBUG] DbsConnection: - Connecting to shard #2
(jdbc:mysql://localhost/hello2)

# The SQL statement is executed against the shard.
   [java] [DEBUG] DbsStatement: - Executing INSERT
INTO person (first_name, last_name) VALUES (?, ?)
{Cory,Isaacson} against shard #2
   [java] [DEBUG] HelloPipelinesDatabaseService: -
updated: 1 row(s)
...
# Transaction committed to the database.
   [java] [DEBUG] DbsConnection: - Committing JDBC
transaction
   [java] [DEBUG] DbsConnection: - Closing connection to
shard #Shard #2
```

```
# Result message returned to client from service.
   [java] [DEBUG] LocalPipelinesConnector: - Put result
message on incoming message queue:
   [java] [Message]
   [java] Destination Service Name:  helloService
   [java] Name:  Software Pipelines Database
   [java] [INFO] HelloPipelinesDatabaseResponseClient: -
Received response:
   [java] [Message]
   [java] Destination Service Name:  helloService
   [java] Name:  Software Pipelines Database
...
```

This debug output shows a trace of the entire process, including some descriptive comments added for clarity. The sequence is as follows:

1. The client sends the transaction to the distributor, which forwards it to the round-robin router and the pipeline named *p_1*.

2. The pipeline invokes the service, then the service calls the sharding database driver.

3. The sharding driver uses the *DefaultShardResolver* to select the appropriate shard for the transaction.

4. The transaction is written and committed to the shard.

5. The service returns the response to the client.

Summary

This completes the example for database sharding. We've also finished our demonstration examples for Pipelines Patterns.

In the next chapter we'll provide more information about the reference Pipelines Framework.

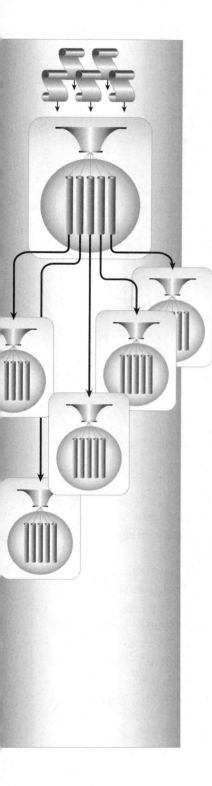

Pipelines Framework Overview

This chapter covers the reference Pipelines Framework we've used and referred to many times throughout the book. It gives you an overview of the framework components and the *Instrumentor* class and is intended to provide a better understanding of how the framework is organized.[1]

The purpose of the reference framework is to demonstrate how the Software Pipelines architecture works and how easily it can be incorporated into your business applications. You can use it for your own work—it's simple, lightweight, and very extensible—but keep in mind there are many available open-source and commercial tools you can integrate with Software Pipelines. You should evaluate the options and select the framework that is the best fit for your pipelines projects.

Interface Overview

There are only a few key interfaces in the reference Pipelines Framework. We'll describe them briefly in this chapter, and if you're interested, you can find the complete Javadoc documentation for all framework classes in the Appendix.

In Figure 21.1 you can see the high-level object model for the main Pipelines Framework components.

---

[1] The source code for the reference Pipelines Framework is available at www.softwarepipelines.org.

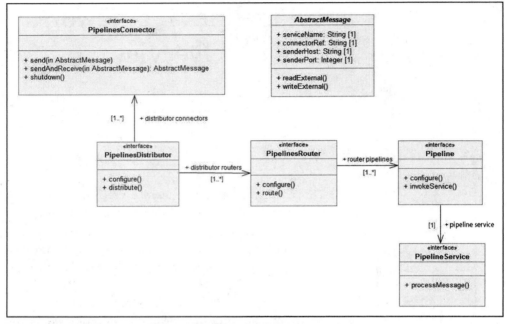

Figure 21.1 High-level object model for Pipelines Framework

The following sections describe each primary interface used in the framework.

AbstractMessage

The *AbstractMessage* class is the parent for all application-specific messages. It contains fields the framework uses under the hood to identify the service being invoked and return any response to the originator of the message.

In addition, this class contains the `readExternal()` and `writeExternal()` methods, which are part of the Java Externalizable interface. These methods provide a customized serialization mechanism for sending messages "over the wire." The mechanism is similar to the standard Java serialization mechanism, but with an added advantage: It allows you to optimize performance.

The `readExternal()` and `writeExternal()` methods are not implemented. You must implement them yourself if you're using certain network protocol connector types, such as the socket connector. However, they're relatively easy to implement.

PipelinesDistributor

This is the interface for all Pipeline Distributor implementations. The two methods that must be implemented are

- **configure():** When an application starts up any of the distributor implementations, or when it uses a custom implementation, it invokes the configure() method and passes in the master configuration object, which defines one or more distributors. Each distributor refers to its matching <pipelines-distributor> element in the object, then uses the child elements under <pipelines-distributor> to define all the services, routers, message types, and pipelines it will support.
- **distribute():** Connector implementations call this method to start the pipelining process.

PipelinesConnector

This interface defines all connectors. Clients send messages to connectors, which then relay the messages to distributors for execution, and distributors listen on connectors for message invocations from clients. The methods you should understand are

- **send():** Used for the One-Way Message Exchange Pattern, where a client uses a service invocation to send and "forget" a message.
- **sendAndReceive():** Used for the Request-Response Message Exchange Pattern, where a client sends a message/invocation to the distributor and receives a response in return.

PipelinesRouter

All Pipelines Routers implement this interface. Routers evaluate incoming messages, then make routing decisions according to the pattern you're using: Round-Robin, Content-Based, or Custom. The methods that must be implemented are

- **configure():** Uses the master configuration object to set up the routing and Pipelines Configuration, which tells the router how to route service messages.
- **route():** Specifies the routing method. The router evaluates each service invocation and message per this method, then places the message onto a pipeline for execution.

Pipeline

This interface defines all pipelines. You can think of pipeline implementations as mini-queues holding messages that are waiting to be processed. When it's time to process a message, the pipeline delegates the execution to the *PipelineService*. Each pipeline "queue" preserves message order. The pipeline also hides the inherent thread management supported by the framework. The *Pipeline* interface supports the following methods:

- **configure():** Uses the master configuration object to configure the pipeline. Contains information for the pipeline, such as which service to invoke.
- **invokeService():** The pipeline calls invokeService() for each message on its internal queue, in the same sequence in which the messages were placed onto the pipeline. The invokeService() method executes the actual business functionality and manages the threads and scalability provided by the framework.

PipelineService

All pipeline services must implement this interface. This component encapsulates the business functionality and has a single method:

- **processMessage():** You've seen this method in all our example services. The pipeline uses invokeService() to trigger processMessage(), which performs all the functionality of your services. This method receives a pipelines message as a parameter and can optionally return a response via the sendResultMessage() method (defined in the abstract *PipelineServiceBase* class, which implements the *PipelineService* interface).

Pipelines Instrumentor

The reference Pipelines Framework includes the *Instrumentor* class, which you can use to measure the performance of *PipelineService* implementations. It's used in *PipelineServiceBase*, the abstract class that all implementations extend, but you can also use it to measure the performance of many types of Java components. We've used *Instrumentor* extensively to generate reports for our examples.

Instrumentor uses a simple set of counters to keep aggregate statistics on the number of times a particular method is called, then uses a timer to output the results, in transactions per second (TPS), to a log file. The frequency of the output defaults to every 2 seconds.

The advantage of using *Instrumentor* to monitor component performance is its low overhead (there is always overhead in any monitoring tool). And because it works on the inside, it's a fairly reliable method for determining how the various pieces of a given system are performing. Of course, it can only monitor the components themselves. It doesn't specifically identify elements such as network overhead, but the output figures do reflect the aggregate result of these other items. All things considered, we think *Instrumentor* might be sufficient for many production applications.

Keep in mind that *Instrumentor* measures how many times a particular component is invoked in a given period, not necessarily the raw speed of the component. For example, if it takes only 1 ms to invoke a particular method, but the method is invoked on the average only once per second, *Instrumentor* will rate the method at 1 TPS, not 1000 TPS, which is the method's actual capability. Therefore, we recommend you set up test harnesses to exercise each component individually, as well as an entire system test framework. Using individual tests with your system tests gives you critical information about your components and how they work together in the actual application.

Instrumentor relies on the *Counter* class, a thread-safe counter mechanism that aggregates invocation results. Let's take a look at the source code for *Counter*:

```
package org.softwarepipelines.framework.util;

/**
 * Thread-safe counter for measuring throughput.
 */
public class Counter {

  private long count = 0;

  public synchronized void next() {
    count++;
  }

  public synchronized long reset() {
    long ret = count;
    count = 0;
    return ret;
  }
}
```

Counter simply increments the counter each time next() is called. The counter can be reset by using the reset() method.

Now let's look at the complete source code for *Instrumentor*:

```java
package org.softwarepipelines.framework.util;

import org.apache.log4j.Logger;
import java.util.Map;
import java.util.HashMap;

/**
 * Instrumentation class for collecting runtime
performance data.
 */
public class Instrumentor {

  /**
   * Logger for outputting instrumentation statistics.
   */
  private static final Logger logger = Logger.getLogger(
Instrumentor.class );

  /**
   * Map of instrumentors.
   */
  private static final Map<String,Instrumentor> map =
new HashMap<String, Instrumentor>();

  /**
   * Name of this instrumentor instance.
   */
  private String name;

  /**
   * Map of named counters which can be used for
tracking arbitrary statistics.
   */
  private Map<String, Counter> counterMap = new
HashMap<String, Counter>();

  /**
   * Configurable log interval.
   */
  private static int logInterval;

  /**
   * Static initializer spawns a logging thread to
output statistics.
   */
  private static Thread loggingThread;
  static {
    loggingThread = new Thread( new LoggingThread() );
```

```
      loggingThread.setDaemon(true);
      loggingThread.start();

  }

  /**
   * Static shutdown method stops the logging thread.
   */
  public static void shutdown() {
    LoggingThread.alive = false;
  }

  /**
   * Private constructor to force use of
getInstrumentor() method to obtain
   * an instance.
   */
  private Instrumentor(String name) {
    this.name = name;
  }

  /**
   * Get an Instrumentor instance for the specified
class.
   *
   * @param theClass
   * @return
   */
  public static synchronized Instrumentor
getInstrumentor(Class theClass) {
    return getInstrumentor( theClass.getName() );
  }

  /**
   * Get an Instrumentor instance for the specified
class name.
   *
   * @param className
   * @return
   */
  public static synchronized Instrumentor
getInstrumentor(String className) {
    Instrumentor ret = map.get( className );
    if (ret == null) {
      ret = new Instrumentor(className);
      map.put( className, ret );
    }
    return ret;
  }

    /**
     * Get a named Counter instance.
     */
```

```java
  public synchronized Counter getCounter(String name) {
    final String key = this.name + ":" + name;
    Counter ret = counterMap.get( key );
    if (ret == null) {
      ret = new Counter();
      counterMap.put( key, ret );
    }
    return ret;
  }

  /**
   * Return the log interval.
   */
  public static int getLogInterval() {
    return logInterval;
  }

  /**
   * Set the log interval.
   */
  public static void setLogInterval(int aLogInterval) {
    logInterval = aLogInterval;
  }

  /**
   * Perform logging in a separate thread to minimize
overhead.
   */
  static class LoggingThread implements Runnable {

    public static boolean alive = true;
    private float total;
    private float oneSec = 1000;

    LoggingThread() {
    }

    public void run() {
      while (alive) {
        try {
          Thread.sleep(logInterval);//LOG_PERIOD);
        } catch (InterruptedException e) {
          logger.warn( "Sleep interrupted", e );
        }
        for (Instrumentor instrumentor : Instrumentor.
map.values()) {
          for (Map.Entry<?,?> entry : instrumentor.
counterMap.entrySet()) {
            Counter counter = (Counter) entry.
getValue();
            total = counter.reset();
```

```
                logger.info( entry.getKey() + " = " + total
+ "(" + ((float)(oneSec*total)/((float)logInterval)) + "
TPS)");
            }
        }
    }
  }
}

}
```

We'll briefly explain the most important points for the *Instrumentor* class.

- The class maintains a static map of all *Instrumentor* instances, so that any *Instrumentor* instance can be referenced. An individual *Instrumentor* instance is created by calling getInstrumentor(). Usually, one instance is created for each class that will be monitored. The class has two getInstrumentor() methods, one for the class object and one for the class name.
- There is a map of *Counter* instances, by name, so that each *Instrumentor* can maintain as many counters as required. You can create a *Counter* for each method you want to monitor by invoking getCounter().
- All the logging is done through an internal class, *LoggingThread*, to ensure that delays in logging output don't create unnecessary overhead for the actual class you're monitoring. There's some overhead, of course, but you can reduce it by increasing the logging interval. To increase the interval, use setLogInterval().

Now let's look at *HelloPipelinesInstrumentorExample*, an example of using *Instrumentor*:

```
package org.softwarepipelines.examples.ch21;

import org.apache.log4j.Logger;
import org.softwarepipelines.framework.util.
Instrumentor;
import org.softwarepipelines.framework.util.Counter;

/**
 * A simple example of using the Instrumentor class.
 *
 */
public class HelloPipelinesInstrumentorExample {
```

```java
private static final Logger LOG = Logger.getLogger(Hel
loPipelinesInstrumentorExample.class);
  private static final int SLEEP_TIME = 50;
  private static final int SLEEP_CYCLES = 10;
  private static final int LOG_INTERVAL = 2000;

  /* Get the Instrumentor instance.*/
  private final Instrumentor instr = Instrumentor.getIns
trumentor(HelloPipelinesInstrumentorExample.class);

  /* Get the Counter instance.*/
  private final Counter helloCounter = instr.
getCounter("helloCounter");

  /**
   * Default constructor
   */
  public HelloPipelinesInstrumentorExample() {
    /* Set the log interval.*/
    Instrumentor.setLogInterval(LOG_INTERVAL);
  }

  /**
   * Write the 'Hello' message contents out to the log.
   */
  public synchronized void sayHello(String name) {

    /* Instrument the method.*/
    helloCounter.next();

    /* Consume some CPU.*/
    eatCpu();

    /* Write the message to the log.*/
    LOG.debug("Hello " + name + " from
SoftwarePipelines, in " + SLEEP_TIME + " ms!");
  }

  /**
   * Consume some CPU time to simulate processor work.
   */
  private void eatCpu() {
    for (int i = 0; i < SLEEP_CYCLES; i++) {
      try {
        Thread.sleep(SLEEP_TIME/SLEEP_CYCLES);
      } catch (InterruptedException ie) {
        LOG.warn("Interrupted while sleeping for " +
SLEEP_TIME + " ms to eat cpu", ie);
      }
    }
  }

  /**
```

```
 * Set up and run the example.
 */
public static void main(String[] args) {

HelloPipelinesInstrumentorExample helloExample = new
HelloPipelinesInstrumentorExample();

/* Say hello in a loop.*/
for(int i=0;i<100;i++) {
    helloExample.sayHello("Cory");
    }


  }

}
```

This class will look very familiar—we adapted it from the Hello Software Pipelines example in an earlier chapter. It calls the main() method to invoke the sayHello() method repeatedly in a loop. For each iteration of say-Hello(), the class uses eatCpu() to simulate processor work.

HelloPipelinesInstrumentorExample class goes through the following steps to use *Instrumentor*:

1. Use the static getInstrumentor() method to get an instance, *instr*, of the *Instrumentor*.

2. Use the getCounter() method to get an instance, *helloCounter*, of the *Counter*. You can get as many counters as you need to monitor your class. You'll usually want to get one for each method you want to observe, but there's no reason you can't monitor portions of a method as well. For example, you might want to see how many times a method invokes a particular code branch.

3. Invoke the counter's next() method. Usually, you'll do this at the top of the method you want to monitor. In our example class, you can see this at the top of the sayHello() method:

    ```
    /* Instrument the method.*/

    helloCounter.next();
    ```

That's all there is to it. When you run your class or application, *Instrumentor* generates its output automatically.

Use the following Ant command to run the example:

```
ant run-hello-instrumentor-example
```

The following output is from the test run:

```
[INFO] Instrumentor: - org.softwarepipelines.examples.
hello.ch21.HelloPipelinesInstrumentorExample:helloCount
er = 1.0(0.5 TPS)
[INFO] Instrumentor: - org.softwarepipelines.examples.
hello.ch21.HelloPipelinesInstrumentorExample:helloCount
er = 39.0(19.5 TPS)
[INFO] Instrumentor: - org.softwarepipelines.examples.
hello.ch21.HelloPipelinesInstrumentorExample:helloCount
er = 40.0(20.0 TPS)
```

Notice that after the logger completes the first iteration, the result is approximately 20 TPS. This is exactly what you'd expect, based on the 50 ms SLEEP_ TIME for each iteration in eatCpu().

Summary

This completes the high-level tour of the reference Pipelines Framework and the *Instrumentor* class. Getting accurate metrics is the key to success for scalable high-performance applications. It's also an important factor in gaining control over the execution of your components.

In the next chapter we'll do one more example—building the PBCOR project—so we can show you how easy it is to combine Pipelines Patterns and pipelines technology into a complex, scalable application.

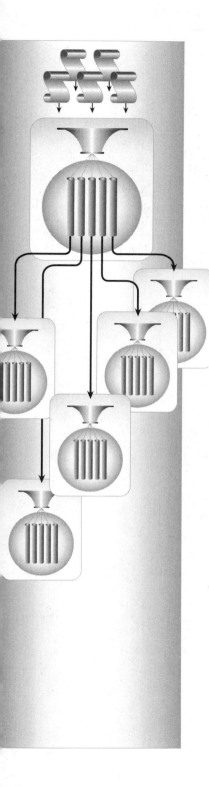

Pipelines Bank Corporation (PBCOR) Example

For our final example we'll build the complex PBCOR example we used earlier to illustrate the SPOC methodology. Figure 22.1 shows the PBCOR demand deposit service flow.

This service flow handles all transactions for both the ATM and DCS systems. To accommodate the load, we'll use several levels of pipelines, with one or more distributors at each level.

In our previous examples we covered the technical details for many of the components we'll be using in the PBCOR example; therefore, in this chapter we'll walk through just a subset of the elements, and we'll highlight any new features.[1]

Account Transaction

We'll start with *AccountTransMessage*, the base class for all message types used in the demand deposit application:

```
package org.softwarepipelines.examples.
pbcor;

import java.io.IOException;
import java.io.ObjectInput;
import java.io.ObjectOutput;
```

---

[1]   The complete source code for the PBCOR example, including all components, is available at www.softwarepipelines.org.

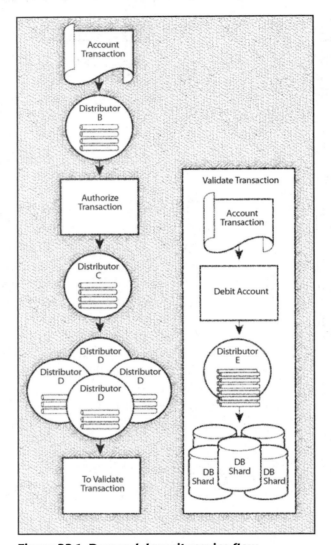

Figure 22.1 Demand deposit service flow

```
import org.softwarepipelines.framework.message.
AbstractMessage;

public class AccountTransMessage extends AbstractMessage
{

  /* Valid transaction flag*/
  protected boolean valid;
```

```java
    /* Field for detailing success, validation, or
authorization errors*/
    protected String msg;

    /* Customer account number */
    public long acctNum;

    /* Branch ID */
    public int branchId;

    /* PIN number */
    protected int pin;

    /**
     * Default constructor
     */
    public AccountTransMessage() {
    }

    public long getAcctNum() {
      return acctNum;
    }

    public void setAcctNum(long acctNum) {
      this.acctNum = acctNum;
    }

    public int getPin() {
      return pin;
    }

    public void setPin(int pin) {
      this.pin = pin;
    }

    public int getBranchId() {
      return branchId;
    }

    public void setBranchId(int branchId) {
      this.branchId = branchId;
    }

    public boolean isValid() {
      return valid;
    }

    public void setValid(boolean valid) {
      this.valid = valid;
    }
```

```java
  public String getMsg() {
    return msg;
  }

  public void setMsg(String msg) {
    this.msg = msg;
  }

  /**
   * Implement writeExternal for efficient serialization
   * of the message. This is used for the socket
   * connector type and only serializes the specific
   * fields required.
   */
  public void writeExternal(ObjectOutput out) throws
IOException {
    super.writeExternal(out);

    /* Write the valid flag.*/
    out.writeBoolean(this.isValid());

    /* If invalid, write the message.*/
    if (!this.isValid()) {
      out.writeUTF(this.getMsg());
    }

    /* Write the account number.*/
    out.writeLong(this.getAcctNum());

    /* Write the branch ID.*/
    out.writeInt(this.getBranchId());

    /* Write the PIN.*/
    out.writeInt(this.getPin());
  }

  /**
   * Implement readExternal for efficient
deserialization
   * of the message. This is used for the socket
   * connector type and only reads the specific
   * fields required.
   */

  public void readExternal(ObjectInput in) throws
IOException {
    super.readExternal(in);

    /* Read the valid flag.*/
    this.setValid(in.readBoolean());
```

```
      /* If invalid, read the message.*/
      if (!this.isValid()) {
        this.setMsg(in.readUTF());
      }

      /* Read the account number.*/
      this.setAcctNum(in.readLong());

      /* Read the branch ID.*/
      this.setBranchId(in.readInt());

      /* Read the PIN.*/
      this.setPin(in.readInt());
   }

   /**
    * Output the message as a string.
    */
   public String toString() {
      return super.toString() + "\n\tAcct Num: " + this.
getAcctNum() +
          "\n\tBranch ID: " + this.getBranchId() +
          "\n\tPIN: " + this.getPin() +
          "\n\tValid?: " + this.isValid() +
          "\n\tMessage: " + this.getMsg();
   }
}
```

Most of the fields and methods in this class are self-explanatory, but we'd like to mention the following points:

- The `msg` field is used for error, validation, and other system messages used by the client and various services.
- This class contains the `readExternal()` and `writeExternal()` methods, which are part of the Java Externalizable interface. The Externalizable interface allows you to provide optimized serialization code.

  These two methods are optional unless you're using network-based connectors, especially if you're using socket connectors. They are invoked when messages cross the "wire" to other services via the socket connector. Therefore, it's good practice to implement these methods for all service message types. If you do, you'll have the flexibility to use any connectors.

  For the PBCOR example, we'll implement these two methods by reading and writing the fields we want to use from/to the UTF format.

Pipelines Configuration

We included the distributor configuration tables for PBCOR in the SPOC methodology section (SPOC Step 3), so we won't repeat them here. However, a review of the Pipelines Configuration (from the `pbcor-full-pipelines-config.xml` file) will help you understand the current example, because it shows how all the components tie together:

```xml
<?xml version="1.0" encoding="UTF-8"?>

<pipelines-config xmlns="http://www.softwarepipelines.org"
  xmlns:xsi="http://www.w3.org/2001/XMLSchema-instance"
  xsi:schemaLocation="http://www.softwarepipelines.org http://www.softwarepipelines.org/schema/pipelines-config.xsd">

  <instrumentor log-interval="2000"/>

  <!-- Authorize Transaction Distributor (Example Distributor B) -->
  <pipelines-distributor
    name="authorizeDistributor" pattern="push">

    <!-- Local Connector -->
    <pipelines-connector
      name="localConnector" type="local"/>

    <!-- Socket Connector -->
    <pipelines-connector
      name="socketConnector" type="socket"
      send-to-host="localhost" send-to-port="8090"
      response-host="localhost" response-port="8091"/>

    <!-- Authorize transaction service, 4 round-robin
pipelines. -->
    <pipeline-service
      name="authorizeService" one-way="false"
      class-name="org.softwarepipelines.examples.pbcor.
AuthorizeTransactionService">

      <pipelines-router
        class-name="org.softwarepipelines.framework.
router.RoundRobinRouterImpl"
        enforce-sequence="false"/>

      <message
        type="org.softwarepipelines.examples.pbcor.
DebitAcctMessage" />
```

```xml
            <pipeline name="p_1" type="local"/>
            <pipeline name="p_2" type="local"/>
            <pipeline name="p_3" type="local"/>
            <pipeline name="p_4" type="local"/>

    </pipeline-service>

  </pipelines-distributor>

  <!-- Validate Service Relay Distributor (Example
  Distributor C) -->
  <pipelines-distributor
    name="validateDistributor" pattern="push">

    <!-- Local Connector -->
    <pipelines-connector
      name="localConnector" type="local"/>

    <!-- Socket Connector -->
    <pipelines-connector
      name="socketConnector" type="socket"
      send-to-host="localhost" send-to-port="8092"
      response-host="localhost" response-port="8093"/>

    <!-- Validate transaction service, 4 content-based
    pipelines by branchId. -->
    <pipeline-service
      name="validateService" one-way="false"
      class-name="org.softwarepipelines.examples.pbcor.
full.ValidateTransactionService">

      <pipelines-router
        class-name="org.softwarepipelines.framework.
router.ContentBasedRouterImpl"
        enforce-sequence="true"/>

      <message
        type="org.softwarepipelines.examples.pbcor.
DebitAcctMessage"
        pipeline-key="branchId" />

      <pipeline
        name="p_0thru10" type="relay"
        send-to="validateDistributor1"
        connector="socketConnector">

        <int-expr match-from="0" match-to="10"/>

      </pipeline>

      <pipeline
        name="p_11thru20" type="relay"
```

```xml
        send-to="validateDistributor2"
        connector="socketConnector">

        <int-expr match-from="11" match-to="20"/>

      </pipeline>

      <pipeline
        name="p_21thru30" type="relay"
        send-to="validateDistributor3"
        connector="socketConnector">

        <int-expr match-from="21" match-to="30"/>
      </pipeline>

      <pipeline
        name="p_31thru40" type="relay"
        send-to="validateDistributor4"
        connector="socketConnector">

        <int-expr match-from="31" match-to="40"/>

      </pipeline>

    </pipeline-service>

  </pipelines-distributor>

  <!-- Validate Distributor 1 (Example Distributor D #1)
-->
  <pipelines-distributor name="validateDistributor1"
pattern="push">

    <!-- Local Connector -->
    <pipelines-connector name="localConnector"
type="local"/>

    <!-- Socket Connector -->
    <pipelines-connector name="socketConnector"
type="socket" send-to-host="localhost" send-to-
port="8094"
        response-host="localhost" response-port="8095"/>

    <!-- Validate transaction service, 3 content-based
pipelines by acctNum. -->
    <pipeline-service name="validateService" one-
way="false" class-name="org.softwarepipelines.examples.
pbcor.full.ValidateTransactionService">
        <pipelines-router class-name="org.
softwarepipelines.framework.router.
```

```
ContentBasedRouterImpl" enforce-sequence="true"/>
        <message type="org.softwarepipelines.examples.
pbcor.DebitAcctMessage" pipeline-key="acctNum" />
        <pipeline name="p_0001thru0999" type="local">
          <int-expr match-from="0001" match-to="0999"/>
        </pipeline>
        <pipeline name="p_1000thru1999" type="local">
          <int-expr match-from="1000" match-to="1999"/>
        </pipeline>
        <pipeline name="p_2000thru2999" type="local">
          <int-expr match-from="2000" match-to="2999"/>
        </pipeline>
      </pipeline-service>

      <-- debitAcctService, single local pipeline -->
      <pipeline-service name="debitAcctService" one-
way="false" class-name="org.softwarepipelines.examples.
pbcor.DebitAcctService">
        <pipelines-router class-name="org.
softwarepipelines.framework.router.RoundRobinRouterImpl"
enforce-sequence="false"/>
        <message type="org.softwarepipelines.examples.
pbcor.DebitAcctMessage" />
        <pipeline name="p_1" type="local"/>
      </pipeline-service>
   </pipelines-distributor>

   <!-- Validate Distributor 2 (Example Distributor D #2)
-->
   <pipelines-distributor
     name="validateDistributor2" pattern="push">
...
   </pipelines-distributor>

   <!-- Validate Distributor 3 (Example Distributor D #3)
-->
   <pipelines-distributor
     name="validateDistributor3" pattern="push">
...
   </pipelines-distributor>

   <!-- Validate Distributor 4 (Example Distributor D #4)
-->
   <pipelines-distributor
     name="validateDistributor4" pattern="push">
...
   </pipelines-distributor>
</pipelines-config>
```

Spring Framework

The next components we'll take up are the services that perform the actual work. Before we look at the services, though, we'd like to talk about the Spring Framework, which we've incorporated into this example.

It's a vital requirement for any architecture, such as Software Pipelines, to be compatible with other software frameworks. This gives the architecture flexibility, enables it to interoperate with many types of environments, widens its applicability, and makes its scalability available to more developers and organizations. Accordingly, you can use Software Pipelines with many other commonly used frameworks. We selected the Spring Framework for this example, because it's easy to configure, and because it's used by a large number of business application developers.

Spring requires its own configuration file to enable "dependency injection," a very effective technique for externalizing object configurations and implementations from your source code. Spring extends this concept to many types of applications, including Web development, Spring JDBC, and others. It's not our purpose to give you all the details on Spring and dependency injection, but we will cover how we've used them in our example.

Spring has an application context configuration document, analogous to the Pipelines Configuration file, in which you set up the components you want to use. We'll look at the sections of this document, `pbcorFullAppContext.xml`, that relate to our example. The first section defines the master Pipelines Configuration:

```
<beans xmlns="http://www.springframework.org/schema/
beans"
  xmlns:xsi="http://www.w3.org/2001/XMLSchema-instance"
  xsi:schemaLocation="http://www.springframework.org/
schema/beans http://www.springframework.org/schema/
beans/spring-beans-2.5.xsd">

  <!-- Pipelines Master Config -->
  <bean id="masterConfig" class="org.softwarepipelines.
config.PipelinesMasterConfig" scope="singleton" init-
method="load">
    <constructor-arg value="source/examples/src/org/
softwarepipelines/examples/pbcor/full/pbcor-full-
pipelines-config.xml"/>
  </bean>
  . . .
```

Our earlier examples require code to specify where the master configuration file is located. With Spring, however, we can use the <bean> configuration, which automatically configures the file location when we access the *master-Config* component.

Database Access

Each demand deposit service needs access to a database to get account information. The following SQL code creates the *account* table in a relational database, such as MySQL (which we're using in our examples):

```
CREATE TABLE account (
account_no integer not null,
branch_id integer not null,
pin integer not null,
balance numeric(12,2) not null,
primary key (branch_id, account_no));
```

The *Account* class is a simple JavaBean, with a class member representing each field in the table, and a setter and getter for each member:

```
package org.softwarepipelines.examples.pbcor.acctdb;

/**
 * Object-relational mapping class for the account table
 */
public class Account {

  /* Account Number */
  protected long acctNum;

  /* Balance */
  protected float balance;

  /* PIN required for authentication */
  protected int pin;

  /* Branch ID */
  protected int branchId;

  /**
   * Default constructor
   */
  public Account() {
  }
```

```java
public long getAcctNum() {
  return acctNum;
}

public void setAcctNum(long acctNum) {
  this.acctNum = acctNum;
}

public float getBalance() {
  return balance;
}

public void setBalance(float balance) {
  this.balance = balance;
}

public int getPin() {
  return pin;
}

public void setPin(int pin) {
  this.pin = pin;
}

public int getBranchId() {
  return branchId;
}

public void setBranchId(int branchId) {
  this.branchId = branchId;
}
}
```

To access the database, we'll use Spring JDBC. The following section from pbcorFullAppContext.xml configures database access:

```xml
<!-- AccountDBJDBC Datasource, used for AccountDBJDBC
implementation only -->
<bean
  id="accountDataSource"
  class="org.apache.commons.dbcp.BasicDataSource"
  destroy-method="close">

  <property name="driverClassName"
    value="com.dbshards.jdbc.Driver" />

  <property name="url"
    value="jdbc:dbshards:source/examples/src/org/
softwarepipelines/examples/pbcor/conf/" />

  <property name="username"
    value="test" />
```

```
    <property name="password"
      value="password" />

</bean>

<!-- Account DB -->
<!-- accountDBMemory, a small mock database in memory
-->
<!--   <bean
         id="accountDB"
         class="org.softwarepipelines.examples.pbcor.
acctdb.AccountDBMemory"
         init-method="init" scope="singleton"/> -->

<!-- accountDBJDBC, for accessing a MySQL database via
dbShards -->
<bean
  id="accountDB"
  class="org.softwarepipelines.examples.pbcor.acctdb.
AccountDBJDBC"
  scope="prototype">

  <property name="dataSource"
    ref="accountDataSource" />

</bean>
```

The *accountDataSource* bean defines our JDBC connection, which uses the sharding JDBC connector (we'll cover the sharding scheme later in this chapter). The *accountDB* bean configures the *AccountDBJDBC* class and attaches it to the *accountDataSource*. That's all we need to configure database connectivity for our example.

We designed the PBCOR example to use the MySQL or other relational database. However, we've included a mock memory database implementation, the *AccountDBMemory* class, in the complete source code, which is available for download from www.softwarepipelines.org.

The *AccountDBMemory* class simulates the approximate processing time we've experienced when using an actual database. You can use it to see how a pipelines implementation performs on various hardware configurations.

If you don't want to set up a full multishard relational database to run the PBCOR example, you can download the source code and use *AccountDBMemory* instead of *AccountDBJDBC* in the application context file. To use the *AccountDBMemory* implementation, uncomment the *AccountDBMemory* section in the application context, then comment out the *accountDBJDBC* section.

The following code shows the *AccountDBJDBC* class:

```
package org.softwarepipelines.examples.pbcor.acctdb;

import java.sql.Connection;
import java.sql.DriverManager;
import java.sql.SQLException;
import org.softwarepipelines.framework.exception.
PipelineException;
import javax.sql.DataSource;
import java.sql.ResultSet;
import java.sql.SQLException;
import org.springframework.jdbc.core.simple.
SimpleJdbcTemplate;
import org.springframework.jdbc.core.simple.
ParameterizedRowMapper;
import org.springframework.transaction.annotation.
Transactional;

/**
 * Implement of the accountDB using Spring JDBC.
 */
public class AccountDBJDBC implements ParameterizedRowMa
pper<Account>, AccountDB {

    /* Spring JDBC template object*/
    protected SimpleJdbcTemplate jdbcTemplate;

    /* Data source for connection to the database*/
    protected DataSource dataSource;

    /**
     * Default constructor
     */
    public AccountDBJDBC() {
    }

    /**
```

```
    * This method is invoked by the Spring JDBC framework
to inject the data source,
    * and initialize the JDBC template.
    *
    * @param dataSource
    */
  public void setDataSource(DataSource dataSource)
  {
    this.dataSource = dataSource;
    jdbcTemplate = new SimpleJdbcTemplate(dataSource);
  }

  /**
    * Map result rows to an Account object.
    *
    * @param rs
    * @param row
    * @throws SQLException
    * @return Account
    */
  public Account mapRow(ResultSet rs, int row) throws
SQLException
  {
    Account dto = new Account();
    dto.setAcctNum( rs.getInt( 1 ) );
    dto.setBranchId( rs.getInt( 2 ) );
    dto.setPin( rs.getInt( 3 ) );
    dto.setBalance( rs.getFloat( 4 ) );
    return dto;
  }

  /**
    * Retrieve an account by number.
    */
  public Account getAccountByNumber(long acctNum) throws
PipelineException {

    // Check if the account map contains our key; if so,
return the account.
    /**
      * Returns all rows from the account table that
match the criteria 'branch_id = :branchId AND account_no
= :accountNo'.
      */
    try {
      Account account = jdbcTemplate.
queryForObject("SELECT account_no, branch_id, pin,
balance FROM account WHERE account_no = ?", this,
acctNum);
      return account;
    }
```

```
    catch (Exception e) {
      throw new PipelineException("Query failed", e);
    }
  }

  /**
   * Save an account.
   */
  public void saveAccount(Account dto) throws
PipelineException {
    try {
      jdbcTemplate.update("UPDATE account SET account_no
= ?, branch_id = ?, pin = ?, balance = ? WHERE account_
no = ?", dto.getAcctNum(), dto.getBranchId(), dto.
getPin(), dto.getBalance(), dto.getAcctNum());
    } catch (Exception e) {
      throw new PipelineException("Update failed", e);
    }
  }

  /**
   * Shutdown method
   */
  public void shutdown() {
    /* Empty implementation*/
  }
}
```

Let's take a look at some of the methods in this class. Two methods are required for enabling the Spring JDBC framework:

- **setDataSource():** Spring invokes this method directly. It sets the data source according to the configuration in the application context, then automatically sets up the required JDBC connection.
- **mapRow():** Spring invokes this method automatically. It performs the object-relational mapping between the JDBC result set and the *Account* object.

The next two methods are the ones that actually do the application work:

- **getAccountByNumber():** Looks up the *Account* object in the database, finds the one that matches a given account number key, and retrieves it.
- **saveAccount():** The *Account* object is passed in as a parameter to this method, which then saves the object to the database.

And that's all there is to our database access. We now have support for each service. Of course, in a real application you'd add methods for inserting and deleting rows in the database, and you might have custom methods for accessing accounts.

AuthorizeTransactionService

Now we can look at the service implementations to see how they work. First we'll examine the *AuthorizeTransactionService*:

```
package org.softwarepipelines.examples.pbcor;

import org.softwarepipelines.config.service.
PipelineServiceConfig;
import org.softwarepipelines.examples.pbcor.acctdb.
Account;
import org.softwarepipelines.examples.pbcor.acctdb.
AccountDB;
import org.softwarepipelines.framework.connector.
PipelinesConnector;
import org.softwarepipelines.framework.exception.
PipelineException;
import org.softwarepipelines.framework.message.
AbstractMessage;
import org.softwarepipelines.framework.service.
PipelineServiceBase;
import org.softwarepipelines.framework.util.
PipelinesHelper;
import org.springframework.context.ApplicationContext;
import org.springframework.context.support.
ClassPathXmlApplicationContext;

/**
 * PBCOR AuthorizeTransactionService
 */
public class AuthorizeTransactionService extends
PipelineServiceBase {

   /* Connector through which we will invoke Validate
Transaction */
   protected PipelinesConnector connector;

   /* Target Service; the next service in the invoke
chain */
   protected String targetService;

   /* Account DB */
   private AccountDB acctDB;

   public AuthorizeTransactionService(PipelineServiceConf
ig config) throws PipelineException {
      super(config);
```

```
    /* Get the Spring application context. */
    ApplicationContext ac = new
ClassPathXmlApplicationContext(
        "pbcorAppContext.xml");

    /* Set the target service. */
    targetService = "validateService";

    /* Load the connector for the validationService
     * from the destination map configured in the
application context.*/
    connector = PipelinesHelper.
getConnectorFromDestMap(ac, getDestMapKey(),
targetService);

    /* Get the AccountDB. */
    acctDB = (AccountDB) ac.getBean("accountDB");
  }

  public void processMessage(AbstractMessage msg) throws
PipelineException {
    /* Validate that we received an AccountTransMessage.
*/
    if (!(msg instanceof AccountTransMessage)) {
      throw new PipelineException("AuthorizeTra
nsaction service requires a message of type " +
AccountTransMessage.class.getName());
    }

    /* And cast the incoming message. */
    AccountTransMessage acctMsg = (AccountTransMessage)
msg;

    /* Get the account with the given account number
from the AccountDB. */
    Account acct = acctDB.getAccountByNumber(acctMsg.
getAcctNum());

    /* Check that we have a valid account. */
    if (acct == null) {
      acctMsg.setValid(false);
      acctMsg.setMsg("Invalid Account Number!");
      sendResultMessage(acctMsg);
    }

    /* And that the PIN numbers match; if so, invoke
Validate Transaction. */
    if (acct.getPin() == acctMsg.getPin()) {
      acctMsg.setServiceName(targetService);
      connector.send(acctMsg);
    }
```

```
  /* If not, set the invalid flag and return. */
  else {
    acctMsg.setValid(false);
    acctMsg.setMsg("Invalid PIN");
    sendResultMessage(acctMsg);
  }
}

/**
 * Finally, implement our shutdown logic.
 */
public void shutdown() throws PipelineException {
  super.shutdown();
  connector.shutdown();
  acctDB.shutdown();
}
}
```

AuthorizeTransactionService ensures the requested account is valid, and that the customer's PIN matches the code for the account. The constructor in the service follows this sequence:

1. Get the Spring application context.

2. Get a connector for the `targetService`, which in this case is the *ValidationService*.

   In this example we're now showing you a service that must invoke another service. After *AuthorizeTransactionService* verifies that the account number and PIN are valid, it must invoke *ValidationService*. To do this, it must have a connector to *ValidationService*.

   To load the connector, the constructor uses a lookup to the *destinationMapBean*, which is defined in the application context (we'll show you the relevant section later, in the snippet for the *destinationMapBean*).

   The *destinationMapBean* is a simple map that links source and target services. Each target service has a corresponding *DestinationMap* in the application context. The map is required because several distributors can host the same pipeline service, and you need a way to specify which target the current source should invoke. You'll learn more about this when we discuss the *ValidationService*.

To perform the lookup and get the connector, the constructor uses the following call:

```
connector = PipelinesHelper.
getConnectorFromDestMap(ac, getDestMapKey(),
targetService);
```

This method retrieves the proper connector. Its parameters include the application context, the destination map key, and the target service.

The getDestMapKey() method, which is implemented in the parent base class by *PipelinesHelper*, builds the destination map key from the configuration for the current service instance.

3.   Get an *AccountDB* implementation—in this case, the *AccountDBJDBC*—by using the Spring getBean() method, which uses the application context to configure the component. Compared to our earlier JDBC examples, this approach requires far less code, and it's a more flexible way to establish database connectivity.

The processMessage() method performs the actual work of the service. The main item we'd like to point out is the connector.send() method inside the service. We're using the connector obtained by the constructor to invoke *ValidationService*, the next service in our flow. This is essentially the same way you'd invoke a service from a pipelines client, so it's very convenient and easy to reuse at any level of your application.

Connect Services

The *AuthorizeTransactionService* class shows how you can integrate Spring or another framework with Software Pipelines, then chain services together in your code. There are many ways to chain or orchestrate services, such as BPEL, and each one has its strengths and weaknesses. We like the inline code approach we're using here for its ease of use, but you can use other methods as well. Whatever method you use, get one that allows you to chain services; it's a vital capability.

When you chain services in conjunction with Software Pipelines, you'll get some interesting options. In the ideal scene, when you invoke a service from a client or from another service, the invoking component doesn't know where the service is physically located. You'll see this in operation when we discuss the

ValidationService. By using Software Pipelines, you can embed a service in a pipeline within a local distributor, a remote distributor, or even a chain of distributors. This requires a level of abstraction between the service invocation and the pipelines' physical configuration—along with the capability of changing the physical configuration. We're using the pipelines connector to get this level of abstraction in the reference Pipelines Framework, but you can use another framework that has similar functionality. The important goal is to maintain independence and flexibility between the service components and the deployment configuration.

The current PBCOR example illustrates this point. If you review the Pipelines Configuration document and service flow diagram for this example, you'll see the following details:

1. The flow uses a round-robin router to invoke *AuthorizeTransactionService* on a set of four pipelines.

2. When the current transaction is authorized, *AuthorizeTransactionService* invokes the *ValidationService* via Distributor C.

3. Distributor C also has four pipelines. Each pipeline uses content-based routing by `branch_ID` to relay transactions to an instance of Distributor D.

4. There are four instances of Distributor D, each with its own set of three pipelines. Each pipeline routes transactions by `account_no` to the *ValidationService.*

This is a relatively complex flow. If we tried to hard-code these physical relationships into the services, our task would be impractical and our code would become unwieldy. However, we're using configuration to gain abstraction, so that any service can invoke another in a very simple manner, regardless of the number of hops between execution points.

To add more configurable flexibility to the pipelines connector architecture, we'll use the *DestinationInfo* and *DestinationMap* objects. The following snippet from the application context shows the *DestinationInfo*:

```
<bean
  id="val1DestInfo"
  class="org.softwarepipelines.config.dest.
DestinationInfo"
  scope="singleton">
```

```
<property name="destinationDistributor"
  value="validateDistributor1"/>

<property name="destinationConnector"
  value="socketConnector"/>

</bean>
```

DestinationInfo identifies a specific destination distributor/connector combination. We'll use this as a lookup mechanism to get references to connectors anywhere in our pipelines implementation.

The *DestinationMap* is also configured in the application context. You can see it in the following snippet:

```
<bean
  id="destinationMapBean"
  class="org.softwarepipelines.config.dest.
DestinationMap"
  scope="singleton">

  <property name="masterConfig">
    <ref local="masterConfig"/>
  </property>

  <property name="destinationMap">
    <map>
    <entry
      key="authorizeService:authorizeDistributor:valida
teService">
      <ref local="valDestInfo"/>
    </entry>

  </property>
...
</bean>
```

DestinationMap defines links between source services and target services. Each map <entry> element defines such a link, using the following information:

- **key (attribute):** Defines the link. Includes the name of the source service, the name of the distributor that hosts the source service, and the name of the target service.
- **<ref> (child element):** Provides a reference to the *DestinationInfo* definition. *DestinationInfo* defines the target service information needed to obtain the connector.

The *DestinationMap* in the snippet links *authorizeService* (the source service) to *validateService* (the target service) and specifies that *valDestInfo*, the *DestinationInfo* object, contains the information for connecting to the target service.

To put it simply, the *DestinationInfo*/*DestinationMap* mechanism defines links between services and hides the complexity of the physical configuration. And so, for the PBCOR example, we can use just one line of code to invoke the right service instance in the correct pipeline on a given distributor:

```
connector.send(acctMsg);
```

ValidateService

ValidateService ensures that an account has enough funds to cover debits. Technically, it's fairly similar to *AuthorizeTransactionService*, so we're not including the code in this chapter. We'll generate multiple instances of *ValidateService*. Each one invokes an instance of *DebitAcctService*, which runs in the same pipeline.

DebitTransactionService

The *DebitTransactionService* performs the final work of debiting funds from an account:

```
package org.softwarepipelines.examples.pbcor;

import org.softwarepipelines.config.service.
PipelineServiceConfig;
import org.softwarepipelines.examples.pbcor.acctdb.
Account;
import org.softwarepipelines.examples.pbcor.acctdb.
AccountDB;
import org.softwarepipelines.framework.exception.
PipelineException;
import org.softwarepipelines.framework.message.
AbstractMessage;
import org.softwarepipelines.framework.service.
PipelineServiceBase;
import org.springframework.context.ApplicationContext;
import org.springframework.context.support.
ClassPathXmlApplicationContext;

/**
 * Service for debit of an account
 */
public class DebitAcctService extends
PipelineServiceBase {
```

```
/* Account Database Communication Service */
private AccountDB acctDB;

/**
 * Default constructor
 */
public DebitAcctService() {
}

/**
 * Required service constructor
 * @param config
 */
public DebitAcctService(PipelineServiceConfig config)
{
    super(config);

    /* Load the account db from the application context.
*/
    ApplicationContext ac = new ClassPathXmlApplication
Context("pbcorAppContext.xml");

    /* Load the AccountDB bean. */
    acctDB = (AccountDB) ac.getBean("accountDB");
}

/**
 * Process the message.
 */
public void processMessage(AbstractMessage msg) throws
PipelineException {
    /* Validate that we have a DebitAccountMessage and
cast it.*/
    if (!(msg instanceof DebitAcctMessage)) {
        throw new PipelineException(DebitAcctServi
ce.class.getName() + " requires message type " +
DebitAcctMessage.class.getName());
    }
    DebitAcctMessage debitMsg = (DebitAcctMessage) msg;

    /* Get the account from the account db.*/
    Account acct = acctDB.getAccountByNumber(debitMsg.
getAcctNum());
    float currBalance = acct.getBalance();
    synchronized (acct) {
      acct.setBalance(currBalance - debitMsg.
getAmount());
    }

    /* And send a successful result message.*/
    debitMsg.setMsg("Successfully debited $" +
debitMsg.getAmount() + " from account #" + debitMsg.
getAcctNum());
```

```
      debitMsg.setServiceName("authorizeService");
      sendResultMessage(debitMsg);
   }

   /**
    * Finally, implement our shutdown logic.
    */
   public void shutdown() throws PipelineException {
      super.shutdown();
      acctDB.shutdown();
   }

}
```

DebitTransactionService uses the *AccountDB* implementation to update the account balance in the database, then returns a result message to the client that originally invoked the entire service chain.

As we mentioned earlier, the *AccountDBJDBC* implementation is configured to use the sharding JDBC driver. *DebitAcctService* is already running on a pipeline within a specific account range. The sharding JDBC driver further distributes the load by sharding on the account number value. Each range of account numbers is stored in a separate shared-nothing database instance. Since we can set up multiple database instances, we're minimizing the end-of-the-line bottleneck.

The following code shows `shard-config.xml`, which defines the account range:

```
<dbshards-config>

  <database
    name="account"
    db-platform="MySQL"
    db-version="5.1"
    driver="com.mysql.jdbc.Driver">

    <table name="account">
      <column name="account_no" type="int" key="true"/>
      <shard-strategy type="range" key="account_no">
        <vshard id="1" start="0001" end="0999" />
        <vshard id="2" start="1000" end="1999" />
        <vshard id="3" start="2000" end="2999" />
        <vshard id="4" start="3000" end="3999" />
        <vshard id="5" start="4000" end="4999" />
        <vshard id="6" start="5000" end="5999" />
        <vshard id="7" start="6000" end="6999" />
        <vshard id="8" start="7000" end="7999" />
        <vshard id="9" start="8000" end="8999" />
```

```xml
                <vshard id="10" start="9000" end="9999" />
            </shard-strategy>
        </table>

    </database>

    <!-- Mapping of virtual shards to physical shards -->
    <shard-mapping>
        <shard id="1"
            url="jdbc:mysql://localhost/pbcor1"
            user="user" password="password"
            vshards="1,5"  />
        <shard id="2"
            url="jdbc:mysql://localhost/pbcor2"
            user="user" password="password" vshards="2,6"  />
        <shard id="3"
            url="jdbc:mysql://localhost/pbcor3"
            user="user" password="password" vshards="3,7"  />
        <shard id="4"
            url="jdbc:mysql://localhost/pbcor4"
            user="user" password="password" vshards="4,8"  />
        <shard id="5"
            url="jdbc:mysql://localhost/pbcor5"
            user="user" password="password" vshards="5,10"  />
    </shard-mapping>

</dbshards-config>
```

We defined ten virtual shards and five physical shards. Each physical shard supports two virtual shards. Using this technique allows us to add more in the future as transaction volume increases.

Configuration files can start piling up in a complex system, and the effort to manage these files manually can turn into a major chore. This is an area of Software Pipelines that can benefit from additional tooling and enhancement. For more details about enhancements, see the final chapter covering the future of pipelines technology.

Run the Test

For this example we configured and ran a test using a configuration similar to the one we've outlined in this chapter. However, we reduced it to accommodate the

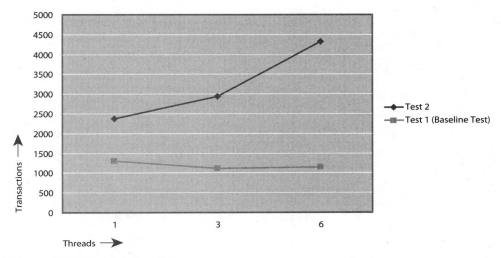

Figure 22.2 Test run results

available hardware in our environment. The chart in Figure 22.2 shows the scalability we achieved in our test run.

In the first test, which served as our baseline test, we ran all components on a single server, with a single pipeline for each service. In the second test we utilized four servers, which supported all pipelined services and two sharded database instances. As you can see, after the number of client threads ramps up, we achieve 4X scalability, even with our limited hardware resources.

Summary

In this chapter we showed you the primary components in the PBCOR demand deposit application. The PBCOR example illustrates how to apply Software Pipelines to real-world applications with multiple services and levels of distribution. What you don't see in the text is the speed of development time; the flexibility of the environment enabled a single developer to complete the entire example in several hours.

In the next chapter we'll look at the future of Software Pipelines and make some suggestions for further enhancements to the architecture.

The Future of Software Pipelines

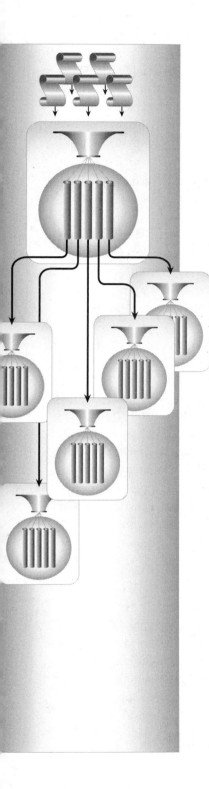

## CHAPTER TWENTY-THREE

The Future of Software Pipelines

We've covered the fundamental aspects of the Software Pipelines architecture, including its purpose, its theoretical foundation, its laws and patterns, and its methodology, and we've provided examples you can use to develop your own pipelines solutions.

We hope you've achieved some understanding of how to use the technology, and in particular, we hope we've communicated how much simpler it is than the complex hand coding required for multi-threaded applications. In fact, as our team developed the examples for this book, the most common remark was how easy and flexible the architecture actually is. Multi-threading is a valid and powerful software tool, and it's here to stay, but any experienced developer knows it's not for the faint of heart—it's quite arduous to develop multi-threaded code, and it's especially hard to test and debug such applications.

Our primary goal, however, was to provide information you can use to solve your own scalability problems. If any part of the book helps you with that, we believe we've accomplished our objective.

Final Words of Advice

In parting, we'd like to recommend some tips to follow if you're working on your own pipelines implementation:

- Get a solid understanding of pipelines theory. You don't have to be an expert in fluid dynamics to appreciate how pipelines function. Instead, use the concepts as a guide when you use the technology. You'll get an even deeper understanding of the principles as you continue to work with them, and most likely you'll be able to contribute ideas to pipelines architecture.

- "Think in pipelines"—in other words, when you tackle a particular performance or scalability issue, look at it in parallel, and figure out how to do more than one thing at a time. Parallel concepts are useful for solving all kinds of software problems. When you start thinking this way routinely, you'll be able to come up with more (and better) solutions.
- Pay particular attention to "doing the math." Use the formulas of Pipelines Law to *predict* and *control* your pipelines implementations. Proper prediction can spell the difference between success and failure, and not just for pipelined applications. The formulas are easy to apply, and they hold up in practice. If you're comfortable with the basic formulas and know how to apply them, you can use them to solve any performance issues you come up against.
- SPOC methodology is very robust but possibly more comprehensive than you need. The analysis steps can prevent a lot of future problems, and it's well worth your time to follow them, but we recommend that you use the parts of SPOC that are truly relevant to the problem at hand, rather than trying to apply every detail to each situation. Simple problems with low risk factors don't require the full-dress methodology; more complex problems warrant more research and analysis before you start development.
- Use the PBCOR case study, the Pipelines Patterns, and the pipelines examples as guides for your own work. When you're faced with a particular set of requirements, find an example that solves a similar problem, then use it as the basis for your own solution.

Ideas for the Future

Software Pipelines architecture is definitely in its infancy as an applied concept in computer science and business application development. There are plenty of opportunities for improving its support and adding to its capabilities. Eventually we'd like to see the architecture evolve into a full-fledged component of the application developer's tool kit. With a mind toward this goal, we came up with a list of features we'd like to add (and we're confident you'll think of more):

- **Robust pipelines frameworks:** Our reference Pipelines Framework is exactly that—a reference. It shows how to apply the architecture, but there are plenty of areas where it can be enhanced and extended. We've included some ideas for those areas in this list.
- **New routing patterns:** Currently we have the simple Round-Robin and Content-Based Routing Patterns, but many additional patterns can be developed. Even the two basic patterns can be extended to accommodate priority scheduling based on transaction type and content, and to add more complex content-based patterns, with multifield Pipeline Keys.
- **Dynamic Pipelines:** This is an idea for a new pattern, similar to a routing pattern, in which an automated analytics engine dynamically creates pipelines and manages the load for each pipeline. Applications would consist of combinations of pipelined services, and the automated performance manager could respond to workload changes on the fly. A business with this capability could gain immense flexibility and competitive advantage.

    We've seen this type of functionality in some sophisticated calculation-intensive grid applications, but not in business applications. Dynamic Pipelines is a brand-new way to apply the same concept to service-oriented technology.
- **Reliable pipelines:** Reliability is vital in any business application, particularly in mission-critical applications. In some industries even minutes of downtime can cost millions in lost revenues and lost customer faith, and more to repair lost transactions. Hours or days of downtime can be fatal. So it's vital to add this capability to the architecture. There are two areas where reliability can be added to Software Pipelines:

    Message reliability: We'd like a function that ensures that all service invocations and message transmissions are delivered and executed. Many messaging technologies already provide messaging reliability, but these solutions are usually centralized services, not distributed and scalable—which we'll need for Software Pipelines.

    Automated fail-over: Hardware redundancy has evolved to a very high state, but software redundancy that provides continuous operation for distributed systems is not yet as robust or available. We'd like to add redundancy to Software Pipelines for all components in the pipelines architecture. This enhancement would provide a backup component or system that automatically continues processing messages or transactions if they don't execute as planned.

- **Pipelines design tools:** Graphical design tools can make it easier to design pipeline services, distributors, and other components. The pipelines concept lends itself well to a graphical approach, so it's a natural area in which to create such an interface.
- **Management tools:** IT operations staff will need reliable, comprehensible tools for controlling and running pipeline systems. The tools should be robust and mesh well with other proven, established operations tools.
- **Pipelines simulator:** In working with pipelines, we realized a simulation modeler would be very useful. We'd like to see a tool into which you can input estimated statistics for various components and services, then test different distribution and routing patterns to determine the best solution for a given problem. The ideal tool would operate dynamically on a live system and incorporate real-time feedback, allowing you to optimize pipelines instantly (which ties in with Dynamic Pipelines).
- **Debugging tools:** A pipelines debugger that traces the entire service flow through all distributors would be invaluable to developers. Remote debuggers are already available, so it would be easy to extend this technology for a Software Pipelines environment.
- **Integration with other frameworks:** Software Pipelines is not a silo technology; it's designed so you can overlay it on top of other proven technologies. We found it easy to use the Spring Framework for our Web service example, and in the future it might be possible to add pipelines to almost any robust development environment. The goal will be to enhance other environments by using pipelines to complement the tools you already use and understand.

We hope we've sparked some interest in helping evolve Software Pipelines to the next level. We also hope you've found the Software Pipelines architecture as fascinating and applicable as we have; the concept and its technology have a bright future.

Pipelines Reference Framework Javadoc

The appendix contains the Javadoc output for the key classes and interfaces that developers need to deal with in the reference Pipelines Framework. We have provided this documentation so you can see all of the supported methods and public class members. The examples section adequately demonstrates the methods you normally need to interact with, but you can get additional information here.

org.softwarepipelines.framework.connector
Interface PipelinesConnector

public interface **PipelinesConnector**
Interface for a client-side pipelines connector; includes methods for sending a one-way message, sending a message and receiving a response message, and shutting down the connector.

Clients use `PipelinesConnector` instances to send messages to a certain `PipelinesDistributor`. Clients should use the helper method `PipelinesHelper.getConnectorByName(String distributorName, String connectorName, PipelinesMasterConfig config)` to obtain a connector with the given name, configured on the distributor with the given name in the pipelines master configuration provided:

```
PipelinesConnector connector = PipelinesHelper.getConnec
torByName("myDistributor", "myConnector", masterConfig);
```

Method Summary	
void	**send**(AbstractMessage msg) Invoke a service from which we do not expect an AbstractMessage in return.
AbstractMessage	**sendAndReceive**(AbstractMessage msg) Invoke a service from which we expect an AbstractMessage returned.
void	**shutdown**() Convenience method to shut down this connector.

Method Detail

send

void **send**(AbstractMessage msg)
          throws PipelineException

Invoke a service from which we do not expect an AbstractMessage in return.

Parameters:

msg - the message to send to the service for processing

Throws:

PipelineException

sendAndReceive

AbstractMessage **sendAndReceive**(AbstractMessage msg)
                                throws PipelineException

Invoke a service from which we expect an AbstractMessage returned.

Parameters:

msg - the message to send the service for processing

Returns:

the message reply sent from the invoked service

Throws:

PipelineException

shutdown

void **shutdown**()
          throws PipelineException

Convenience method to shut down this connector.

Throws:

PipelineException

org.softwarepipelines.framework.distributor
Class PipelinesDistributorRunner

```
java.lang.Object
   └─ org.softwarepipelines.framework.distributor.
PipelinesDistributorRunner
```

public class **PipelinesDistributorRunner**
extends java.lang.Object
Simple utility to start a `PipelinesDistributor` instance locally from the command line.

Constructor Summary

PipelinesDistributorRunner()

Method Summary

protected void	**finalize**() Shut down the singleton distributor instance.
static void	**main**(java.lang.String[] args) Start a `PipelinesDistributor` instance, configured in the configuration file whose path is provided.

Methods inherited from class java.lang.Object

clone, equals, getClass, hashCode, notify, notifyAll,
toString, wait, wait, wait

Constructor Detail

PipelinesDistributorRunner

public **PipelinesDistributorRunner**()

Method Detail

main

```
public static void main(java.lang.String[] args)
                  throws java.lang.Exception
```
Start a `PipelinesDistributor` instance, configured in the configuration file whose path is provided.

Parameters:

`args` - in order, the configuration file path and then the name of the distributor to start

Throws:

`java.lang.Exception`

finalize

```
protected void finalize()
                  throws java.lang.Exception
```
Shut down the singleton distributor instance.

Overrides:

`finalize` in class `java.lang.Object`

Throws:

`java.lang.Exception`

---

org.softwarepipelines.framework.message
Class AbstractMessage

```
java.lang.Object
    └─ org.softwarepipelines.framework.message.
```
AbstractMessage
All Implemented Interfaces:
java.io.Externalizable, java.io.Serializable

```
public abstract class AbstractMessage
extends java.lang.Object
implements java.io.Externalizable, java.io.Serializable
```

Base class for all messages sent through the pipelines framework.

Custom messages must extend this class, and must set `serviceName` to the destination service as configured in the `PipelinesMasterConfig`. Custom messages may also specify the `opName`, to allow for different operations, and thus different behavior, in the destination service.

If a custom message is to be sent, at any point, via a socket connector, the custom message class must override the java.io.Externalizable interface methods write-External and readExternal, and must call into its parent implementations of these methods first. See the documentation for the Externalizable methods in this class for further details and examples.

See Also:
> Serialized Form

Field Summary	
protected java.lang.String	**opName**
protected java.lang.String	**serviceName**

Constructor Summary
AbstractMessage()   Default constructor; allows for setter injection of message attributes.
AbstractMessage(java.lang.String aServName)   Constructor that injects the service name at construction.

Method Summary	
protected java.lang.Object	**decodeObject**(java.io.ObjectInput in)
protected void	**encodeObject**(java.io.ObjectOutput out, java.lang.Object obj) Messages mostly know what types they are writing but we still need to encode user-supplied objects e.g.
boolean	**equals**(java.lang.Object obj) Checks for message content equality.
java.lang.String	**getConnectorRef**() Internal use only.
java.lang.String	**getOpName**() Set the operation name, to be used by the destination service.
java.lang.String	**getSenderHost**() Internal use only.
int	**getSenderPort**() Internal use only.
java.lang.String	**getServiceName**() Get the name of the destination service.
void	**readExternal**(java.io.ObjectInput in) See the java.io.Externalizable interface.
void	**setConnectorRef**(java.lang.String connectorRef) Internal use only.
void	**setOpName**(java.lang.String opName) Set the operation name, to be used by the destination service.
void	**setSenderHost**(java.lang.String senderHost) Internal use only.

void	**setSenderPort**(int senderPort) Internal use only.
void	**setServiceName**(java.lang.String serviceName) Set the destination service.
java.lang.String	**toString**() Outputs a somewhat readable string representation of the message.
void	**writeExternal**(java.io.ObjectOutput out) See the java.io.Externalizable interface.

Methods inherited from class java.lang.Object

clone, finalize, getClass, hashCode, notify, notifyAll, wait, wait, wait

Field Detail

serviceName

protected java.lang.String **serviceName**

opName

protected java.lang.String **opName**

Constructor Detail

AbstractMessage

public **AbstractMessage**()
Default constructor; allows for setter injection of message attributes.

AbstractMessage

public **AbstractMessage**(java.lang.String aServName)
Constructor that injects the service name at construction.
Parameters:
aServName - the name of the destination PipelineService

Method Detail

getServiceName

`public java.lang.String `**`getServiceName()`**
> Get the name of the destination service.
> **Returns:**
> the destination service name

setServiceName

`public void `**`setServiceName`**`(java.lang.String serviceName)`
> Set the destination service.
> **Parameters:**
> `serviceName` - the destination service

getSenderHost

`public java.lang.String `**`getSenderHost()`**
> Internal use only.
> **Returns:**

setSenderHost

`public void `**`setSenderHost`**`(java.lang.String senderHost)`
> Internal use only.
> **Parameters:**
> `senderHost` -

getSenderPort

`public int `**`getSenderPort()`**
> Internal use only.
> **Returns:**

setSenderPort

public void **setSenderPort**(int senderPort)

> Internal use only.
>
> **Parameters:**
>
> senderPort -

getConnectorRef

public java.lang.String **getConnectorRef()**

> Internal use only.
>
> **Returns:**

setConnectorRef

public void **setConnectorRef**(java.lang.String connectorRef)

> Internal use only.
>
> **Parameters:**
>
> connectorRef -

getOpName

public java.lang.String **getOpName()**

> Set the operation name, to be used by the destination service.
>
> **Returns:**
>
> the operation name

setOpName

public void **setOpName**(java.lang.String opName)

> Set the operation name, to be used by the destination service.
>
> **Parameters:**
>
> opName - the operation name to set

writeExternal

```
public void writeExternal(java.io.ObjectOutput out)
                throws java.io.IOException
```

See the java.io.Externalizable interface. An example of how to implement this method is given below, for a sample custom message class, `MyMessage`.

```
public class MyMessage extends AbstractMessage {

...
// custom message members and methods, for example:

// some integer
int someInt;

// some required string
String reqdString;

// some optional string
String optString;
...

public void writeExternal(ObjectOutput out) throws
IOException {
super.writeExternal(out);

// write ALL custom message members, checking for
NULL values where necessary, for example:

// write the integer
out.writeInt(this.getSomeInt());

// write the required string
out.writeUTF(this.getReqdString());

// and write the optional string, if it is defined
final boolean hasOptString = this.getOptString() ==
null;
```

```
out.writeBoolean(hasOptString);
if (hasOptString) {
out.writeUTF(this.getOptString());
}
}
}
```

Specified by:
writeExternal in interface java.io.Externalizable
Throws:
java.io.IOException

readExternal

```
public void readExternal(java.io.ObjectInput in)
             throws java.io.IOException
```

See the java.io.Externalizable interface. An example
of how to implement this methods is given below, for
a sample custom message class, MyMessage.
The example below assumes that the writeExternal
method is implemented as described in the documentation for that method in this class.

```
public class MyMessage extends AbstractMessage {

...
// custom message members and methods, for example:

// some integer
int someInt;

// some required string
String reqdString;

// some optional string
String optString;

...
```

```
public void readExternal(ObjectInput in) throws
IOException {
super.readExternal(in);

// read ALL custom message members, checking for NULL
values where necessary, for example:

// read the integer
this.setSomeInt(in.readInt());

// write the required string
this.setReqdString(in.readUTF());

// and write the optional string, if it is defined
final boolean hasOptString = in.readBoolean();
if (hasOptString) {
this.setOptString(in.readUTF());
}
}
```
Specified by:
readExternal in interface java.io.Externalizable
Throws:
java.io.IOException

encodeObject

protected final void **encodeObject**(java.io.ObjectOutput out,
                                    java.lang.Object obj)
                                throws java.io.IOException
Messages mostly know what types they are writing but
we still need to encode user-supplied objects, e.g.,
parameters bound to prepared statements. Using this
method of encoding objects is much more efficient
than calling writeObject(). However, this method will
call writeObject if it does not have an optimized way
of writing a particular type.

Parameters:
out - output stream
obj - object to write
Throws:
java.io.IOException - if an i/o exception occurs

decodeObject

protected final java.lang.Object **decodeObject**
        (java.io.ObjectInput in)
    throws java.io.IOException,
        java.lang.ClassNotFoundException
Throws:
java.io.IOException
java.lang.ClassNotFoundException

equals

public boolean **equals**(java.lang.Object obj)
    Checks for message content equality.
    Overrides:
    equals in class java.lang.Object

toString

public java.lang.String **toString**()
    Outputs a somewhat readable string representation of
    the message.
    Overrides:
    toString in class java.lang.Object

org.softwarepipelines.framework.router
Interface PipelinesRouter

`public interface` **PipelinesRouter**

Interface for a `PipelinesRouter`. Includes methods for configuring the router and routing a message to the appropriate pipeline.

Custom routers should extend `org.softwarepipelines.framework.router.PipelinesRouterBase` class, which implements this interface, and override the `route(AbstractMessage msg)` method to implement custom routing logic.

Method Summary	
`void`	**configure**(`PipelinesRouterConfig` config) Configure the Router instance according to the given `PipelinesRouterConfig`.
`void`	**route**(<u>AbstractMessage</u> msg) Route the incoming message to the appropriate Pipeline.

Method Detail

configure

`void` **configure**(`PipelinesRouterConfig config`)
            `throws PipelineException`
   Configure the Router instance according to the given
   `PipelinesRouterConfig`.
   Throws:
   `PipelineException`

---

route

`void` **route**(<u>AbstractMessage</u> msg)
            `throws PipelineException`
   Route the incoming message to the appropriate Pipeline.
   Parameters:
   `msg` - the `AbstractMessage` to distribute
   Throws:
   `PipelineException`

org.softwarepipelines.framework.service
Interface PipelineService

`public interface` **PipelineService**

Interface for a generic `PipelineService`. Includes a method to process an incoming `AbstractMessage`.

Custom `PipelineServices` must extend the abstract `PipelineServiceBase` class, which implements this interface.

Method Summary	
`void`	**processMessage**(**AbstractMessage** `msg`) Process an incoming message.

Method Detail

processMessage

`void` **processMessage**(`AbstractMessage msg`)
                    `throws PipelineException`
Process an incoming message. If you wish to return a message from this service invoke to the invoking connector, call the

`PipelineServiceBase.sendResultMessage(AbstractMessage result)`

method in the base service class (which custom services must extend).
Parameters:
`msg` - the message to process
Throws:
`PipelineException` - in case of error or failure

---

org.softwarepipelines.framework.util
Class `PipelinesHelper`

```
java.lang.Object
  └─ org.softwarepipelines.framework.util.PipelinesHelper
```

```
public class PipelinesHelper
extends java.lang.Object
```

Helper class with convenience methods for getting pipelines framework components.

Constructor Summary
`PipelinesHelper()`

Method Summary	
static `PipelinesConnector`	**getConnectorByName**(java.lang. String distName, java.lang. String connName, PipelinesMasterConfig masterConfig) Build and return a new `PipelinesConnector` instance, configured by name on the given distributor in the master config.
static `PipelinesConnector`	**getConnectorFromDestMap** (ApplicationContext ac, java. lang.String baseKey, java. lang.String targetService) Get a `PipelinesConnector` from a `DestinationMap` configured in a Spring ApplicationContext.
static `PipelinesDistributorBase`	**getDistributorByName**(java. lang.String name, PipelinesMasterConfig masterConfig) Build and return a new `PipelinesDistributor` instance, configured in the given master config with the given name.

Methods inherited from class java.lang.Object

```
clone, equals, finalize, getClass, hashCode, notify,
notifyAll, toString, wait, wait, wait
```

Constructor Detail

PipelinesHelper

```
public PipelinesHelper()
```

Method Detail

getDistributorByName

```
public static PipelinesDistributorBase
getDistributorByName (java.lang.String name,
                      PipelinesMasterConfig masterConfig)
                              throws PipelineException
```
Build and return a new `PipelinesDistributor` instance, configured in the given master config with the given name.

Parameters:

`name` - the name of the distributor we wish to instantiate

`masterConfig` - the master pipelines configuration

Returns:

the new `PipelinesDistributor`

Throws:

`PipelineException`

getConnectorByName

```
public static PipelinesConnector
getConnectorByName(java.lang.String distName,
                   java.lang.String connName,
                   PipelinesMasterConfig masterConfig)
                           throws PipelineException
```
Build and return a new `PipelinesConnector` instance, configured by name on the given distributor in the master config.

Parameters:

`distName` - the name of the `PipelinesDistributor` on which the desired `PipelinesConnector` is configured.

`connName` - the name of the `PipelinesConnector`

`masterConfig` - the master pipelines framework configuration in which both the distributor and connector are configured

Returns:

a `PipelinesConnector`

Throws:

`PipelineException` - if no such connector or distributor is configured, or something else goes wrong

getConnectorFromDestMap

```
public static PipelinesConnector
getConnectorFromDestMap(ApplicationContext ac,
                        java.lang.String baseKey,
                        java.lang.String targetService)
                               throws PipelineException
```

Get a `PipelinesConnector` from a `DestinationMap` configured in a Spring ApplicationContext.

Parameters:

`ac` - the ApplicationContext

`baseKey` - the base map key, attained in a service through the `PipelineServiceBase.getDestMapKey()` method.

`targetService` - the name of the target service

Returns:

the `PipelinesConnector`

Throws:

`PipelineException`

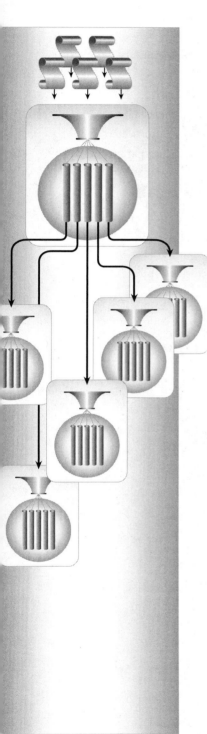

Index

Register
Your Book

at informit.com/register

You may be eligible to receive:

- Advance notice of forthcoming editions of the book
- Related book recommendations
- Chapter excerpts and supplements of forthcoming titles
- Information about special contests and promotions throughout the year
- Notices and reminders about author appearances, tradeshows, and online chats with special guests

Contact us

If you are interested in writing a book or reviewing manuscripts prior to publication, please write to us at:

Editorial Department
Addison-Wesley Professional
75 Arlington Street, Suite 300
Boston, MA 02116 USA
Email: AWPro@aw.com

Visit us on the Web: informit.com/aw

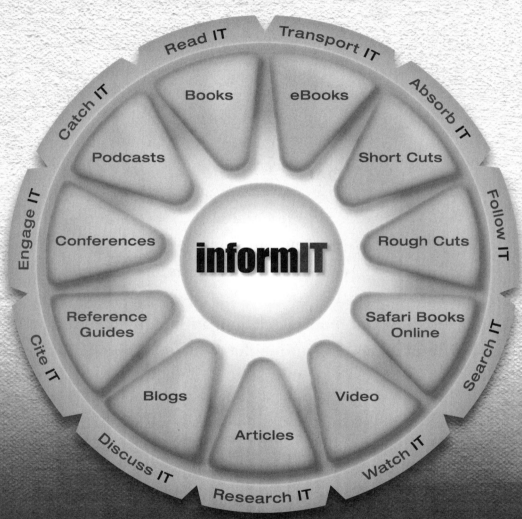

Go Beyond the Book

informIT

Read IT · Transport IT · Absorb IT · Follow IT · Search IT · Watch IT · Research IT · Discuss IT · Cite IT · Engage IT · Catch IT

Books · eBooks · Short Cuts · Rough Cuts · Safari Books Online · Video · Articles · Blogs · Reference Guides · Conferences · Podcasts

11 WAYS TO LEARN IT at **www.informIT.com/learn**

The online portal of the information technology
publishing imprints of Pearson Education

FREE Online Edition

Your purchase of **Software Pipelines and SOA** includes access to a free online edition for 45 days through the Safari Books Online subscription service. Nearly every Addison-Wesley Professional book is available online through Safari Books Online, along with more than 5,000 other technical books and videos from publishers such as, Cisco Press, Exam Cram, IBM Press, O'Reilly, Prentice Hall, Que, and Sams.

SAFARI BOOKS ONLINE allows you to search for a specific answer, cut and paste code, download chapters, and stay current with emerging technologies.

Activate your FREE Online Edition at
www.informit.com/safarifree

> **STEP 1:** Enter the coupon code: EDCDBWH.

> **STEP 2:** New Safari users, complete the brief registration form.
> Safari subscribers, just log in.